AF574133

David Canther's life and words offer a consistent biblical message. *First Response* is an inspired work filled with great encouragement and practical details that equip readers to be a very real blessing to others. A man of prayer and action, Canther champions the message that even the smallest act of caring has the potential to turn a life around.

—Dr. Joel C. Hunter, Senior Pastor
Northland, A Church Distributed
and Becky Hunter

Serving and *loving* are not two separate words; they form a unit. Together they form the nucleus about which the individual, or church, can have its greatest impact. This book features the thoughts and experiences of David, who has dedicated his life to this vision and who wishes to share his journey with you. Studied as a personal devotional or the subject of group discussion, a vision will emerge—a vision of what is possible through a life of service directed by prayer and empowered by the Holy Spirit. May that yearning to serve be brought to fruition as you experience *First Response.*

—Warren Lovett, MD

Over four decades in the humanitarian profession have taught me that catastrophe, both personal and collective, is often the best springboard for positive change. Human nature is more motivated to commit to and achieve change for the better through relationships of trust forged in the crucible of crisis. Life takes on new meaning and provides great fulfillment when we are able to influence others for good in the worst of times. David Canther brings this truth to life in his provocative book *First Response.*

—David C. Taylor,
Executive Advisor World Vision International

I am amazed. This is great stuff, and it's for everyone! *First Response* can turn your problems into your blessing. The problems of others are nothing more than opportunities, so the bigger the problem, the bigger the opportunity. Whoever solves big problems is really a big servant.

—Dr. Ed Thornton

Love your book! Couldn't put it down. The love of our dear Savior is wonderfully and practically expressed.

—Dr. Thomas Andrews, Psychiatrist

David Canther intimately understands and applies a fundamental principle of human interactions, and this is that we can only meet the most pressing needs of people when we build relationships with them. Beyond this, he fully comprehends the importance of compassion, respect, and teamwork in fostering and maintaining relationships. On a practical basis, his skillful leadership and creative allocation of resources have enabled many volunteers to become involved in unique and satisfying ways to help meet the needs of others. Truly, this book is a reality check; it extends an invitation to take the walk from the dump of selfish pursuits to the triumph of selfless service. *First Response* is a walk to experiencing fulfillment. Let's start walking together.

—Richard M. Greene, PsyD
Clinical Psychologist

First Response reminds us that "faith without works is dead." David Canther's style of bringing out biblical themes through his personal experiences and stories will inspire you to do great things for God. Reader beware! After reading this book, you may find yourself desirous of an "out of my comfort zone" experience. David is a man of God whose sincere desire is to extend the healing ministry of Christ to a hurting world. Read the book, be inspired, then get out there and serve! I have used his nine keys to experiencing the power of the gospel serving others over and over in my presentations because they have changed my life.

—Jason Shives, MD
Family Medicine Physician Medical Director,
ACTS World Relief—Haiti First Response

I first met David Canther in 2004 when several hurricanes devastated Florida. During Hurricane Katrina, when ACTS was deployed in Waveland, Mississippi, I got to know David on a personal level. Not many people have been able to grasp the simple mission that Jesus Christ followed and emulated to the world. He verbalized His mission in Luke 4:18–20, "The Spirit of the Lord is on me, because he has anointed me to preach good news to the poor. He has sent me to proclaim freedom for the prisoners and recovery of sight for the blind, to release the oppressed, to proclaim the year of the Lord's favor."

Every aspect of David Canther's life demonstrates that he's "got it." His vision for both relief work in times of disaster and service to the needy during times of calm reflects this. David not only uses ACTS to serve in times of disaster but distributes ACTS resources to churches and organizations to use in times of calm. Unbelievable global vision! This book, *First Response*, will feed the reader from the rich fare that constitutes David's vision. What a feast!

—Pastor Andrea Van Heerden
President, Mercy Network

David Canther and ACTS have helped thousands worldwide. David's devotion to his fellow man was evidenced by his time in Haiti. Working alongside David was inspirational. His grace under extreme circumstances brought dignity to those in need. I encourage anyone interested in the non-profit arena to read this book.

—Kenneth R. Lukins
Cofounder, Relief and Development International

Being available for others is a call from God. It is good to be responsible and always charitable toward others as He is to us every day. This book brings to us a deep insight on a lot of issues related to what ordinary people are facing in their everyday life, in good time as in bad, in rich environments as in poor, in well developed countries as in the most backward. It shows our fragile reality as humankind and Christian challenges in a fast-changing world.

Haiti is not the first country to be hit by such a natural disaster. It will not be the last. Life is a particular type of gift that has the ability to face risks and challenges. The most important question is: What do we do when such circumstances happen? The Haiti earthquake on January 12, 2010, reminds us of the wisdom and the beauty to be a servitor to others. ACTS World Relief and other NGOs, volunteers, and friends rushed to Haiti as servitors of God. I will always remember Dave Canther, with his notepad, noting and coordinating everything, day and night, until all people were served. On the ground, when all looks like chaos—dust, sadness, despair, discouragement, death, tears, and pains—through their passionate words, cares, and prayers with those who have lost all, through these teams of volunteers, God made the light of hope shine again. The road to rebuild Haiti will be a long one, and many share the responsibility to get the job done. The great community of Haiti's friends and the Haitians themselves will continue to work hard and repeat "thank you" again and again to God and all of His servants for listening to His call by helping Haiti with your own means.

—Dr Jean P. Mathurin
Chief Economic Advisor to the Prime Minister of Haiti

You hold in your hands a book that will not only thrill your soul but will also inspire you to reach out to the millions of lost and hurting people. David's book proves that God is still working through those who have willing hands and an open heart.

—Crystal and John Earnhardt

I am truly blessed by your ministry! I pray we can work together to change the world!

—John Louis Muratori,
Best-Selling Author, Senior Pastor, and
Executive Director of Turning Point Christian Center

Our goal at Heritage Academy is to develop a character in young people that mirrors the servant leadership so strongly exemplified in Christ's life and ministry. The profound partnership, divinely inspired, between Heritage and ACTS World Relief has provided a platform for such servant leadership in action. Nothing impacts a young person's life like experiencing the face-to-face ministry that disaster response provides. We are grateful for the numerous opportunities we have had to work closely with David and the ACTS World Relief team. While the circumstances that bring us together are unfortunate, we are blessed to be a part of this ministry. Thanks for the opportunity to share the blessings ACTS has been to us!

—Debbie and Doug Baker, Principal, Heritage Academy

The capabilities and outreach of volunteers from ACTS World Relief are inspirational to say the least. I was proud to deploy and train with them in Haiti following the earthquake.

—Rich Wales,
Assistant Fire Chief, Orange County, Florida

First Response reveals an in-depth look into real accounts that followed the devastating earthquake that rocked the island of Haiti in early 2010 through the eyes of a man who has committed his life to serving his Savior and mankind. It demonstrates what our Maker can do through us when we are determined to "find, follow, and fulfill" His purpose and plan for our lives. It was an honor to serve the people of Haiti with David Canther and the ministry of ACTS World Relief.

—Mickey Agostini
District Fire Chief
Orlando International Airport Fire Rescue

God has blessed David with the vision and ability to organize and utilize large numbers of people effectively in times of disaster. High school and college age students find his approach of using them to directly meet the needs of disaster victims to be an effective method of recognizing and utilizing their talents and skills, fulfilling their need for adventure and most importantly to be the hands and feet of Jesus. I have never seen a more positive and effective life-changing experience for young people. They invariably leave each experience being worn out and with a desire to come back and do it again as soon as possible. ACTS World Relief has a training program that gives students knowledge of how to safely involve themselves in effective emergency response. I look forward to working with David in future times of disaster using young people to meet the needs of victims whenever and wherever possible.

—Jim Ingersoll, Education Superintendent

David Canther has been a friend and a colleague for many years. He walks out what he teaches, serving and loving all along the way. It has been an honor and a pleasure to serve alongside David locally, nationally, and internationally. Serving the hurting in Haiti has been a life-changing experience for me. It has impacted the lives of many Northland responders, congregation members that followed our journey remotely, and so many who prayed for our mission and the people of Haiti.

—Gretchen Kerr, Emergency Response Director
Northland, A Church Distributed

We met David Canther when our non-profit emergency response organization worked in Haiti under the ACTS umbrella. David's organization offered us food, shelter, safety, and spiritual guidance. We are truly blessed by his leadership. David trusted in our ability to carry on his mission and provided connections to other resources. His book is a reflection of his deep devotion and commitment to a life serving others through God with practical advice for disaster response . David's book inspires us to hope for a better world.

—Dr. Rebecca Thomley, CEO,
Headwaters Relief, River of Hope

A good friend and colleague, Judith Bunker, once shared, "I believe emergency response work is the most Christlike thing anyone can do." David exemplifies this through his selfless acts to alleviate the pain and suffering of those impacted by disaster. *First Response* shares example after example of this Christlike work and offers all the opportunity to realize and engage in the joy(s) of service. Good work(s)!

—Jody Hill, Executive Director
Florida Interfaith Networking in Disaster (FIND)

First Response reveals an awesome inspiration of how God desires to work in our lives in service for others. We are truly living in the End Times, and it is imperative that we learn how to help others in times of need as we see more and more disasters come upon us. This book can be used as a manual for personal or church growth in community service. Manuals typically make us think of dry, point-by-point, tedious instruction. Not so with this book! Witty, funny, and filled with stories, it will inspire every reader to pursue a personal walk with God and instill in every heart a burning desire to serve others. I plan to use this book as a guidebook and inspirational tool for the students I train.

—Michael Duehrssen, MD
Program Founder, International Rescue and Relief,
Associate Professor, Union College
Emergency Room Physician

I met David Canther about ten years ago as we were both involved with the Dream Center in Los Angeles. Later we worked together on his Fountain of Hope project in Florida. I have served David and his ministry for the last four years as a member of the board of ACTS World Relief.

Knowing and working with David has been an honor, and it is clearly an experience of faith in action. He is a man of faith, prayer, and action. When David feels a leading from the Spirit, he consistently puts himself in harm's way to help others as he demonstrates the meaning of the gospel.

The day of the earthquake in Haiti I received a phone call from David indicating that ACTS World Relief was going to deploy in response to the disaster. The original plan was for a small group of experienced people to travel to Haiti, meet with governmental officials, and implement a plan of action. If you know David, the previous description is not consistent with who David is. Instead, four days later, I arrived at a small executive airport in Florida, and there were nearly one hundred medical and emergency response personnel, medical supplies, food, and blankets and transportation arranged to move this army of God's responders to Haiti. A couple of days later, late at night, as David and I sat in a hospital with thousands of people who had been helped by ACTS World Relief, David told me that he couldn't accept the notion of going to Haiti to see what could be done while people were dying, so he simply raised up the volunteers to address the suffering as directly and soon as possible. God has always honored David's response, and this book chronicles just some of what extraordinary tasks God achieves with ordinary people.

—Douglas A. Lowe, FAIA
Principal, Cuningham Group Architecture, P.A.

This book brings together faith and compassion in a powerful, life-changing mix! There is much hard data that demonstrates that people become stronger Christians as they do concrete, practical things that demonstrate God's love in the real world; it makes His power present in secular settings where there are hurting people, and it ups the temperature of His power in their own hearts at the same time. This is why the whole concept of faith-based charitable work is so explosive. It has demonstrated its usefulness time and time again and most recently in Katrina and in Haiti. People of faith responding rapidly to human disasters—the secret is out; secular agencies depend on them! You can be part of this phenomenal experience. David Canther has laid out the basic knowledge you need.

—Monte Sahlin
Former President,
National Organizations Active in Disaster (NVOAD),
and Former Member of the FEMA Advisory Board,
Chairman, Center for Creative Ministry

FIRST**RESPONSE**

CHANGE YOUR WORLD THROUGH **ACTS** OF LOVE

FIRST**RESPONSE**

CHANGE YOUR WORLD THROUGH **ACTS** OF LOVE

DAVID CANTHER

First Response by David Canther
Published by Excel Books
A Charisma Media Company
600 Rinehart Road
Lake Mary, Florida 32746
www.strangbookgroup.com

People and incidents in this book are composites created by the author from his experiences in counseling. Names and details of the stories have been changed, and any similarity between the names and stories of individuals described in this book and individuals known to readers is purely coincidental.

Design Director: Bill Johnson
Cover design by Marvin Eans

Visit the author's website: www.actswr.org

Library of Congress Control Number: 2010940917
International Standard Book Number: 978-1-61638-362-6

First Edition

11 12 13 14 15 — 9 8 7 6 5 4 3 2 1
Printed in Canada

ACKNOWLEDGMENTS

Writing a book is an exciting journey of God using a team of diverse talent to share how we can be more effective in serving Him with unconditional love.

First, I want to thank the many people who have poured prayers and spiritual wisdom into my life to challenge me and ACTS World Relief to grow in areas that are truly miraculous.

Heartfelt thanks to: Gwyneth Joy, who helped teach me how to write and edit with descriptive word pictures; Dr. Warren Lovett, who edited from a medical perspective; Cecelia Gordon, a grammar expert; my mother, Shirley, an encourager who let me know God was using me; and my dear wife, Sherri, who kept reading the manuscript over and over and offering suggestions. God has richly blessed me through each of you.

CONTENTS

INTRODUCTION

How do you give love, energy, hope, service, and finances more effectively? How can you love yourself enough to believe in your self-worth and have a healthy identity? How can you become involved in helping others even when you are hurting, so that it miraculously allows you to become more unselfish and healthy? The world is searching for those answers, and Jesus has them. The approach of Jesus was always the same: His first response was always to meet the needs of people, build relationships, accept them for who they were, and then provide hope for who they could become! In simple terms Jesus' model was relational first, theological second.

Jesus defined the Golden Rule and then showed us how to love others as we would want to be loved. He demonstrated how powerful the gospel is when His *unconditional love replaced traditions of "conditional" love.* Jesus lived every day in a way that summarized all of the Ten Commandments in one: love and serve both God and others unconditionally!

Christianity spread like wildfire through the implementation of a fresh, unseen kind of unselfish love. Early Christians shared their resources, gave the shirts off their backs for one another, and died for God and each other. Jesus told His disciples, "Love your neighbor as yourself" (Mark 12:31), and the early Christians understood this principle. Paul wrote to the Galatian church, instructing them to, "serve one another in love" (Gal. 5:13).

Their personality gifts and self-worth exploded with new possibilities, because every worldly failure was now viewed as only an opportunity to display the power of God. Some of the disciples, like the "sons of thunder" (James and John), who had quite the tempers and swore like sailors, realized that their challenges—once they were sanctified—became their strengths when serving others. They unlocked the power of the gospel in their lives by serving others with unconditional love. Every challenge they faced became an opportunity to glorify God through their service to God and those around them.

Readers of this book will learn how First Response unconditional love is essential to unlocking the power of the gospel and changing the world in seemingly nontraditional ways. When you unlock the power of the gospel, two things happen:

- First, you desire to serve God because you understand how much He loves you.
- Second, you grow in God's love by serving others and find fulfillment in doing so from now throughout all eternity (Rev. 22:3).

This book moves you from intellectualizing, impersonalizing, and theorizing about love to inspiring you how to do it. It shares effective, creative, realistic, achievable ways of how to become involved in "loving others as ourselves." These methods are urgently needed worldwide for personal, institutional, and church growth. This book will challenge the way you view others locally, regionally, and globally. To unlock the power of the gospel is one of the best solutions for assisting Christianity to grow in every denomination, beginning with helping just one person at a time. Loving unconditionally also helps to prevent and overcome depression. Through the process of helping and blessing others, you will be blessed even more than they will! The time to provide practical solutions for making a difference for others and ourselves is long overdue. Through ACTS of love, God has special plans for your life of hope and a future (Jer. 29:11). God is looking for opportunities to show Himself strong through individuals just like you (2 Chron. 16:9)!

As a pastor, I have learned that unconditional love through serving others unlocks the power of the gospel: 1) to you and me individually, 2) to each other, 3) to our church, 4) to our world, and 5) to our God. Biblical doctrine wrapped in unconditional love through nontraditional service brings healing in many ways to divided, bickering churches suffering with a decline in growth. It also brings healing to broken relationships. Through my years of leading volunteerism in disaster-relief efforts around the world, I have learned this, too, is an extremely effective way for personal and institutional growth. A by-product of people serving together is that the server often becomes more blessed than the ones being served, and together people develop strong bonds that at times are even stronger than the bond of family ties.

Start living to love and serve others! Don't give up hope on others, because deep down most people want to be loved and forgiven and given a new chance in life. Painful experiences must be shared. No one is alone in this journey of life. God will continue to birth in you new gifts you never knew you had as you love unconditionally.

In this book true-life stories illustrate the transformational principle of "give and it will be given to you!" (Luke 6:38). It will show you how to become radically transformed by learning how to help others inside and outside church walls. *First Response* is an invitation to join the adventure of letting your legacy multiply love for others, whether in everyday life or serving in catastrophic worldwide events. You will be challenged with a new model to meet the needs of others in the same way that First Response emergency personnel are willing to lay down their lives for you!

Love Is Action

> Faith [is] activated and energized and expressed and [works] through love.
>
> —Galatians 5:6, amp

ACTS World Relief began in 2004 with four hurricanes that were devastating Florida. This created an opportunity to unite Christian volunteers to make a difference demonstrating love in action. Since then, youth and adults continue to change their world through ACTS of love with both inner city work and emergency response. ACTS World Relief has remained focused on a unique model of extremely low overhead and administrative costs.

Through years of serving people in our local community and around the world, the ACTS World Relief volunteers and I have experienced that our faith in God grows in proportion to how much love we are willing to give away.

A sign of an ultimate relationship with Jesus comes by our faith demonstrating actions of love (James 2:14–19), not through a statement of beliefs.

This book is all about encouraging you to break away from the spirit of empty religion that controlled the Pharisees and Sadducees, who taught biblical doctrine but had little relevance in practicing it. Begin experiencing the law of liberty of God providing His assurance of love for you and eternal salvation!

This book can be used as a personal devotional or for group study. The study guide can assist you with the contents of this book by stretching your imagination to serve. This book will ignite that internal yearning to experience the power of the gospel, and you'll discover how it grows by putting it into action! Every chapter is filled with parables and actual experiences, many of them from my twenty-seven years as a pastoral minister and as the founder and president of Active Christians That Serve World Relief (ACTS World Relief) organization. I pray that each page will teach you how to love unconditionally, how to attract love from others around you, how to keep love, and how to share it in new, fulfilling ways. The world is waiting for people who really show their love through their actions. Jesus has shown us how to be those people! Now is the time to join those who believe in ACTS's acronym by being "Active Christians That Serve." Invest an hour a day helping someone in need. Go on a mission trip, or join an emergency response team. The rewards are eternal, and give purpose and perspective to your life.

Chapter 1
"FIRST RESPONSE"— EMERGENCY PERSONNEL

THE FIREMEN WHO responded to 9/11 looked in horror as two of the tallest buildings in New York City were ablaze with thousands of lives at stake trapped inside. They did not first try to establish five committees to decide if responding might be the right thing to do; instead, they did not hesitate to respond! They did not merely announce on sound systems, radio, or TV, that if you wanted to find safety, you needed to give money to their union and then your seed of faith would become your deliverance. They acted quickly, putting on all their safety equipment and joined together as a team. They ran into the inferno of smoke and heat, feeling the very foundation of the buildings shake and give way, determined to save every life possible. Many had fleeting thoughts of their families as they pressed up the stairwells, only thinking of saving others lives before their own.

How can "First Response" emergency personnel such as firemen, policemen, rescuers, EMT's, paramedics, and medical providers inspire you to change your world through ACTS of Love? Every time you see emergency personnel, you will be challenged to realize that they are responsible for allowing you to feel safe, provide hope, and to be inspired to think of the needs of others before your own. The Gospel inspires you to become a "First Response" world changer to others in need with commitment, quickness, and efficiency. This produces deep relationships. You can experience the same fulfillment in life as emergency personnel through ACTS of Love.

Jesus says, "I command you to love each other in the same way that I love you. And here is how to measure it: the greatest love is shown when you lay down your life for your friends, neighbors, and your enemies. You are my friend if you obey me. I command you to love each other as I have loved you" (John 15:12–17, author's paraphrase).

Why is it that many times when I share this passage with some, they respond by saying "that is only a parable" or "what a challenging thought?" By not following this command, aren't they breaking God's command? No friend of His would refuse to follow it!

Some Christians emphasize rules, standards, and doctrine, while others ignore them; both potentially missing the fruit of genuine ACTS of love. "If you love me, keep my commandments" (John 14:15). Your "First Response" lifestyle means being willing to lay down your life for others when needed. I have heard some define this command of Jesus, by calling it a "Social Gospel," or trying to save yourself through social justice. The good news is that the only way you are saved, is by faith in Jesus' death on the cross, not by works. That is grace.

A prayer for changing your world through ACTS of love could be: Lord, by faith I accept that You have given Your life to save me. Each day I release my sins and failures to You and believe You will change my heart into one of unselfishness by helping others in need! Empower me to now change my world through ACTS of love, by helping someone who is in need today.

Haiti Aftershocks

The ground shook violently under my feet. The walls on either side of the hospital hallway moved and swayed as I watched in horror. It was an aftershock measuring 6.1 on the Richter scale, only one of 29 aftershocks I experienced within three weeks of the January 12, 2010 infamous earthquake that devastated the small island. Three hallways looked like an ant farm as patients ran for their lives; acute-care patients frantically dragging their IV's, more ambulatory patients climbing over bodies, and still others hobbling on crutches, all desparate to reach the main front door and safety. Interspersed in the chaos were those from our medical staff trying their best to maintain order and calm, trying to keep them from stampeding like frightened animals. The Haitians had seen so many of their loved ones perish by falling cement roofs that these memories now etched in their minds filled them with terror. Horrified, I watched Adule stumbling on his two recently amputated stumps. The clean white gauze had turned bright red with fresh blood soaking through his bandages. He managed to make it to the doorway, but patients were leaping over him causing him to get stuck in the doorway opening. Without thinking I ran to the doorway, stooped down from behind and picked him up under his armpits and carried him out the door. Once outside I quickly turned to the left where I was able to gently ease him back down to safety, away from under the roof structure. The look of gratefulness in his eyes is etched in my mind forever. My first response was to save someone else's life before my own. Praise God, I now had gained a life-long friend! Ten minutes following the aftershock, our medical director issued the care providers a mandatory directive. In no uncertain terms, she let them know that if anyone bolted again, rather than calming and staying with their patients, they would immediately be relieved of their positions. They must be willing to lay down their lives for those entrusted to their care, even if the roof fell on them in the process.

Prostitution Ministry

A group of seven leaders and I were struggling to figure out how to help meet the needs of prostitutes in the red-light district of Los Angeles. It was forty-six degrees out and about two o'clock in the morning; you could see your breath. It was my goal to stretch our new group of church leaders to think of loving unconditionally as Jesus would. Some individuals in religious circles would consider prostitutes as trash, treat them like trash, or simply put, define them as having trashed their lives beyond repair. But each year our church budgeted money to travel the U.S. to learn how God was using powerful, growing ministries to meet the needs of hurting individuals in their communities. This gave our leaders a new vision of how God was calling them to lead and serve others.

That day, noticeable goose bumps marred the exposed flesh on the prostitutes' bodies as they paraded the streets trying their best to attract a unique service industry market. We noticed many pimps in their fancy Cadillacs and luxury cars circling the area to keep an eye on their employees, who were caught in a web of slavery and self-destructive survival behavior. Well-meaning Christians had faithfully handed out religious tracts thinking this was the solution to turn the prostitutes' lives around, but because We noticed piles of religious tracks creating garbage on the ground from many well-meaning Christians. They thought this was the solution to turn the prostitutes' lives around, but because they had been handed out as a "greater-than-thou" spectator sport, the ladies had easily discarded them and they now lay in piles of worthless garbage.

Calling the group back together I asked, "What would Jesus' first response be?"

Our new female head elder, Rhoda, said, "I am cold and just watching them makes me shiver. They must be freezing!"

"Great idea. What could we do to meet that need?" I asked.

"Why don't we pass out hot chocolate, tea, or coffee from a local vendor?"

she replied. It was amazing to see how receptive the shivering, exposed ladies were, and the looks of penetrating thankfulness in their eyes.

Next we discussed a game plan. Offering to meet the prostitutes' needs first, we would invite them to jump aboard our blue van, picking up any along the curbside who wanted an emergency escape. We would take them to the well-known Dream Center in L.A. The rehabilitation center was a converted, abandoned hospital, and those running the compassionate ministry were always receiving those who desired to have their lifestyles changed by the power of God through practical Christianity.

As we made a rolling pass down the busiest section of the street at four o'clock in the morning, eight young girls jumped into the open doors of our van and into the arms of the welcoming ladies inside as they responded to the invitation, "Jump inside." Blankets were shared and through tears, Natalie, one of the ladies from the street, said to one of our volunteers, "You'll never know how thankful I am to you for saving my life." As the volunteer embraced the young girl a bond between them was instantly formed. The kind of bond that only comes through a brief, seemingly by chance encounter, one where the practical needs of someone others would have judged and shunned were met with love and acceptance. The pimps did not have a chance to beat them up or kill them as we sped off to the place that would become their new transitional home. Both their lives and ours were changed forever!

We created an opportunity for love to express itself through our unconditional actions.

The keys presented in this book will stimulate you to discover solutions to these personal questions:

- Am I aware of—and willing to listen to—the needs of my community?
- Am I seeing the needs of others as problems or opportunities?
- Can I meet the needs of others with relevant solutions?
- Is prayer a key to changing your world through acts of love in order to anticipate daily miracles and overcome persecution and discouragement?
- Am I meeting needs with my resources and gifts at my work, home, school, church, community, or during domestic and international catastrophic events?

Five biblical examples illustrate that ACTS of Love in Christianity are more than saying we love Jesus, following His commands, or looking or acting a certain way:

1. Isaiah 58: Describes a religious group that appears to be seeking His will and keeping His laws, but is only superficial (vs. 1–7). Next, the signs of His true followers are identified as those who feed the hungry and care for the poor (vs. 8–11).
2. Matthew 25: Sheep are the only ones described who enter the kingdom of heaven. Not because they say they are Christians or have membership in some denomination, but because their actions reveal true Godliness. They act in loving ways toward the poor, the sick, and the imprisoned, while the goats did not.
3. First John 2:3–6: We are called to "Walk as Jesus did". A fuller explanation is given in I John 3:16–20 "Let us not love merely with words, but in actions and in truth." If you have money, share it with someone else in need.
4. John 14:15 says, "If you love me, keep My commandments." But also adds, "My disciples are those who produce much fruit. This brings glory to My Father and as a result, fills you with joy!" (John 15:5–11, author's paraphrase).
5. Ephesians 2:8–10 "Salvation is a gift from God because you are saved by grace alone."

Now that you are saved, your good works will demonstrate it! (author's paraphrase). When our first response to others is an act of love, it offers them a life-changing process towards ultimate fulfillment and will change your world!

Chapter 2
HAVING A HEALTHY IDENTITY

D*O YOU HAVE a healthy identity? You must be able to love yourself first in order to love others unconditionally and successfully!*

Let's begin the journey of loving others unconditionally by thinking of the idea of putting on the whole armor of God, illustrated by a fireman's Personal Protection Equipment (PPE) or bunker gear. In order to have a positive identity and self-worth, you must put on the armor of Christ, which enables you to be successful in resisting Satan's attacks in your life of both self-destructive thoughts and actions. The alternative is to put on the false armor of self-centeredness, righteousness by works, and materialism to make you look and feel good on the outside. This only creates false security. Every day as you get dressed with each of the items listed in Ephesians 6 as part of the armor of God, remind yourself of your unique value in Christ! Loving others unconditionally will cause you to explode in growth both spiritually and emotionally! You will anticipate greater opportunities, avoid burnout, and experience fulfillment and greater miracles in your life as a result!

Spiritual Empowerment

The reason I am strong in Your power is because I prepare, dress, and am equipped to resist attacks with my: belt or suspenders (integrity and faith); coat and breathing apparatus (confidence of righteousness by faith); boots (peace); shielding gloves (grow faith); helmet, face shield (salvation), and fire hose, halligan, pike pole, and ax (God's Word).

—Ephesians 6:13–15, author's paraphrase

Our society has bought into the blond-haired, blue-eyed, Malibu-looking Jesus. Most all of the pictures depicting Jesus show Him as a Caucasian; some show Him with brown hair and brown eyes, but He is still definitely of white descent. But that is not true. He was Middle Eastern and therefore looked like Middle Easterners do today, with black hair, dark eyes, and brown skin. He was Jewish. He would have looked Jewish right down to the physical features that distinguish Israeli Jews from all other ethnicities.

In addition, we have also been taught that when Paul wrote to the Ephesians about putting on the whole armor of God, he likened that armor to that of the armor worn by the Roman soldiers, perhaps the very one standing guard outside his jail cell. What we sometimes forget, though, is that Paul was born and raised a Jew. He was raised up in the Jewish culture and studied the Torah, which we today know as the first five books of the Bible: Genesis, Exodus, Leviticus, Numbers, and Deuteronomy. He had the best in every level of the Hebraic educational system; otherwise he would have gone into the family business, like Peter, James, and John were when Jesus found them. In addition, Paul apprenticed under the rabbi Gamaliel. Paul knew the scriptures backward and forward because he had gone through the entire Jewish educational system.

When Paul tells us to put on the breastplate of righteousness and the helmet of salvation, he is quoting the prophet Isaiah (Isa. 59:17). And Isaiah never saw a Roman soldier in his entire life! In Ephesians 6:15 (KJV) when Paul tells us to shod our feet with the preparation of the gospel of peace, he is quoting from Isaiah 52:7. The sword comes from Paul quoting Isaiah 49:2.

It is very likely that when Paul was writing the letter we now refer to as the Book of Ephesians, he could see the Roman soldiers. However, I suspect that Paul was like you and me in that when he was facing trials by being imprisoned, he found inner strength through what he had been taught and lived and studied rather than what he saw at the present. Think about it. When you and I are in a crisis, whether you are Christian or not, where do you get the strength to continue? A remembered encouragement your mother spoke to you as a child, a favorite saying of yours, something a teacher or mentor said that sparked determination within you, or for those of us who know that God is our source, a cherished passage of Scripture.

Paul used something from his background to appeal to the Ephesians. His description of the armor of God didn't come from a Roman soldier's armor but from the garments of the High Priest. As you read on, I ask you to look at the armor of God through new eyes and realize how this armor is essential to wear daily in order to successfully serve others.

A Parable

The identity of a fireman is, in part, revealed by their uniform, or personal protective equipment. They also need uniquely designed equipment that not only enables them to do their jobs effectively but also provides for their safety while doing it. Everything they use in their trade, from protective gear to smashing and preventive gear, makes them successful. They understand that their mission is "First Response!"—to save lives of the hurting and the dying.

Individual Identity Crisis

> By faith I believe in the power of the Holy Spirit to change my life now because I am in Christ. I am a new creation!
>
> —2 Corinthians 5:17, author's paraphrase

God does not see you soiled through your mistakes, failures, or misery. Instead, He sees you as perfect in Christ. He is not disappointed in you, though you may be disappointed or discouraged in yourself. Every day He sees you as perfect and forgiven through His eyes of love. He loves fixing broken lives and restoring them to their fullest potential. You are saved by grace through faith, manifested by love. Ephesians 5:2 says, "Live a life of love."

The negative experiences in your past undoubtedly make an impression on your life, which are only opportunities from which to learn and grow. These experiences do not have to determine who you will become. The Law's intent is to condemn you with guilt and point you to the Savior, who has "redeemed us from the curse of the law" (Gal. 3:13)!

The sooner you identify the areas of your pain, the sooner you can "overcome evil with good" (Rom. 12:21). (See my family's life journey in Appendix A.) Your self-worth and undiscovered gifts will grow as you share love with others. I used to administer personality assessment tests for individuals to help them discover their hidden gifts so they were able to align themselves with their strengths and get connected in their correct areas of service. I later discovered that God explodes an individual's personality with miraculous new areas of giftedness because of his or her commitment to serve others first. God will set you free from your insecurities and low self-esteem the more you keep loving others unconditionally.

Today there is a great need for self-worth, which affects how you express your God-given greatness! In order to "love your neighbor as yourself" unconditionally, you have to be able to love yourself first. Do you love life and the fulfillment it brings? The self-worth of countless people has been destroyed through personal failures, fractured homes, broken relationships, and misconceptions of how to live a fulfilled life. You can benefit greatly by developing long- and short-term personal visionary goals and objectives for your gifts. This process forces you to think about how you are uniquely blessed with gifts you may not yet have recognized.

Visionary Goal

Do you have a personal visionary goal? If you do not, take a moment right now to write down what it might be. What do you want to accomplish in life? Where do you want to be in twenty years? When you have spare time, what do you enjoy doing most with it? What are your interests and passions? Who are your heroes? What is your purpose? (Use the lines below to write your visionary goal.)

____

____

____

When you understand your purpose, you understand how you can effectively be involved in serving the needs of others through acts of love. When you serve their needs, you empower them to become all God wants them to be. Then you are fulfilled by helping in that process and experience the great joy it brings!

It's OK to frequently change or modify your visionary statement as you assess the importance of your initial goals, and the steps outlined to achieve them. As you begin to understand yourself more fully, your goals will become more refined. If you cannot write your visionary statement, then become involved in a variety of volunteer opportunities and you will discover which one or ones you enjoy the most. This will help you discover your interests or gifts. I struggled with my own identity until my visionary statement became clear:

> There is no miracle in small plans. When I think of ministry, my vision is adults mentoring youth, serving the world. Anything less is not worthy of Christ, or His will for my life.

I challenge you to write down your visionary goals. It is a biblical thing to do. Habakkuk 2:2 says to record your vision and make it clear. The time will come when your vision will be fulfilled! This will help to develop your identity and give you focus on where to best spend your time and energy.

Overcoming your perception of low self-worth and dwelling on the mistakes, inadequacies, and hurts of your past can be the foundation stone upon which you start to build your life. Until you do this, you will not be equipped to meet the needs of others. Wrong perceptions of yourself will prevent you from ever rising up to take the first step of the gospel seriously: "Love your neighbor as yourself" (Luke 10:27). The Bible is clear; Jesus said, "Because I gave My life in love for you, your past is forgiven, and you are now free to love others!" (John 3:16, author's paraphrase). He paid the debt for your sins. Those who can now love the most are those who choose to accept how much He has forgiven them. Whoever has been forgiven much, loves much (Luke 7:47). The greatest accounts of miracles in the Bible are given to remind you of how much God loves to use those who are seen by their peers as the most ungifted and unworthy (1 Cor. 1:27). That sounds like an opportunity. By faith, you are a new creation now in Christ Jesus! You are redeemed!

Today the greatest need begins with understanding. Why does God have a special plan for my life for greatness? How can I accomplish it? Encouragement is found in Philippians 2:13: "God is at work within you, giving you the will and power to achieve His purpose" (my paraphrase).

A friend once reminded me of four things that Jesus promised—peace, power, purpose...and trouble. God doesn't promise your victorious life will come easily. Right now Satan desires to steal, kill, and destroy. We have been redeemed and restored through Jesus' death and resurrection, but this world is not our home. We live in enemy territory. Bad things happen to good people. It's not right, and it's not fair! Our lives are a daily battle between good and evil. But God has given us the necessary tools in order to be victorious in this life. God promises peace and joy in the midst of your troubles (John 16:33), and we are perfect in Christ. You are one of God's incredible investments! How can you be perfect in this Christian life? On your own it's impossible! But in Christ, you have a perfect report card, regardless of your past or the extent of your sins. If you could succeed through your own accomplishments, you wouldn't need God's grace.

How can you move from an understanding of salvation defined as what

God has already done for you (head knowledge) into an experience of what God is doing in you now (heart experience)? You need to see yourself not as who you are or what you look like now, but rather as who you are willing to become. All you need is what you already have. And what you have is what He is! He does not give you strength; He IS your strength! He promises that you can do ALL things through Christ who strengthens you (Phil. 4:13). Speaking God's promises in a personalized, "Now Faith" paraphrase has proven very helpful to me. I encourage you to say these promises out loud with me:

> "The joy of the Lord is my strength!" (Neh. 8:10).
>
> "I can do all things through Christ who strengthens me!" (Phil. 4:13).
>
> "His strength is made perfect in my weakness!" (2 Cor. 12:9).
>
> "I am God's masterpiece" (Eph. 2:10).
>
> "I am blessed and highly favored, daily increasing in favor with both God and man" (Luke 1:28, 2:52).
>
> "All Your promises are mine, and they are 'yes' and 'Amen'" (Gal. 3:29, 2 Cor. 1:20).
>
> "I am Your son/daughter" (Gal. 4:5).
>
> "Because I am in Christ, I am a new creation" (2 Cor. 5:17).

What you look like or what you wear on the outside is only a part of what gives you your *identity*. One of the greatest ways you can overcome the insecurities you face daily is to know who you are in Christ. This provides you with an inner security or identity. When you speak God's Word and confess it from your mouth, it activates God's sanctification process within you (Rom. 10:9–10)!

> Faith grows in us by hearing and then speaking God's Word (Rom. 10:17, author's paraphrase).

Having a Healthy Church Identity

If you are a member of a church, do you have the healthy identity of someone who is ready to be a positive contributor of meeting needs where you are attending? Is your church really meeting your community's needs and growing?

Here are some successful keys for church growth:

1. Focus on answering, How would Jesus meet the needs in my community?

2. Involve youth more in helping others through serving. It is contagious! They remain practicing Christians and go on to attend college at a much higher percentage than those who do not. The key is adults mentoring youth in serving others!
3. Quickly integrate those who come to church into more outreaches by mentoring them. When you reach out to help someone else, it blesses you the most by helping overcoming materialism, depression, discouragement, and burnout.

If you belong to a church, what is your church's visionary mission statement or motto? Many answers arise, such as, "to preach the three angel's message," or "to be like Christ," or "to keep all the commandments." It is crucial to move your doctrine into practical application of the needs in your community!

How do you enjoy meeting the needs in your community? That is a revolutionary question to most. When you begin accomplishing what God asks you to do, a visionary statement arises out of the need to clarify your identity and to understand the needs of the community. These two items must harmonize. This happens when you discover the unique gifts within your congregation. If congregations do not define their purpose, they are unable to unite to become a force or movement in their community.

Andre, a pastor in Florida, expresses how implementing the keys explained in *First Response* have impacted his ministry:

> I really appreciate your inspiration to me to keep plugging away at networking in the community. It has re-energized my ministry and my church!

Modern-Day Gideons

To move beyond a survival mode (merely maintaining service positions and monetary needs within the congregation), as a pastor I came to find that a minimum of three hundred active members are needed to make a major impact in your community. It does not matter how many are on the church books, since about half are missing from active participation in most church memberships. The larger the number of active members reaching out to the needs of its community, the larger the explosion of growth from within! When you implement programs solving your community's needs, your church will never have to fear closing its doors. God wants three hundred faith-filled ambassadors united with a cause to bring hope to the hurting who will overcome all the power of the enemy in every community!

There is nothing wrong with continuing to modify a church visionary statement, as long as you are being challenged to get out of the pew and become involved with a real, tangible plan for helping those in the community who are hurting.

Four Goals of a Healthy, Growing Church with Identity

1. **Visionary meetings**—Let leadership meetings become visionary meetings. Allow more time for prayer, asking God where He wants to lead you. The more you catch a vision of how God wants to use you, the more you empower smaller committees to solve internal needs, like leaky faucets. This allows you to become a united, dynamic force of love in action in your community.
2. **Measurable goals and plans**—Require one-, three-, and five-year goals from each leader, including a budget, for fulfilling some need in your community. Your areas of gifting will be defined and challenged when a plan for serving is submitted. Annual or periodic evaluations of your goals and of the total vision are necessary.
3. **Mentor, rather than maintain**—Spend intentional time casting your vision to committed, positive individuals who are meeting others' needs. Become a provider of resources, allowing others to succeed! When others succeed in ministry, you have accomplished your goal. Mentoring requires leading by loving others. Youth especially love to be mentored, if they sense that you care for them. Your main goal is to put yourself out of a job—not to become jobless—by mentoring others to become your next leaders.
    - Some pastors confuse their congregations by preaching on what their congregations should be doing rather than leading by mentoring them. This results in many within their congregation feeling guilty because they aren't living up to the pastor's expectations, yet these are often things such pastors do not practice themselves. This prevents the pastors from developing close relationships or loyalty among the members.
    - I often challenge church leaders to dedicate six months to praying for God to reveal the outreach ministry to which

He is calling them to lead and mentor others. The biblical model of a leader is that they are to disciple and train others, not just pray over the offering and/or congregation. Some think that leadership is only being seen or heard in front of the congregation once a week. If after a period of prayer they cannot discover what outreach ministry they should be leading or mentoring others in, they should voluntarily step down from their office. This plan infuses the congregation with a tremendous surge of life-blood, and congregations will begin to see themselves through the example of their church leaders.

4. **Freedom to fail**—Developing identity needs room to keep trying to succeed through trial and error. The only real failure is when you quit trying or give up. You best succeed by encouragement and support in a positive environment at home, church, or work.

The most exciting paradigm shift in evangelism is from predominately receiving head knowledge to releasing love in action through effective utilization of your gifts. In other words, live to love! When you reach out and meet the needs of others rather than thinking primarily of your own needs, you become "recycled." This creates contagious Christianity in your life and also develops long-lasting relationships!

How to Prevent Churches from Losing Their Identity

Many sermons are preached on why churches are declining in membership. Some say it is because the doctrines and standards of the church are not being stressed enough. Others say denominations have lost their identity and are not preaching enough prophecy. *The solution is to emphasize through practice and shared testimonies how relevant the power of the gospel is in meeting the needs of others and providing them with hope!*

When Christians develop relationships outside their inner circle, they no longer see others as being outside the walls of their fortress or exclusive denomination. They come to realize the power of the gospel breaks down walls of prejudice, judging, and hypocrisy. When Christians unite their resources together in serving others yet maintain their uniqueness, it evangelizes non-Christians and meets the world's greatest needs. This occurs by denominations breaking free from the fortress-mentality of primarily serving their own needs and instead joining together to help meet the needs of others.

The solution for Christian churches desiring growth and identity is to focus on what true greatness is in a church. Jesus placed a strong emphasis on serving the needs of others first. Somehow God's church continues to believe greatness is in measuring how many churches you can plant or how many people are on the church books. Jesus' main emphasis was on practicing a radical kind of love whether at work, home, or in His community. Growing churches that place more emphasis on developing relationships will spend less focus on theological differences.

Challenges of Identity Can Provide Opportunities to Refocus Within Religions

Baptists give a strong financial commitment to serving their communities, especially in emergency response volunteerism, hospitals, and schools. Internal divisions have multiplied growth under various names.

Seventh-day Adventists have experienced outstanding growth through a worldwide emphasis in public evangelism (which is becoming less effective). Establishing private schools and hospitals has been a strong emphasis for them. A search for doctrinal relevancy in the 1980s has multiplied their diversity and challenged clarity.

> "Their traditional humanitarian endeavors are supported through ADRA (Adventist Development Relief Agency), which gets more money from government grants than it does from the donations of Christians. This too often ties it to government policies instead of a purely Christian analysis of needs and development strategies."
>
> —Monte Sahlin

Catholics run some of the oldest Christian institutions and are well known for their private schools and hospitals. In my experience, Catholic Charities donate more to inner city and emergency response than any other denomination. The Catholic Church has struggled in recent years to retain members due to doctrinal relevancy and because of negative media exposure, though this is producing more accountability in the denomination.

The Mormons have experienced phenomenal growth in America because of their strong emphasis on family values and serving others through establishing community centers. I can testify that they are number one in personal and emergency response, having worked with them for years. They are modifying their theology because of the media challenging their doctrinal soundness.

The Jehovah's Witnesses also have experienced outstanding growth in spite of controversial theology.

Liability is a growing concern for any organization that is self-insured, because it can dictate and paralyze service. This will ultimately destroy its mission.

Many churches are searching for fulfillment and relevancy in untraditional ways. Christianity is growing most rapidly outside North America, where there is a strong emphasis on meeting the needs of others.

In the 1700's to 1900's, many new denominations were formed. These included the following in chronological order: Presbyterians, Lutherans, Baptists, Methodists, Episcopalians, Mormons, Southern Baptists, Seventh-day Adventists, Salvation Army, Jehovah's Witnesses, Pentecostals, Nazarenes, and the Assemblies of God.[1] These groups often focused on their unique doctrines—what made them different from other denominations—with less emphasis on implementing the relevancy of their doctrines to the greatest commandment of loving your neighbor as yourself.

Healthy identities are a result of focusing on changing lives and healing broken spirits, loving them unconditionally through serving others! Denominations, churches, and individuals who evangelize by intellectual, impersonal Christianity alone experience short-term growth because this perspective develops a superior, legalistic attitude toward others and is only religion. Revelation 3:14–17 says these churches are like the church at "Laodicea, and God will spit them out of His mouth because they are content, comfortable, and already have all the truth!" (author's paraphrase). Loving your neighbor as yourself is a Christian movement that multiplies, relying on the power of the Holy Spirit to accomplish miracles while serving others in need! Only those churches that refocus their doctrinal uniqueness on serving others will grow. This builds long-term relationships and loyalty.

Pentecost grew as the result of people becoming united in serving others. The early Christians literally pooled their money and helped those in need. Likewise, today the Holy Spirit empowers you because of your need to serve in a miraculous way, but Satan produces a counterfeit based on self-interest. Love-motivated manifestations of the Holy Spirit are what Paul means by saying, "You should desire the most helpful gifts" (1 Cor. 12:31, NLT).

Churches that practice doctrinal soundness and loving others unconditionally are experiencing sustained growth! This is why Christianity is the fastest-growing religion in the world. Percentages vary between many articles and statistics given when you Google "fastest growing religions" and/or "declining denominations." In actual conversions, Christianity still is first and growing worldwide! A simple summary shows the following in order from highest to lowest percentages of newly forming growth, which is different from actual conversion growth: secularism (no religion), Wicca (satanism), paganism, scientology (who have marketed themselves in a huge way in disaster-response), Islam (because of more offspring being born, and immigration), all Protestant churches who focus on their community's needs, Pentecostals and Charismatic Christians (who offer a strong emphasis on hope and relevancy).[2] Christianity is growing rapidly because of its foundation in showing unconditional love. God's last-days remnant church will meet the relevant needs of a hurting generation both doctrinally and practicing what we believe by what we do! Many are shocked when I invite them to help in catastrophic events to help save lives. They tell me, "I never thought of actually helping these people who I saw in need on TV or heard about in need. I thought someone else or the government would take care of them. I thought only government employees were first responders." Youth, in particular, love to be involved in reaching out to the needs of their communities and it keeps them connected to their churches. I can testify that this was one of my greatest blessings as a youth. Being a part of singing groups, going to nursing homes, or feeding the homeless kept my mind focused on unselfishness. The most powerful motivator for lasting change is becoming involved in each other's struggles, thereby creating witnessing opportunities. When your head knowledge turns into love in action, your prayer grows from, "Lord, please give me strength," which is technically a prayer of unbelief, not accepting what He's already promised in Philippians 4:13, to, "Thank You, Lord, for being my strength!" That is a prayer of faith, personalized into a confession.

God turns our mistakes, or life's unfair misery, into life's treasure not because of what we do but because of what He has already done for us. He turns our greatest fears into faith-building opportunities. Are you willing to become involved in the life of someone who needs you? When you do, you will discover that you are being helped the most. Listen to their needs by telling them, "I don't know how you feel. Please tell me." Do you sometimes fear that you must have all the answers theologically, emotionally, or physically to fix all of life's problems? You must realize God created you to gain healing by helping others, and sometimes just by listening.

Emergency Response Identity

As first responders, what we wear and carry as identification is essential for our protection. It identifies who we are to survivors, emergency personnel, and others around us and inspires volunteers to unite. It gives us a clear, positive identity.

Late one night after Hurricane Katrina, I drove my white, dual-axle truck to the disaster zone. All around me the evidence of massive destruction was clear. Large oak trees that once stood tall and strong, covered with hundreds of years of Spanish moss, were now stripped of their lofty foliage standing vulnerable and naked. Others lay in piles, mangled and splintered as if mere twigs.

A 6:00 p.m. curfew was in place to prevent looters from having free access to the area and, subsequently, the victims' personal belongings. Because it was after the curfew, I really shouldn't have been driving in the area. At one house where the garage had once stood, but was now entirely gone, an expensive collection of Snap-on tools lay out in the open, unprotected. It would have been easy to justify that God had provided me a free set of good-quality tools, but instead I thought, "How would I wish to be treated if these were mine?" I quickly pulled my truck over to the side of the road and parked. Taking a tarp that I had in the rear of the truck, I covered up the tools and secured the corners with some rocks that were lying nearby.

Continuing on my drive, the flashing blue lights of police cars up ahead let me know that I was approaching another check point. When I stopped, officers shined their flashlights into my vehicle, looking for suspicious looters. The outside of my door proudly displayed the ACTS Disaster Response decal, so when I showed my I.D. and said, "I'm with ACTS Disaster Response," they waved me through. My identification was the most important item in helping me get through there quickly. Now, I was allowed to continue helping a hurting community. Identity with a cause is important!

What if I had an ACTS decal on my truck and yet had a bunch of stolen tools in the back end? What kind of a witness would I have been? Later, I was able to meet the devastated owners of those tools and offer further help by sorting and cleaning their tools.

Lesson Learned

Some people mistakenly think that you communicate your identity and effectively witness by the tracts you give out or by the decals displayed on your bumper. But when others *see* your love in action by helping, it is more important than *telling* them.

Saved by the Tub

They knew of the tornado warning, but no one really thinks it is going to come to their house! By the time the storm was on its way, there wasn't much they could do. They lived in a mobile home. If the tornado hit, and their home was in its direct path, boarding up the windows wouldn't save anything.

Mary was scared. It might not be much by higher standards, but it was their home, filled with memories of laughter and tears and family. Things that were precious to her, like photographs, her favorite frying pan, the crocheted afghan on the couch—these things had much sentimental value.

Mary and her husband, Chuck, huddled together watching the news. The continuing weather reports forewarned them of the veracity of the storm. They could hear the wind roar outside like an angry, wild animal sent to devour them. The sky had grown dark. Tree limbs began snapping and crackling in the distance. Metal banged against metal, though they couldn't tell exactly what was making the sounds. Was it trash cans? Was it the metal porch awning of their neighbor's house coming loose?

Suddenly Chuck grabbed Mary's hand and pulled her as he ran toward the bathroom. For a split second, Mary only heard complete silence, but just then she was thrown quickly into the bathtub by her husband as he landed on top of her, protecting the most cherished love of his life. Immediately the tornado passed over them sounding like a freight train thundering right through their bathroom. The roar was deafening as the ferocious wind destroyed their home. Mary could feel the walls caving in around them, as if they were made from cardboard. She hears glass breaking and metal clanging and the heavy thuds of heavier furniture being rammed into each other. Next, she felt everything being sucked away from around her like a gigantic vacuum cleaner on steroids. She was terrified that she and her husband would be sucked away too. She could only listen, helpless, as she lay beneath her husband, the smell of his shirt, sweat, and fear upon him. Thankful for Chuck's protectiveness, Mary cowered beneath him, her face practically buried in the drain of the fiberglass tub. Her husband's weight heavy upon her, she heard him breathing hard as he tried to cover her for protection. Her own heart was beating so hard it hurt. It was the strangest moment, one in which she felt safe and terrified all at once.

And then it was over. Gingerly, Chuck moved off of his wife and she looked up and then around, astonished at the emptiness where her home once stood. They had lost everything, but had each other. Her husband's bravery and protectiveness had cost him a broken arm and shoulder and broken ribs. Mary had a broken wrist. But they were thankful they had their lives!

"I Have Lost My Wedding Ring"

It was in Paisley, Florida, where a Category 5 tornado had just swept through a mobile home park. It had either leveled or swept away everything in its path. Twenty-five students from Heritage Academy in Tennessee trained by ACTS World Relief's best first response teams arrived at the scene. They were all CERT (community emergency response teams) trained and dressed in ACTS maroon T-shirts. (These students plan time out of every school year to respond and to deploy within six hours to hurricanes, tornados, or flooding wherever needed across the U.S.)

When they encountered her, Mary was sitting on a log with tears streaming down her cheeks as she surveyed the empty yard where her mobile home had once stood. Ever since it had happened, she had been replaying the recent events over and over in her mind. Her loss loomed large, and her future seemed insurmountable. Hopelessness threatened to consume her. She was still somewhat in shock. That's when Doug, a member of our team, approached her with a smile on his face asking, "How can we be of help to you?"

"My husband is at the hospital lying in ICU with a broken arm, shoulder, and several ribs," she cried, "but he survived. He saved my life by throwing himself on top of me in the bathtub as the tornado, which sounded like a freight train, ran right over us. We had only a few seconds to get there. I was never more frightened in my life!" The horror was still very real and was reflected in her eyes. There she was with a cast on her broken wrist, the hopelessness and despair showing vividly on her face.

There was only one item standing nakedly in the middle of what used to be their mobile home: the bathtub. How would any of us feel in a momentary flash if we heard a tornado approaching our house like a freight train? The scenario is something we could only imagine, but in doing so, we could also sympathize emotionally.

"See over there," Mary continued and pointed to a pond behind her yard, "the fire department just pulled three of my neighbors out of there that didn't make it." She had lost everything but was thankful to be alive! The shock of such sudden and complete devastation, along with extreme emotional loss, was unmistakable in her eyes. Death had come much too close to home for her. She looked lost, as though she didn't know where she was or how she had gotten there.

"I have lost my wedding ring," she replied with a melancholy look on her face and despair in her voice. "I set it on the table next to my bed, and now it's gone." For a moment she looked puzzled, as if she thought perhaps she should be concerned about something of greater value than a ring, but the look passed, as if she had reconciled within herself that nothing could be as important as her marriage and the symbol of their union—her wedding ring. She paused a moment, then added with a resigned look and quiet sigh of defeat, "Homes can come and go, but I don't even have any family pictures left. I feel like I have lost my identity."

That's when Doug called to the group of students, "Let's come on over here and pray for a miracle to find Mary's lost ring." He began, "Lord, You know how much this token of their love means to her right now, especially since she has lost everything. Because we know You watch even the sparrow fall, lead us to find the impossible."

After reviewing some basic instructions with the student volunteers on search-and-rescue techniques using their rakes, wheelbarrows, and large shovels, together they set out to work in rows covering her property. The students began to get excited as they found buried family pictures and coins from an antique coin collection that belonged to a neighbor across the street. Julie, a member of the ACTS team, held up a diamond ring and squealed with pure delight, "I found it!" She came running, flying through the air to happily present Mary with her missing wedding ring.

Someone else had found a family photo album belonging to one of Mary's neighbors who lived one and a half miles away. It was returned to him still intact. This was all he had left with which to reconstruct the dreams of his life.

CBS featured Mary on national news holding up her ring, happily declaring, "I love all of you!" She wrapped her arms around the youth helpers, whose lives had also been changed forever. They demonstrated the identity of love in action! Love in action was worth far more than only telling Mary that they were praying for her or hoped she would trust in the Lord to get back on her feet. They released love, and their love was increased. They turned her debris into the only dream she had hoped for—finding her lost ring, which was one of the few things she had left in life to give her identity. (You can watch this feature on the www.actswr.org website. The clip is titled "Faster than FEMA.")

God wants to remind us that our identity is found in Him! We may feel like we are merely debris, but God looks at us as His treasure. Remember, God is searching the world to find anyone who desires to have a loving Father-child relationship with Him. He throws His arms around us in complete joy and delight when we choose Him, for He is the best Father you'll ever have!

PRAYER FOR TODAY:

John 17:1-4, My Prayer to Jesus

Glorify me today so that I can give glory back to You. You have given me authority over all circumstances. Thank You for giving me eternal life, because I know how much You love me! In everything I do, I want to bring You glory!

Chapter 3

SIX KEYS TO CHANGING YOUR WORLD

You have seen how these six pieces of armor, or a fireman's personal protective equipment or bunker gear, give you identity because Christ is living in you. Now let's look to see how each piece is essential in providing empowerment in serving others. By wearing each essential piece, Satan will never be able to defeat or discourage you!

Integrity is the most important foundation for success and self-worth in every individual. This reveals your inner soul, or what you are made of. Sooner or later you will be tested in this area, and *your* response to this test will demonstrate *your* self-worth and *your* value in serving God and man.

Spiritual Empowerment

"The reason I am strong in Your power is because I prepare, dress, and am equipped, to resist all the attacks of the enemy with my: belt or suspenders (integrity and truth), fire coat and breathing apparatus (confidence of righteousness by faith), boots (peace), shielding gloves (grow faith), helmet, face shield (salvation), and fire hose, halligan, pike pole and ax (God's Word)."

—Ephesians 6:13–15, author's paraphrase

A Parable

The suspenders are one of the most important pieces that hold up the fireman's pants. They reduce the probability of his pants falling down, which could be fatal if he tripped and fell. These are far superior to a belt, which causes restriction.

THE NUMBER ONE KEY TO CHANGING YOUR WORLD: the Belt or Suspenders of Integrity

First, the belt or suspenders represent God's character of integrity and truthfulness. This is vitally important for us to put on at the beginning of each day. Integrity is the most valued possession in life. You can't buy it. By making this a high priority, self is forgotten, and we will think of the needs of others. Many think that integrity comes automatically. When we believe that, the old devil can slip up behind us and knock us right off our feet. It brings us helplessly to our knees in humiliation. Our character and reputation are worth nothing without integrity and truthfulness integrated into our actions.

From the Hebrew perspective, the belt of righteousness represented girding yourself up so you were mobile and therefore ready for the onslaught of the wiles of the devil. In other words, you tucked up your garments into your belt, thereby allowing your legs freedom of movement from the long robes that were the customary fashion of that day. You were then able to position yourself in the stance of readiness as a fighter, prepared to withstand anything the devil could aim at you. Today, you have the authority of God and heaven behind you, so when the wiles of the devil come at you, first touching the magnetic field of God around you (because you are wearing the whole armor of God), nothing can get past you.

You can own a fancy car, have a big house, and a bank account; but without a reputable character of integrity and truthfulness, your deceit or sins will catch up to you. About the only thing valued in this life or the one promised is our character development.

If you think it's too late, the good news is, you can begin again! Put your belt back on; it's your black-belt weapon.

In all that you do, remember to be filled with integrity. If you lose sight of this, the consequences are great. Thankfully, God's grace is available, and this enables Him to help us overcome addictions, evil habits, and consequences for our actions.

Airborne!

In high school my brother Dennis and I, ages seventeen and sixteen respectively, were part of a gymnastics team called the Olympians. We were preparing for an upcoming performance, and I was very determined to master doing a back flip off the rings in a gymnastic routine. Normally, it was Dennis who performed the ring and high bar routines, and I performed on what we called a side horse. My brother was better than I was on the rings and high bars, but because of his frequent nose bleeds and his shoulder, which often became dislocated; I wanted to be able to substitute for him in an emergency.

For this particular performance, I was working up a routine that included a back flip off the rings, and Dennis was doing a high bar routine. My coach made it very clear that we were never to perform flips without wearing our safety spotting belts, and we had to have at least two spotters, one holding a rope on each side. The coach adamantly instructed us to follow his directions, even though we may have felt differently. He drilled this safety procedure into our heads so frequently that sometimes I thought I heard him in my sleep. For an added safety measure, I also positioned two four-inch-thick crash pads underneath me in case I fell.

A few days before the performance, Dennis and I went to the gym for extra practice. My brother went to an area about twenty feet away from me to practice his high bar routine, while I got on the rings. Mom had come to watch, and she sat on one of the benches along the wall where she had a good view of both my brother and me.

I was determined this would be my best routine yet! Intent on perfecting my moves before the performance, I decided to try the routine without my safety belt or spotters. It was a quick, impulsive decision, not one that had been made with much premeditation. After all, I had done this routine so many times that surely I was good enough to forego the safety equipment. Quickly convincing myself that I didn't need any spotters and ignoring the sound of my coach's voice and his many warnings in my head, I approached the rings, feeling quite confident in my skills.

Higher and higher I swung, adrenaline coursing through my body as I prepared for my back flip. In addition to all of the physical practice, I had practiced this routine a thousand times in my head. I could almost hear the applause of awed spectators and the heartfelt congratulations of my teammates and coach as my imagination projected a 3-D picture of the competition in my mind.

Now was the moment! This was the moment when body, time, and space came together. Without conscious thought, I had effortlessly mastered the physics of speed and distance, and the moment of "now or never" had arrived. With one last push, I let go of the rings. Airborne! I tucked my legs in tight; my knees pressed against my chest as my body rotated quickly into what I thought was the perfect back flip. Oh the feeling of defying gravity, of being suspended in thin air, that split second of weightlessness before the inevitable descent. This was exhilarating! This was what fun was all about!

However, when I let go of those rings, I had flown through the air so high and so far that I completely missed the safety crash pads! *Thud! Crack*! The sound of my body, head, and at last my feet slamming into the hard wooden flooring echoed throughout the openness of the gymnasium.

My brother and I shared a very close bond with each other, and being older, he felt responsible for not protecting his little brother. He told me later that feelings of guilt raced through his mind, thinking of what he should do next as I lay there unconscious in a fetal position.

My mom raced to my side, landing next to me as if sliding into home plate on all four hands and feet, shouting frantically with sheer panic in her voice, "David, can you hear me? David, it's Mom. Can you hear me?" I couldn't hear it. I remained silent and unmoving. As emotional and traumatic as that moment had to be for my mother, she did what any other mother would have done. She rose above her own emotional terror as certain calm came upon her, and she began to take charge of the situation. Without leaving my side and with one eye focused on me, anxiously waiting for any slight movement, she called out to anyone listening to phone Dr. Warren, who was the school physician and also our family doctor. He lived just up the street from the school. He was there within ten minutes, arriving just about the same time I regained consciousness. After a quick evaluation, I was then loaded into a car and taken to my father's x-ray clinic.

For years later, at times the pain in my back would totally incapacitate me. One day I woke up and quickly got out of bed. My morning was going to be busy, as it was time to do a final run-through of my notes for the two sermons I would be preaching that day. When I went to stand, I fell to the floor on my knees in excruciating pain. "Lord, I need Your strength!" I cried out with a tear in my eye as I broke into a cold sweat. Although sorely tempted to call the church and say, "I can't make it," I chose to believe God would give me strength through the pain. And He did! At the end of that day, I felt like I had just run a marathon. My entire body ached with the pain that had started in my back, but I praised God through it. With each recurring episode, it usually took about three days until the pain subsided.

When I turned the wrong way or tried to lift something too heavy, it brought back a quick reminder of that accident when I was a teenager. The residual pain I experienced every so often seemed proof enough that I would have to live with the consequences of my mistake for the rest of my life. Or did it? Yes, I had reaped what I had sown by purposely disregarding my coach's advice. Yes, it was most definitely my own fault, and the law of cause and effect declared I deserved to live with it. However, I chose to believe something more radical. God's Word says that by the stripes of Jesus I am healed

(Isa. 53:5). There are no "ifs" in that promise. It doesn't say that I was healed by His stripes, as long as I haven't disobeyed or made an unwise choice. If He says I'm healed, then by faith, I'm healed! By faith I knew that regardless of my present condition or the reason for it, God's Word was more powerful. I not only believed that He could heal my back but that He would! *I would simply leave the timing of His will up to Him.*

God's will for our lives is for us to prosper and be in health (3 John 2), so I claimed God's Word in Isaiah and 3 John and all throughout Scripture regarding my healing for: 1) instantaneous, 2) gradual, or 3) delayed until the second coming of Jesus. Yes, we are to pray according to God's will; therefore it was important for me to find out what the will of God was regarding the healing and then claim it according to His promises and leave the timing up to Him! During the entire time Jesus walked this earth, did He ever tell anyone, "No, you can't be healed"? He only asked them, "What do you want me to do?" He never went through a list of qualifiers either, like, "Do you attend the synagogue regularly?" (remember, Jesus was a Jew), or "Have you returned a faithful tithe?" For every person who came to Him desiring healing and believing that He would grant their request, they were healed. God is the same yesterday, today, and forever.

Here's something to think about: if I'm sick and I'm not certain that God wants me to be healed, would it be disobedience for me to go to a doctor or hospital to get well? It would be if I thought it wasn't God's will for me to be healed! God uses doctors and hospitals to bring healing. Faith is exercised when we seek God first, not others. Our only role in healing is simply to believe. Leave the timing to God. Our role is to trust God for physical, emotional, and spiritual healing, not to figure out all the *whys* and *whens*—just believe!

I knew that in Matthew 18:19 Jesus talks about the power of agreement, so I drove some distance with my associate pastor to believe together with someone we knew who practiced speaking and living by faith as well. He asked me, "Do you believe God can heal your back?"

Confidently I replied, "According to Mark 16:18 Jesus says that in His name, believers will lay hands on the sick, and the sick will recover. We just leave the timing up to God! I know you're a believer, so lay your hands on my back. Yes, God can bring healing to my back!"

God's Word is sure! Encapsulated in His Word is the power to bring it to pass in my life—and yours. The only thing God asks for us to do is believe and let Him work in the way that is best. Where two or three are gathered together in His name, His presence lives to love us in a powerful way.

From that day on, I have been a living testimony to God's grace of healing by faith, despite of the fact that my accident was the result of being disobedient to the coach. Many times we can turn our worst valley experiences into learning opportunities as we practice speaking God's Word by faith. Speaking God's Word by faith is very important. More than any other voice on Earth, our subconscious believes our own voice and thoughts. Faith also accepts when it seems our prayers are not answered in the way for which we believed. But we learn to glorify God anyway through the challenges of life, for His blessings!

An extremely successful person and one who is depressed have thought processes that are completely opposite from each other. One continues to visualize success and feeds his or her mind with positive, life-changing thoughts and words regardless of any setbacks or failures, whereas the other constantly tears themselves down, dwelling on the negatives and hurts in life regardless of any potential or positive choices available to them.

Lesson Learned

Without the safety belt and spotters, I had lost my protection, and it nearly cost me my life. It also caused me to realize that my coach's instruction was important for me to follow. He had only been trying to keep me safe. Integrity is doing what you know to be right when no one is watching. I had chosen to do something I knew to be wrong. Integrity can save your reputation and your life, even when you are tempted to feel otherwise.

In this life, faith is the victory for overcoming the world's challenges. There have been many times in life when I claimed God's Word by faith for something I thought I needed, but more times than not, He usually gives me something different that is better for me in the long run.

Love in Action: Finger Lickin' Good!

Rhoda had a real burden on her heart for outreach ministry. She and her husband, Ross, wanted to make a difference in our community. Even in the small town of Mount Dora, Florida, there were people who were hungry and having to do without the necessities of life, like several changes of clothes. Rhoda went to the local police chief and asked, "What area of town would you consider to be the most in need of transformation?" They told her it was an apartment complex called Oakwood Village. It was the highest crime, highest drug trafficking area in the community at the time.

Rhoda invited a few other young adults to begin a Friday night ministry with her called the Chicken Ministry. It was called Chicken Ministry for two reasons. First, she visited the local Kentucky Fried Chicken store and asked if they would donate four buckets of chicken every Friday night to give away to the teens who gathered at Oakwood to sell drugs in a darkly lit part of the complex. Second, she challenged our youth class by inviting only those who felt God would protect them and were not "chicken" to minister for God in an unusual way, by handing out chicken. Week after week, about seven from our youth class would go out with her (some acting as bodyguards), and they would pass out chicken late on Friday nights. Each week, trust grew in this drug community as they realized that these church people were not undercover narcs but seemed to be genuine people who would not rat on them.

How do you apply the principle of integrity to this situation? One Friday night about eleven o'clock as they were passing out chicken, Rhoda and several others overheard plans being made for a major robbery that would bring in some additional revenue for an extra large drug purchase. She quickly pulled one of those gathered around Oakwood who she had befriended to her side and put her arm around his shoulder. "Please encourage your friends to think very carefully before becoming involved. This is not good. It could turn real bad for them."

The next day in church we prayed for God to move mightily in the hearts of those who were contemplating a robbery that night somewhere in town. It weighed heavily on our hearts. Should we try to find out where and when? Should we alert the authorities and perhaps try to prevent it? Our minds battled back and forth, churning in the struggle to determine the course we should pursue. How should we apply integrity in this unique situation?

Sadly enough, that night the home invasion robbery occurred and Steven, a young man who was only eighteen years old died instantly in the gun battle that ensued when the homeowner defended his property. The four other teens fled the scene, leaving the police trying to identify them from the homeowner's description.

Rhoda, three youth from our church, and I attended this very sad funeral. We were the only white faces amidst the dark ones at this particular church funeral, with me being honored to sit up front with the other black pastors of that community. Many came up to us afterward and thanked us for coming and for showing our compassion. The young man's death weighed very heavily on Rhoda's heart, and she became more determined than ever to intensify her efforts of ministry among this hurting, self-destructive part of our community.

Lesson Learned

Steven learned the consequence that a lack of integrity was fatal. Rhoda learned that integrity was vital to continuing to be accepted and trusted to the next level in ministry to her community.

Tykes and Bikes

Rhoda and I visited Waterman Village, a local retirement and assisted living facility, to request their leftover food on Saturday afternoons. She also made arrangements with a local Publix supermarket to get their bread, cakes, and pies just shy of expiration. With these donations, Ross and Rhoda started a weekly feeding ministry in the middle of the worst crime area in our community.

The many children that were growing up in the project community of Oakwood Village were surrounded with drug deals and either witnessed or were a part of the numerous, regular altercations with law enforcement. Ross and Rhoda were burdened by this, for more than anything else, they wanted to teach principles of integrity by example. In addition to bringing free food for the residents, Rhoda set up large speakers for a program called Kidz Club with songs and games. Ross began an additional ministry of repairing bicycles and giving away many donated bicycles to all the children who could not afford one.

One day while driving to the church, Rhoda noticed an aluminum step-van two miles south of our church. Sale price: only seventy-five hundred dollars. The van was worth about ten thousand dollars. Enthusiastically, she shared her find with me. We had money to purchase this vehicle, but I encouraged her to go to God in faith and ask God to show Himself big on her behalf and for His ministry. Rhoda met with the owner and told her of the ministry at Oakwood Village, sharing some of their success stories with her. The owner was interested in this ministry but didn't feel that she could do any more than she already had. After all, the price was well below current market value.

After meeting with the owner several more times and asking a few more questions and inquiring each time whether she would lower the price, she finally agreed to reduce the price to five thousand dollars. Rhoda quickly shared this new information with me, her excitement contagious, until I encouraged her to pray that the Holy Spirit would impress Rose to just *donate* the van! The initial look on her face was about as bewildered as when a baseball coach looks at his team and says, "You can do it. Go out there and win!" even though they are losing two to ten.

Sure enough, the owner finally said, "I believe in what you are doing for our community. I believe you are an individual of integrity and certainly are exemplifying it too. I have not been to a church in many years, because I believed churches were very hypocritical, only talking about what should be done to help others but really doing very little. Let me donate the van to your ministry."

Praise God! One morning before I gave the sermon we shared this blessing with our congregation. Then I asked if anyone knew of someone who could paint the van for Kidz Club ministry. A hand rose in the back, and Rudy introduced himself as an artist and painter who owned a local art gallery. "I would be glad to paint the van for free," he offered. Ingeniously, Rudy used the children from Oakwood as his models, and the van sported their smiling faces with the words "Kidz Club" lettered on each side. It was quite the masterpiece! In the back we placed a large, upright stainless steel warmer, donated by the head elder, who owned a commercial kitchen company, to help with the weekly hot meals program.

Lesson Learned

When the foundation of integrity is used in serving others, opportunities and blessings abound! When parents entrust their children to your care, integrity is the most important responsibility that will ever be placed on you in serving others!

Five Hundred to Thirty-Five Thousand in Eight Months

Our church believed in community service and wanted a bigger community center. We had a room in the not-very-often-used part of the church that was five hundred square feet. In it were some old clothes and canned goods that a few elderly ladies stood guard over, as if they were treasured keepsakes. The clothes smelled like they had been in storage for years and were fashions from decades past and not wanted by anyone, including the homeless. The food items were canned carrots, asparagus, and many other items you had to be really hungry to want. Okay, maybe it wasn't quite that bad, but it was close. There was a standard procedure to being able to be a recipient of any item from our community service room, and the interrogation process seemed worthy of military proportions.

God wanted to expand the influence of Life-Changing Ministries in our community. Because of our current thriving ministries, He knew we could be trusted in serving the needs of others with integrity. I'm sure God smiled as He miraculously provided larger and larger opportunities of serving others' needs in our community. The people in our church were mostly retired people who were skilled in a trade, and we needed space to capitalize on them—our strongest asset. After looking at several smaller buildings, our leadership decided to take a huge step of faith and set our sights on a building with thirty-five thousand square feet. It was the size of a Kmart and had been empty for fifteen years. It needed a lot of work. But in faith we met together, placed our hands on the building, and prayed for God's miraculous blessings.

We put in one hundred eighty thousand dollars of sweat equity, thereby reducing the rent for the first three years. The night before we officially opened its doors, I went into the facility, knelt down on the bare tile floor surrounded by the empty vastness of the space, and prayed, "Lord, the exciting thing is, it has to be a miracle to work!" There was no merchandise in the outreach center as yet, but God showed it to me by faith. Three days after opening, we had so much donated merchandise that we had to hire an auctioneer to liquidate the surplus items to make room for more. The auction brought in ten thousand dollars!

Did They? Or Didn't They?

Our church had a very active community outreach center that God was blessing financially, spiritually, and emotionally as we helped many people six days a week.

One man had observed the routine of the sales staff for a few days without being too obvious. After all, he was one of them. They knew him by name. They were creatures of habit, he learned, including the store manager, who went home within a thirty-minute window of the same time every night. It really wasn't something he was used to doing—breaking into a store—but the voice on the phone had told him that something was going on in the store that bothered him; he had to know the truth! If not, they would continue getting away with it, and he couldn't allow that to happen.

He waited until the outreach center had closed for the night and everyone had been gone for hours. He dressed in dark clothing and rubber-soled shoes, packing a small bag with essentials necessary for his task at hand. Although he had checked and didn't think the store had an electronic surveillance system, he couldn't be 100 percent sure, and it was bothering him. He didn't want to get in trouble with the police. After all, his purpose wasn't to vandalize or steal but to find out the truth. Information was his goal.

Early the next morning, I received a phone call from our store manager. "David, someone has broken into the center!" The intruder had also broken into the office, and strangely enough, it appeared someone had downloaded all the store computer files. The store manager said he could not find anything stolen. Nothing was damaged, and no other evidence of a break-in was found. He asked if I wanted to file a police report. "Let's hold off on that for just a bit," I told him, wanting some time to pray and let God lead in this situation.

About an hour later, I received another phone call. It was from Danny, a close friend of mine and an elder at our church. "David, I'm sorry, but I was the one who broke into the store last night." When asked why, he explained that someone from the church had told him that my associate pastor and I had possibly been taking money from the store, and he planned to investigate the matter himself. He had broken in so that he could obtain the financial records without fear of them having been altered. For the past few hours he had been looking at all the transactions but could not find any evidence of personal gain by the pastors.

The Bible tells us to first go to someone alone (Matt. 18:15) in hopes for restoration and for correction of misunderstandings, so I confronted him in private and asked, "Why didn't you just ask the manager to view these?" Carefully I explained that what he had done was not only unbiblical but illegal, and we could have him arrested for breaking and entering. "You have really shocked and hurt me with your actions," I told him, still having a hard time comprehending he had actually done such a thing. We were good friends; in fact, I thought he was one of my closest friends. I had even been best man at his wedding. "Couldn't you have trusted me enough to come to me personally and ask me any question you thought appropriate?" Because of using the biblical approach of confronting in love, he apologized, and our fractured relationship was restored. We became closer through this pain.

Do not become discouraged when confronting in love does not work. There will be times when you will feel frustrated when our humanity prevents healing from taking place.

Lesson Learned

For you to be a visionary leader, integrity must be the most important principle of your life. Be ready for others to look at your life through a magnifying glass. Some are unwilling to pay the price. Most do not wish to bear the responsibility of effective leadership. The cost of leadership is great, considering the stress on a leader's personal life. In my non-medical opinion, this is one of the reasons why I believe a number of pastor's wives I've known have an unusually high incidence of poor health. The stress of living in a glass house, trying to defend their husbands against those who create false accusations while overcoming animosity against those same people, can literally be detrimental to their health. They must learn to daily forgive those who do not know what they are doing. Jesus understands this very pain.

When you practice a life of successful service, you can be assured there will be plenty of opposition. The good news is that God is faithful, and He provides the strength needed to face the storm. Satan may knock you down, but not out. Resolve to keep coming back up with the determination of a bobber on a fishing line. When you are fishers of men, get ready for backbiting piranhas. Another benefit is that your character and integrity will be refined as pure gold and stretched to levels where only God can take you.

> Though I have fallen, I will rise!
>
> —Micah 7:8

Belt-less Blunder

Johnny was seventeen years old when he came from Tennessee in 2004 with a group from his school to help after Hurricane Francis hit in Florida. One night after we had eaten supper, a convoy of trucks pulled in with more supplies. The truck drivers asked, "Could you please unload us tonight? We are volunteers and are late getting back to our jobs." I called out to the group, "I need fourteen volunteers to help unload seven more semitrucks." Johnny was the first to raise his hand.

We passed out safety back brace supports, but Johnny exclaimed, "I don't need to wear one. They don't look macho!" We all jumped into the back of the trucks, and everything was going well. Suddenly Johnny cried out, "Oh, my back!" He had been unloading boxes of canned goods, and while turning to hand the box to the next person, had experienced severe back pain.

We helped him off the truck and he sat down on the ground. "I feel like I'm fifty years older. I think I'll listen and follow instructions next time and from now on wear that back support." He reached out to put on something that previously did not look macho but now looked great. It also strengthened and supported his back. Integrity comes by listening and following what we know to be right. After a good night's sleep, his back felt good as new.

Lesson Learned

When you are feeling a little overwhelmed with being tempted to take shortcuts in life by not doing what you know to be right, remember you have on your belt of integrity! Let God fight your battles for you in a preventive way. I like to remind my son, Andrew, that the most important thing people will remember about us is our belt of integrity. Don't leave home without it. Integrity is something we have to learn. It is what we do and how we act when no one else is looking. People without integrity are guaranteed one thing: eventually, their sins will be discovered, and they will feel as lonely as Judas did when he betrayed Jesus, his friend.

PRAYER FOR TODAY: Ephesians 3:14–20

I pray on my knees before You, because You are my Father. I pray that Your glorious, unlimited resources will cause me to grow strong by the power of the Holy Spirit. I pray that I may be rooted and grounded in love and to experience for myself how great Your love is for me. I want to be filled with Your fullness.

Glory be to God, who, because of Your power at work within me, is able to do far more than I would ever dream of asking for or thinking of.

THE NUMBER TWO KEY TO CHANGING YOUR WORLD: Fire Coat and Breathing Apparatus

We must overcome fear factors in life in order to feel safe in service. Do you experience fears that prevent you from serving others freely?

Three big fear factors paralyzing and holding some individuals captive are: fear of the unknown, fear of what people think, and fear of liability. God has freed you to get outside the fence of these false securities and experience the "law of liberty" that sets you free to live!

Spiritual Empowerment

The reason I am strong in Your power is because I prepare, dress, and am equipped, to resist all the attacks of the enemy with my: belt or suspenders (integrity and truth), fire coat and breathing apparatus (confidence of righteousness by faith), boots (peace), shielding gloves (grow faith), helmet, face shield (salvation), and fire hose, halligan, pike pole and ax (God's Word)."

—Ephesians 6:13–15, author's paraphrase

God has not given me the spirit of fear, but of power, love, and a sound mind.

—2 Timothy 1:7, author's paraphrase

From the Hebrew perspective, God was very specific in His instructions for the garments worn by the high priest. You can read those specifications in Exodus 25 and 28. On the breastplate were twelve stones representing the twelve tribes of Israel. Paul quoted Isaiah 59:17 regarding putting on the breastplate of righteousness. The Bible says that our righteousness is like filthy rags (Isa. 64:6), yet we were made to be the righteousness of God in Christ Jesus (2 Cor. 5:21) We have right-standing before God! We can come boldly before His throne because we have right standing with Him. We can stand before Him unashamed, regardless of our past, because in Jesus Christ we have a perfect report card or 4.0 grade-point average in life. Because of Jesus we can stand before God, and He doesn't see us the way we are; He sees us through the blood of Jesus, as perfect in Christ.

Fear is one of the greatest deceptions paralyzing individuals today. One of the main reasons fear has kept people from accomplishing great things in life and for God's kingdom today is because they don't understand that we are free in Jesus! Your salvation is secured when you accept it by faith! "You may know that You have eternal life" (1 John 5:13).

Do you live in a state of feeling unworthy, unsure, or doubting whether God accepts you? Do you speak false statements of humility like, "I am so unworthy," or "I can never be sure God will save me. That would be presumptuous." If so, you need to know God has rescued you from the curse of the Law (Gal. 3:13). He promises never to leave us or forsake us. In fact, the Amplified Bible says in Hebrews 13:5, "[I will] not, [I will] not, [I will] not in any degree leave you helpless nor forsake nor let [you] down (relax My hold on you)! [Assuredly not!]"

A Parable

Firemen wear fire coats or bunker clothes and a breathing apparatus over their chest area, which is essential in providing protection to overcome their fear of fire. The coat is designed to withstand temperatures of 275 degrees for short periods of time. The self-contained breathing apparatus (SCBA) or protective breathing apparatus (PBA) is designed to provide life-saving oxygen for ten to thirty minutes depending upon the amount of physical output in fighting a fire. If you are not active for ten seconds, an alarm sounds from the device, letting others know that you may be in trouble.

FEAR FACTOR NUMBER ONE: Fear of the Unknown

When you understand your unique identity and gifts, this helps you to overcome the fear of the unknown. Have you ever not stepped out to try something new because fear of the unknown paralyzed you?

In my journey of life, I have written a lot of sermon outlines, but this is my first time writing a complete book. As I began to write my thoughts down and ask others for their comments, some were very diplomatic, saying, "Keep struggling, and your thoughts will eventually become clear." There were times when my thoughts just seemed to become paralyzed, and I would have to let the book sit for a few weeks at a time. Others would encourage me by saying, "Your book must be written. There is a huge need for it!"

Maybe you just didn't want to try something new because you first needed to be shown or mentored how to do it. Most occupations do an excellent job in preparing you against the unknown through an internship or orientation program. If you were given that same opportunity in serving others, you would have the training necessary to build your confidence. You would successfully meet many new needs in your church and community. Disaster response teaches you how to overcome the fear of the unknown, because you will never do the same thing twice in your life. You learn the keys to making quick and life-saving decisions. Successful service requires decisive decision makers!

One day, ACTS volunteer youth were cleaning homes that had been filled with the mud that Hurricane Ike left when it struck Texas. Sue, one of the neighbors, watched us work for a while before coming over to where we were working. With tears in her eyes she said, "I have renewed hope in our youth." She glanced around our group, making eye contact with each of us. "I see all of the ACTS volunteers in their maroon shirts and vests helping serve throughout the community. They seem confident and sure of themselves, in a positive way. This is far different from how youth are often portrayed on TV, as being without direction and as being negative, selfish, or disrespectful."

Lesson Learned

Disaster survivors are given hope to overcome their fear of the unknown when they identify volunteers with unique clothing, realizing they are there to help them, not to loot or steal. Survivors take comfort in the fact that trained volunteers are there to help them with emergency supplies, instruct them in receiving financial assistance from the United States Federal Emergency Management Agency (FEMA), and even help them overcome their fear of the unknown or to cope with the desperate feelings and wondering how they are going to survive.

Volunteers who wear identifying shirts or vests automatically act more professional and with a higher degree of self-worth and inner confidence than volunteers who don't. Safety is also increased when some see you as part of a larger team, rather than acting alone.

All ACTS volunteers are required to wear either a shirt or vest identifying them to be with ACTS Disaster Response. ACTS vests accomplish the same thing as our maroon shirts did. The advantage of vests is that they can be passed on from volunteer to volunteer, regardless of what they are wearing, yet still provide the elements of safety and unique identity. Regardless of the task, whether it is serving a hot meal, handing out water, or working in the field removing debris or demucking, vests can be used by everyone and anyone on the team.

Vests, Vests, and More Vests

Two years ago, ACTS needed to make another purchase of three thousand shirts, totaling about fifteen thousand dollars. Rather than purchasing these, I believed that God would provide a new direction—wearing vests, which could be reused much more effectively than shirts.

In the world of emergency response, there are many great organizations that help each other by networking resources. I let some of them know of our immediate need of vests. I reminded myself of what Paul says in Philippians 4:19: "And this same God who takes care of me will supply all my needs from his glorious riches, which have been given to me in Christ Jesus" (author's paraphrase). It says that God will provide from His glorious riches, not from my bank account.

One day I received a phone call from the Convoy of Hope gifts-in-kind director. "One of our suppliers needs us to pick up a semi load of new red vests. Can you use them?" he asked.

"Yes!" I practically shouted with joy. The entire shipment was valued at six hundred thousand dollars! Quite the extravagant gift from God, I'd say! We only needed to pay for shipping, which came to sixteen hundred dollars! The very day we needed to pay this expense, God provided a donor who paid this amount in full. Not only did God provide the vests we needed, but because He is an extravagant God and able to do exceeding abundantly above anything we ask (Eph. 3:20), there were also new police-style safety shirts for security, about one thousand new medical uniforms for our medical teams, and two hundred tropical shirts, which we used for appreciation banquets held at the end of ACTS deployments with the community. The best surprise was that only one box contained red vests, while the rest were a dark royal blue—our new color and the color of our website!

Lesson Learned

God is always just one step ahead of you! Praise Him! He assures you that He knows what your needs are even before you ask (Matt. 6:8)! God knew what color vests we needed and knew just how to provide them. Don't let fear of the unknown keep you from believing for the best blessing of your life today!

FEAR FACTOR NUMBER TWO: Fear of What Others Think

Are you afraid of displeasing someone? Do you believe that if you took time to listen, understand, and barter or sometimes compromise on your position, you would make everyone happy?

Many times it is good to barter or give-and-take to arrive at a solution when you've come to an impasse. This is actually a sign of strength, as long as moral principles are maintained. (Many issues have nothing to do with immorality.) But it can be difficult at times to imagine standing up to people, even when you are carrying out your God-given leadership vision.

For years I was guilty of the fear of rejection or criticism. As a visionary leader, I thought if I could adequately explain all the reasons why change was not only important but vitally necessary, or why a new concept should be implemented, then people would agree. However, it doesn't work that way. People bickering back and forth over trivial issues, such as the color of the carpet or walls in the church, created a very heavy burden for me. Some struggled for power and positions, forgetting to realize that "it is not by might or by power, but by God's Spirit" (Zech. 4:6, author's paraphrase) that great movements of God take place.

Thinking perhaps my diplomacy skills were lacking or that I needed to be more of a servant leader, I took the blame upon myself when others balked at new ideas because of their own fears and/or unbelief. My desire was not only to be the best pastor I could be but to also make a significant impact on the world for Jesus, starting with my own church family. In order to improve my leadership skills, I even took a course in implementing change effectively, which is where I learned that one of the greatest signs of an effective leader is that as change occurs, others take ownership of the idea from the beginning, just one person at a time, until momentum grows to a movement.

What others think of you may be a very real fear in your life. One definition of failure is trying to please everybody, and in the process you please no one. Refrain from allowing a minority of outspoken, critical individuals to hold necessary change captive. Positive, effective individuals are willing to make necessary changes. You will do so because you know that the end result is worthwhile.

Some let unbiblical principles, such as "the church must maintain what the majority finds acceptable or comfortable," bring their demise. Growing churches are not controlled by the traditions of their past but rather focus on what is needed to be relevant in the present.

In global disaster response quite often I am faced with some denominations feeling threatened by ACTS World Relief responding so quickly and effectively. They say, "You are a maverick," in a negative light, because I am not under the control of a slow-moving institution filled with so many levels of bureaucracy that it is difficult to make decisions in an emergency. I let them know that if there were one hundred more emergency response agencies tomorrow, there would not be enough in light of the increasing amount of catastrophic disasters occurring around the world.

Jesus faced the very same issue with the institutionalism of His day and said, "You are destroying the gospel by making your traditions more important!" (Mark 7:13, author's paraphrase). In ministry, one principle is clear: you need to be free to fail. The more we stretch for our best, the more we risk failure. Fear of failure and people's judgment chokes us, and freedom to fail encourages us. Paul says, "I'm not trying to be a people pleaser. No, I am trying to please God. If I were still trying to please people, I would not be Christ's servant" (Gal. 1:10, author's paraphrase).

Your ambitious failure is better than no attempt at all. In 1 Thessalonians 2:4 we read as Paul writes, "You don't understand us; we come not to please men, but to please God" (author's paraphrase). And to quote Richard Needham, "Strong people make as many mistakes as weak people. The difference is, they laugh at them, and learn from them. That is how they become strong."[1] The opposite is also true: if you aim at nothing, you will probably hit it. To say it another way, whether you believe you can or you can't, you're right.

A leader over a denomination's state disaster response agency once told me, "If we had all the money you have, we would be doing as much as you are."

I laughed and looked him directly in the eyes and said, "Every time we leave on a deployment, it is by faith!" His plan was to wait until there was enough money to cover expenses. "We serve a *big* God," I reasoned, "and money always follows ministry, not the other way around."

Living by faith in God's righteousness gives you an inner confidence that moves you from being worried about what others think of you to serving others more effectively. When God is for you, who can be against you (Rom. 8:31)?

FEAR FACTOR NUMBER THREE: Fear of Liability

Is the fear of political or legal liability or personal insecurity preventing you from serving others? This results in the tendency to serve others only if it doesn't involve anything more risky than to attend meetings or share stories about what others are doing. Make a difference by risking being human and knowing liability is very real.

One of the most challenging deployments of ACTS World Relief for adequate volunteers was to Haiti, because some self-insured denominations informed their members, saying, "Do not go to Haiti because it is unsafe." "You do not want to deploy to Haiti on your own without a clear logistical plan, or you will become the disaster as well," they were told. This protected them from being sued, and if they went anyway they were not covered. While some were banning their members, others were sending them by the thousands. Did Jesus say, "Everyone will know that you are My disciples if you demonstrate love to one another, but only if it is safe to do so," in John 13:35? Or in Galatians 6:3, "If you think you are too important to help someone in need, you are only fooling yourself. You are really a nobody"?

Jesus was quite radical when He demonstrated serving with unconditional love by willingly giving up His life for us: "And so we ought to give up our lives for our Christian brothers and sisters (and neighbors)" (1 John 3:16, author's paraphrase).

One of the greatest challenges that I've had to overcome is when my critics say things like, "Youth are too young," or when they express their concern that "youth should not be used, because it is too unsafe," or "no one is needed." It seems as if these people seek to create fear using the guise of expressing concern regarding safety in the form of accusations such as, "You are not practicing being safe," or, "You are placing yourself in unsafe environments." These critics are correct in recognizing that there is indeed a real risk with first response ministries. Yet in most of these cases, the ones appearing to offer their superior counsel were feeling guilty for not doing enough to help the hurting. God has not called us to spend the majority of our time justifying our jobs in committee meetings; instead He asks, "What did you actually do to help the hurting. Did you live to love others?" The greatest miracles in history have occurred when someone was willing to take a risk for God's kingdom! From a practical standpoint, emergency response liability fears are best overcome through providing training in safety and group team techniques. ACTS utilizes nationally recognized accreditation in CERT and a range of seven different Homeland Security Incident Systems courses. ACTS is also accredited with the Department of Health as emergency health professionals. Collaborating with others helps create a barrier of separation of direct liability from those seeking to sue institutions. We also require others to carry an additional private liability insurance policy, which is only about twenty dollars per deployment.

George, from Southwestern University, said after serving in the aftermath of Hurricane Ike in Texas, "Thank you so much for providing me the opportunity to serve. Years ago, I wanted to help with Katrina survivors, but my previous school chaplain told me other volunteers were more qualified. Now at last you have given me this opportunity to help feed and help those in need, empowered me to realize my dream, and helped me overcome the fear that I would be a liability to my school and not be good enough!"

Lesson Learned

George learned to overcome a fear that others saw him as a liability in serving others. Do you see yourself as a liability in serving God?

Your greatest training comes from learning that you are the righteousness of God, or complete, in Christ Jesus. When you fill yourself with God's Word, you realize how God empowers you to meet the needs of others, overcoming all fear of personal liability or inadequacy.

Let's Celebrate!

When we were first beginning our thrift store ministry at Life-Changing Christian Center, we had radically stepped out in faith by committing ourselves to lease a building the size of a Kmart. We knew there were those who seemed more comfortable looking at the bottom line rather than working out the vision by faith. I understood where they were coming from, but it didn't get us anywhere. Believe me, if God hadn't confirmed His Word to me for this, we wouldn't have stepped out in faith.

Don, a leader in my denomination's community service program, came to me, saying, "The Bible says I am to come to you first if I have a problem with you." Immediately I sent up a prayer for a fresh anointing of love as he continued, "I'm just letting you know that I don't think beginning such a large community outreach center is a very good idea. If it fails, it will not reflect well to God's church and this community." I thanked Don for his counsel. Of course, I knew there was a great risk for failure by opening this thirty-five thousand square foot facility with no inventory or real funding, but I believed this was what God was leading us to do.

After our first three years we had helped forty-three thousand people, doubled the membership of our active church, funded fifty-seven new ministries, and grossed over one million dollars (including that which we gave away), which went right back into helping the needs of our hurting community. God had been faithful, and we were abundantly blessed.

It had been such a significant year—going from nothing to something terrific—that we decided to hold a special celebration service to mark our one-year anniversary. By then Don had heard of the tremendous impact we'd had in the community. Once vehemently against the whole idea, he now asked me, "May I speak at your first year anniversary celebration ceremony?" Don asked me to forgive him for his skepticism and asked if I would teach other churches throughout the state how to replicate this concept. I wanted to laugh, not at him but from sheer joy at the goodness of God. As much as Don was against us in the beginning, he was now passionately showing his support of our ministry to others.

This community outreach center has inspired others to open their own centers. We have also used it as a training center for many youth, adults, and retired individuals to find true fulfillment.

Lesson Learned

Learn to listen with two ears: one ear to listen to God, and the other ear to hear the cries of hurting people and well-intentioned counsel of others. This helps lower the risk of various forms of liability in serving others so God's kingdom can be glorified! Do you listen with both ears?

PRAYER FOR TODAY:

Romans 8:37

Lord, I thank you that today overwhelming victory is mine!

NUMBER THREE KEY TO CHANGING YOUR WORLD: Boots Bring Peace

How can the boots or shoes you wear help bring peace to serving others?

When you put on the boots or shoes of peace described in Ephesians 6, it prepares you to run swiftly and effectively with confidence! You need peace to run through the hot coals of potential disasters in life and have protection on your feet when you step on them. When you get wounded enough times, you learn what not to do more effectively. Inner peace provides one of the greatest blessings during your journey.

Spiritual Empowerment

The reason I am strong in Your power is because I prepare, dress, and am equipped, to resist all the attacks of the enemy with my: belt or suspenders (integrity and truth), fire coat and breathing apparatus (confidence of righteousness by faith), boots (peace), shielding gloves (grow faith), helmet, face shield (salvation), and fire hose, halligan, pike pole and ax (God's Word).

—EPHESIANS 6:13–15, AUTHOR'S PARAPHRASE

Thank You Lord, for being with me always.

—MATTHEW 28:20, AUTHOR'S PARAPHRASE

I run the race of life that You have provided for me. I am successful, because I keep my eyes on You.

—HEBREWS 12:1–2, AUTHOR'S PARAPHRASE

I am in perfect peace, because I am fully committed to You.

—Isaiah 26:3, author's paraphrase

I have peace with God.

—Romans 5:1, author's paraphrase

I have peace in You.

—John 16:33, author's paraphrase

Your peace will guard my heart.

—Philippians 4:7, author's paraphrase

To this day soldiers are required to wear boots at all times, whether in combat or in the barracks. They practice how to jump into them quickly if necessary in order to be ready to take immediate action to protect their lives and the lives of others. Many have heard the rhythmic sound of military-issue boots as soldiers who have bravely defended their country's freedom march in parades, eliciting the grateful cheers of the people. For others, boots illustrate being on the frontlines of battlefields literally or spiritually. This illustrates that the most important thing for us to realize is that we must be prepared to run the race of life with swiftness and effectiveness. Being confident that your feet are protected also brings a peace of mind.

The only way to begin and finish any kind of race is to try to be prepared the best way you know how. Once I entered a race running on a blacktop oval track next to someone who thought they could run faster without shoes. It may have been a good idea at first, but very quickly the pain of running across the hot, black, asphalt coupled with the tender sensitivity of growing blisters slowed him down, and I was able to beat him effortlessly. It was because he was not properly prepared. Run each day by claiming the gift of peace in your hectic day!

A Parable

A fireman's boots are hazardous-materials resistant, with steel shanks and steel toes to provide protection. If their feet get hurt, they will be unable to get in or out of the fire.

In disaster response, we insist that volunteers wear boots, especially if they are going to be removing any kind of debris. The risk of stepping on glass, nails, or dropping a couch or chair on one's toes is very high.

Sarah learned firsthand just how vitally important it was to have steel-toed boots. She came running up to me with a big smile on her face, "Look at these boots of mine," she said as she pointed at her leather- and steel-encased feet. "They just saved my toes from getting crushed! I was loading a case of water from the distribution line into that car over there when the driver accidentally ran over the tips of my toes!" Rejoicing with her, I was thankful that she had come prepared to meet the unexpected. Because of her preparedness, she avoided what could have been a very painful and potentially debilitating experience. What might have happened if she had not had on such good safety boots? She was able to serve others with confidence!

Born to Ride!

"Could you please give me the best motorcycle boots money can buy?" I asked the saleswoman at the motorcycle store. I had just purchased a 250cc two-stroke Suzuki motorcycle, which had enough power to pull wheelies about as long as I ever dreamed of. "I would like steel-toed boots in case I dump the motorcycle over onto my toes to keep them from breaking." It was important the saleswoman understood how critical it was to obtain the right pair of boots.

"They're not going to be cheap," the saleswoman warned. The best never are. While watching as she added the price of the boots to the appropriate tax, the final price displayed on the cash register. I swallowed twice. "Wow, are you sure you didn't include an insurance policy with those boots?" I asked jokingly. However, I felt certain I had purchased the best protective boots they had to offer.

With the motorcycle engine revving, I felt pretty confident and at peace wearing my new boots at an advanced motorcycle track designed for jumping hills called burms or moguls. I went around the first lap of the track slowly, learning where the turns were and mentally preparing myself to gauge how much throttle was needed to clear from landing one jump to the next. It was about twenty feet that I needed to be in the air between each hill. I began jumping from one hill to the next, gaining more confidence with each jump. After sailing through the air on a long jump, I then had to make a quick turn around a corner, preparing for the next jump. All of a sudden I landed in some very deep sand, which began turning my handle bars sharply. I countered by giving full-throttle and throwing sand fifteen feet into the air, trying to power through the corner.

The next thing I knew, the motorcycle dumped over, and I was lying next to the motorcycle with my foot twisted and stuck beneath the weight of the frame and the ground. It was embarrassing, as several spectators had watched me fall. Quickly I pushed the motorcycle off my leg and foot, stood up, and got back on my motorcycle. As soon as it revved back to life, I sped off again. What a freak accident!

I could have smashed into the side of a hill in mid air or something more dramatic, but actually I was mad at myself for dumping the motorcycle on my foot because I had miscalculated the deep sand—a motorcycle racer's worst nightmare come true. I was also mad because of the sharp pain in my one foot. When I drove the motorcycle back to where my son, Andrew, and his friends were standing, they noticed the look on my face was more of a grimace than a smirk. I removed my new boot and gingerly tried to wiggle my toes. *Youch!* It appeared all five of my toes were broken—and while wearing the best safety boots money could buy! That wasn't supposed to happen. It was not like I had flown two hundred feet through the air and landed wrong. This was a simple turn gone awry. Carefully I put my boot back on and seriously felt like demanding a full refund. I refused to let this finish what started to be a perfectly good day, so I rode for another three hours, grimacing every time I shifted.

Three months later I decided to go to the doctor and have my foot x-rayed because it was still painful to walk on. "Well, it's amazing that all five toes are healing in place," he said as he pointed to the cracks on each toe on the X-rays. "Normally in order to speed up the healing process, we recommend using crutches and maybe a cast to keep you from walking on broken toes!"

Lesson Learned

Keep on beginning each day with God, even when everything seems to go wrong and you almost lose your peace. Keep searching for God, and you will find Him when you search with all your heart (Jer. 29:13). This will give you confidence to overcome all the power of the enemy and challenges that arise in your life!

Do you think when bad things happen to you that even though you pray each day for God to protect and deliver you from all evil and accidents, your prayers are not heard? Have you ever made the best plans to be well-prepared spiritually, financially, physically, and emotionally for whatever battle this old world might throw your way and had them go terribly wrong? Did you lose your peace halfway through the journey? Remember, God doesn't promise to keep everything bad from coming your way, but He does promise to lead you out on the other side victorious and stronger for it! Psalm 23 says, "Even when I go through the valley, I will fear no evil because I am confident that You are there with me!" (v. 4, author's paraphrase). That's a great insurance policy!

Remember to thank God for the gift of peace He has given you, the peace that passes all understanding (Phil. 4:7), the kind of peace that doesn't make any sense considering present circumstances. Because of this gift, you can confidently claim by faith as you begin each day, "I have peace, because I am hidden away in the secret place of the most high God where no evil will harm me" (Ps. 91:1, author's paraphrase).

PRAYER FOR TODAY:

The Prayer of Aaron, Numbers 6:24-26

Bless and protect me. Smile upon me and be gracious to me. Show me Your favor, and give me Your peace.

NUMBER FOUR KEY TO CHANGING YOUR WORLD: Gloves Grow Faith

Big faith accomplishes big miracles in serving others!

Gloves are today's contemporary parallel of a shield of faith. When you hold up a shield, it protects you from objectionable objects. Gloves are one of the simplest and most useful items you can have. Every day, practice putting on imaginary or real gloves and exercise your faith to accomplish the impossible!

Spiritual Empowerment

The reason I am strong in Your power is because I prepare, dress, and am equipped, to resist all the attacks of the enemy with my: belt or suspenders (integrity and truth), fire coat and breathing apparatus (confidence of righteousness by faith), boots (peace), shielding gloves (grow faith), helmet, face shield (salvation), and fire hose, halligan, pike pole and ax (God's Word).

—Ephesians 6:13–15, author's paraphrase

Lord, I live by faith by putting You first before doctors, lawyers, beginning the day, and eating.

—Matthew 6:33, author's paraphrase

Without faith it is impossible to please You.

—Hebrews 11:6, author's paraphrase

The victory which overcomes every obstacle is faith!

—1 John 5:4, author's paraphrase

Whatever is not of faith is sin.

—Romans 14:23, author's paraphrase

Work gloves are probably the most important clothing item in disaster response work. It seems we never have enough work gloves around. Gloves allow our volunteers to handle unloading thousands of bags of ice, along with a wide variety of emergency supplies. Most importantly, they protect their hands from nails and sharp objects during cleaning operations.

One day I was with a commercial tree farmer who was donating five vans and pickup trucks to ACTS. He then asked, "Do you need any gloves?"

I responded enthusiastically, "Yes!"

He continued, "I would like to give you about five thousand pairs of new gloves as well." God was trying to let me know that He was equipping ACTS with what it needed to serve effectively!

Lesson Learned

God says to you today, "I not only have called you to serve others needs, but I will also provide you the tools necessary to succeed!"

A Parable

Firemen's gloves are invaluable in providing both the protection and confidence to save those trapped in a fire.

Tommy and Big Faith

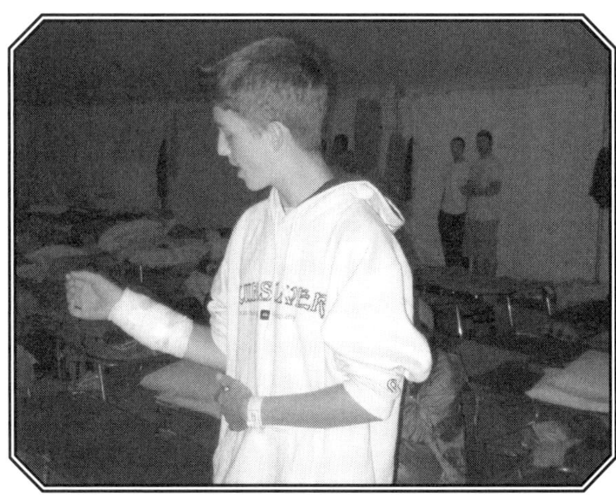

One day in Purvis, Mississippi, Tommy was helping to remove debris from a house that had been flooded with four feet of water from Hurricane Katrina. Everything was going just great until he had the brainstorm to do something that he had seen in a *Die Hard* movie. Feeling quite invincible with his leather gloves protecting his hands and being full of the fun-loving, arrogant cockiness of an adventurous teenage boy, Tommy walked over to a nearby window with a Bruce Willis strut and proceeded to smash it with his fist. Of course, this wasn't the set of a blockbuster movie, and there were no stunt doubles or computer-generated graphics. Special effects are not as simple as Hollywood would have you think, especially in real life. Tommy expected the window to simply smash into pieces. His fist did go through the window all right, but a big, jagged piece of glass remained intact, cutting a very deep gash about six inches long right up his arm. The laceration had severed an artery, and blood was pumping out profusely.

Thankfully, both Tommy and the adult leaders reacted quickly, creating a tourniquet. They brought him over to me. "Please pray for Tommy not to have permanent injury," they asked.

I looked at the teenager, all bravado and arrogance gone from his demeanor. "Tommy, do you believe God wants to bring miraculous healing to your arm?"

Not hesitating a bit and with child-like faith he exclaimed, "Yes!"

"Let's believe for your miracle together," I encouraged Tommy. Then bowing our heads, we prayed, "Lord, You have said that by Your stripes we can receive healing by faith. We know You did not come to steal, kill, and destroy everything good from Tommy's life, but rather You have promised to give Him life and healing in Jesus' name. Amen!" Then he was rushed off to the hospital.

The emergency room doctor told Tommy that he was a very fortunate young man. "If you had not acted as quickly as you did, you would have bled to death." About a year later Tommy told me that he had complete use of his arm. It was if his accident had never happened—well, other than learning some valuable lessons and getting a long scar.

Lesson Learned

When you leave off certain pieces of your God-given protective equipment, like gloves, you leave yourself more susceptible to ongoing setbacks. And, even though you may put on all of God's protective gear, it does not guarantee you a life free from attacks. The good news is that God promises, "[I will] not, [I will] not, [I will] not in any degree leave you helpless nor forsake nor let [you] down (relax My hold on you)!" (Heb. 13:5).

Tommy's faith was rewarded because he first sought out the Great Physician, who says, "I will never fail you or forsake you!" (Heb. 13:5, author's paraphrase).

PRAYER FOR TODAY:

1 John 5:4

Thank You, Lord, for giving me victory to defeat temptation today, because I trust in You.

NUMBER FIVE KEY TO CHANGING YOUR WORLD: the Helmet, Face Shield of Salvation

When you serve others knowing that your salvation is secure, it makes you successful! Today you should put on your helmet or face shield, real or imagined. Remind yourself that you are blessed and highly favored. Your salvation is secure!

The helmet represents the security of salvation as long as you continually accept it by faith. It is probably one of the most important items in life. Without it, you're headed for certain destruction. If you forget what Jesus has accomplished for you, you're in trouble! Justification describes how we have already been made righteous, which is right-standing with God. Jesus, who knew no sin, was made sin in our place. We who knew no righteousness were made the righteousness of God in Christ Jesus. We are righteous in Christ

(2 Cor. 5:21). This is what you receive instantly as a free gift when you make Jesus Lord of your life.

The second aspect of salvation is sanctification. This is the process of becoming more like Jesus in everything you say and do. It is a life-long process.

> Even while you were yet sinning, you were considered valuable enough for Jesus to pay the price of your sins.
>
> —Romans 5:8, author's paraphrase

We've always been His treasure, and when we accept what He has already done for us, we recognize our worth in Him. Yes, He loves us just the way we are, but He is unwilling to leave us that way. The Father wants us to become more like Jesus, and the more we become like Him, the more valuable we are to His kingdom. One of the easiest ways to become more like Him is to reach out to help someone else. This is the process of releasing the unique gifts with which God has blessed you.

Spiritual Empowerment

> The reason I am strong in Your power is because I prepare, dress, and am equipped, to resist all the attacks of the enemy with my: belt or suspenders (integrity and truth), fire coat and breathing apparatus (confidence of righteousness by faith), boots (peace), shielding gloves (grow faith), helmet, face shield (salvation), and fire hose, halligan, pike pole and ax (God's Word).
>
> —Ephesians 6:13–15, author's paraphrase

> I am made right in God's sight because I trust in Jesus to take away my sins.
>
> —Romans 3:22, author's paraphrase

In ancient Hebrew attire, the turban was made of white fine linen. Generally, fine white linen signifies righteous deeds (Rev. 19:8). Here the emphasis is on our mind, the covering of our thought processes, "taking every thought captive to the obedience of Christ" (2 Cor. 10:5) by taking "the helmet of salvation" (Eph. 6:17). Our mind is the big problem. Thoughts become words, words become actions, actions become habits, and habits become character. It all starts in the mind.

Attached to the Hebrew turban and upon the forehead of the high priest was the crown, a gold plate on which "Holy to the Lord" was engraved (Exod.

28:36–39). This seal of God is legitimately there on the forehead of our Lord Jesus Christ, our great High Priest. But for us, whom He has also made priests (Rev. 1:5–6), there is a clear indication that we are not just to be outwardly dressed up in Christ; He must transform us by the renewing of our mind, that we may prove the will of God our sanctification (Rom. 12:2; 1 Thess. 4:3). We need to be renewed in the spirit of our mind, to put on the new man created in righteousness and true holiness (Eph. 4:23–24).

One of the fastest ways to develop your spirituality is to volunteer alongside someone involved in jail ministry. If you minister to the inmates thinking you are there to help them because they are so bad and you're so good, they will see right through you. They can read you like a book. If you go to minister with a willingness to also listen, they will share with you some of the profound truths that Jesus has revealed to them, which will last for a lifetime. They will also expose traces of hypocrisy or a judgmental attitude that you may have.

I am very thankful that God is so patient with us in this journey of life. The more we decide to trust in ourselves and leave off our helmets, the more knocks-on-our-head consequences we experience. A head wound creates a major bleeding problem. You don't have to experience major blood loss to know that this is true. Jesus says, "I've already done that for you."

Don't allow your sins, not even the one over which you desperately want to gain victory, to get you discouraged! Endeavor to help others gain victory in that same area. This is sowing seeds. God promises that we reap what we sow (Gal. 6:7). Give and it shall be given back to you (Luke 6:38). Together you will be blessed, and in the process, you will become more like Jesus.

A Parable

The fireman's helmet and bill, or overhang, is what keeps falling debris and hot melting tar from causing a fatal head injury. The face shield (or Nomex hood) is a separate piece of equipment. When worn together, these pieces join to protect the head and shoulders. This provides protection over the face and neck when objects fly or explode.

Father-Son Outing

My son, Andrew, and I went for a motorcycle ride together driving our new 250cc dirt bikes. After gaining the confidence and skill with our previous 125cc bikes, we had decided we were ready to push the envelope a little more and stepped up the adrenaline factor. By that point we had been driving motorcycles that had the capability of popping wheelies much easier and sustaining the ride on one wheel longer, which seemed to be an effortless and achievable goal.

My wife clearly let me know that I should set the right example for safe riding, and more importantly, I'd better bring our son home in one piece.

We pulled the motorcycle trailer out to a special place where there were some good mogul jumps. Before starting out, we put on the most important item of protection, our helmets.

Leading the way, I turned to issue a last-minute warning to my son: "Andrew stay behind me and try to control yourself!" Having grown up racing motorcycles, I knew how great the temptations were for speed. I didn't want him to be unsafe and end up going too fast.

Things were going quite well. It was a beautiful day, and the wind was whipping across our faces. The vibration of the more powerful engines beneath us, combined with the crucial necessity and sheer thrill of purposefully choosing a jump, mentally calculating speed, distance, and timing fueled our excitement in anticipating that perfect speed rush. I zoomed up the incline to find myself sailing through the air with the feel of that glorious freedom one can only experience in free flight. The moment was over far too soon, as the bike and I hit the ground as one on the other side with precision balance, and I raced on to the next adrenaline thrill. It was exhilarating! The natural competition between two men, combined with the camaraderie of father and son, made this time worthy of capturing as one of those unforgettable mental movies that we each hold dear, etched in the recesses of our minds.

Every so often, and with the eternally protective instincts of a father, I continued to look over my shoulder at my son. As he gave me the thumbs up sign, my heart was practically exploding with the joy of the Lord for giving us this opportunity for such great fun and for the blessing of Andrew, whom I love dearly. This was the life!

I knew my wife would be so proud of me for heeding her words. I could almost see myself on a giant poster ad: The Greatest Dad—A Role Model for Safety. The next thing I knew, I looked back, and he was gone. Quickly turning my motorcycle around, I raced back to where I had last seen him. I was thinking there was perhaps a complication with the motorcycle. I can't even find words to describe to you the utter shock and terror that filled my heart when I found him lying unconscious about ten feet from what used to be a perfectly good motorcycle. (Later I learned that he had dropped back to allow enough room between himself and me so there would be plenty of space for him to pop a good wheelie over two of the moguls and fly through the air with the greatest of ease.)

I jumped off my motorcycle, barely coming to a complete stop before it fell to the ground with a thud that couldn't even begin to match the thud of my heart.

Frantically, I looked around the area trying to assess what had happened. There were three pine trees with their bark removed where Andrew must have grazed them. Pieces of his motorcycle were strewn about the area. Simultaneously, I prayed from the depths of my heart, "Father! We need a miracle here!"

Immediately, something changed in my spirit, and I was able to think a little more clearly. I did what no parent should ever have to do and placed my fingers on his neck to see if he was still alive. With a whoosh of relief that reached down to my toes, I let out the breath I didn't even realize I'd been holding. "Oh, praise God!" I breathed without conscious vocal utterance, when all of a sudden Andrew's eyes fluttered open. "Don't move!" I cautioned him, now fully back into my father role. I knew that if his neck were broken, any kind of movement could cause paralysis, if he wasn't paralyzed already.

"Try to wiggle your toes," I encouraged, willing them to do so with such intensity I could almost see my desire reach out to move his toes for him.

"I can't feel them," he responded weakly. My heart pounded in my chest, a different type of adrenaline rush pulsating in a deafening rhythm within me.

"Can you move your fingers?" There was a slight pause as his brain reacted to my question and slowly sent the correct impulses to his fingers in compliance.

"Yes, I can move them."

"Can you move your head?" This was the critical part.

"No," he said after mentally going through the motions of trying to move his head from left to right and vice versa.

A newfound sense of calm and trust I knew could only have come from God had replaced the sheer horror and fear I had felt just moments before. "Let's pray for God to send us a four-wheel-drive pickup truck," I suggested. Somewhere deep inside I knew even this was an opportunity for me to model faith to my son. The spirit within my subconscious breaking through reality and reaching for the impossible caused me to add, "… and before it gets dark."

My cell phone didn't get any reception where we were, so I was unable to call for emergency help. We were far from any of the well traveled trails. In fact, we were way out in the middle of nowhere, and with only forty-five minutes of daylight left. What was supposed to have been a fun, short, quick ride together had turned into a father's worst nightmare.

"Lord," I began, sensing the strength of my faith rise with every tick of time. After all, God is a Father too. He understood! "We want to thank You for providing a pickup truck because You have promised that if we ask, we receive, for You love to give good gifts to your children."

Andrew then said, "Dad, I can move my head now." The physical shock of his body slamming against the trees at such a high velocity was starting to wear off. With a tenderness that was as much caution against any physical damage as it was love flowing freely from my heart, I proceeded to help him remove the helmet that had surely saved his life. There was a large crack in it from the impact. For a split second I couldn't help but think what he might have looked like if he had not been wearing one.

One of Andrew's gloves had literally been torn off his hand and now laid over with a part of the clutch handle, close to one of the trees he had hit. "I can now move my toes," Andrew's voice interrupted my thoughts, and I noticed his voice was a bit stronger, sounding more like himself.

"But I can't move my shoulder," he continued.

All of a sudden, Andrew said excitedly, "Listen, I can hear someone coming!" This was only about ten minutes after the accident.

Jumping to my feet, I began waving wildly with both arms and yelling, "Over here! Over here!" I wanted to cry for joy and utter amazement at the goodness of God, for He had provided not one but two four-wheel-drive pickup trucks. Four strapping, muscle-bound men in their twenties loaded Andrew's mangled motorcycle, along with the various parts that had broken free upon impact, in the back of one pickup. They then laid Andrew in the back of the other pickup.

"How did you ever find us?" I asked incredulously.

"I don't know," the driver merely shrugged. They followed as I led the way out of the forest on my motorcycle to where our vehicle was parked, about two miles away. By then it was dark as I laid Andrew down in the large back seat of our Lincoln Town Car, making him as comfortable as possible. Then I drove to the hospital emergency room as fast as I dared.

The emergency room doctor explained that it was Andrew's helmet that had protected him from receiving more serious injuries from the accident. Thankfully he only sustained a broken wrist and shoulder.

Lesson Learned

Wearing a helmet can save your life! This provides a limited sense of security when riding something that goes fast.

Money cannot buy the best security, which is God's salvation, but He offers it freely as a gift to everyone who asks for it. Are you that person today? Then His free gift of salvation is for you too! Now that you have accepted Him, put on your helmet of your security of salvation by faith each day.

PRAYER FOR TODAY:
Hebrews 10:22-23

Lord, I come into Your presence with:

1. **A sincere heart,**
2. **Full assurance of faith,**
3. **Freedom from guilt because of Your sacrifice.**

I thank You that because of Calvary I am born again! I hold fast to the hope I profess because You are faithful, according to Your promises!

NUMBER SIX KEY TO CHANGING YOUR WORLD: Fire Hose, Halligan, Pole, Ax—Defeating Satan with God's Word

Do you use faith in God's Word to fight your battles of living an unselfish life?

All of the other items listed in the armor of God were protective in nature. Now you get to the fun part of Christianity—using God's Word by faith! This is when you see God do awesome things *through you*! People get excited about God when they see His miraculous power. God's Word is the aggressive side of life, where you can literally watch Him crush every obstacle in your path. Those habits that seemed insurmountable become only a memory, and impossibilities are made possible when you take God seriously by faith. Remember, God's Word is more than just reading about history. It tells you who you are and what you can have and do as well. It's about what He wants to do in your life now! "Jesus is the same yesterday and today and forever" (Heb. 13:8).

Spiritual Empowerment

> The reason I am strong in Your power is because I prepare, dress, and am equipped, to resist all the attacks of the enemy with my: belt or suspenders (integrity and truth), fire coat and breathing apparatus (confidence of righteousness by faith), boots (peace), shielding gloves (grow faith), helmet, face shield (salvation), and fire hose, halligan, pike pole and ax (God's Word).
>
> —Ephesians 6:13–15, author's paraphrase

> Your Word is full of living power.
>
> —Hebrews 4:12, author's paraphrase

Years ago I published a Bible promise book called *Experience Big Faith*. This pocket-sized book simply took God's promises and rephrased them into personalized, "now-faith" confessions. Your faith will rise by confessing, or speaking to others, what God's Word says. By speaking His promises over your life, your future, and your family, it helps build your faith, plus it activates the power encapsulated in each promise, which brings it to pass. The main challenge we face as Christians is to focus on the good. This is why reading and claiming Bible promises is a blessing. It helps give you an anchor and turns your focus to how good will ultimately rule in spite of the bad. Bible promises also remind us that the battle has already been won in our defense if we claim it by faith!

Experience Big Faith shares six spirits that kill the miracle of God's Word being activated in your life.[2] The Spirit of:

1. Fear (2 Tim. 1:7)
2. Doubt (the way one speaks and thinks that expresses faithlessness, and surrounding oneself with well-meaning but faithless friends; Matt. 21:21; Prov. 13:20)
3. Pride (Mark 7:13)
4. Loving sin (Ps. 66:18)
5. Selfishness (James 2:17)
6. Unforgiveness (James 5:16; Mark 11:25)

The big faith promise book uses this method of applying God's Word to your life to allow you to experience miracle-working transformations.

God loves to bless you with His gifts. Why? Because His Word is sure. God says we are "heirs according to the promise" (Gal. 3:29), and He tells us, "All My promises are 'yes' and 'amen'!" (1 Cor. 1:20, author's paraphrase).

A Parable

Firemen use either a one and three-quarter-inch hose for most fires, or a two-and-a-half-inch hose for large fires. These are manned by two firemen working together as a team. If the hose nozzle is set on fog spray, this is usually to protect those close to a fire by lowering the temperature, if set on straight tip the water can shoot seventy to ninety feet. If you adjust the nozzle to the left it means "life." If you adjust it to the right, the stream reaches out for distance to quench the fire. The water from the hose represents the power of the Holy Spirit to calm the raging inferno of challenges around us. The halligan or hooligan is the smashing pole, which is used many times in place of the ax. Many times an eight-foot-long pipe pole is used to smash through ceilings to find out where the fire might be originating. God's Word smashes through any stronghold or douses any fire that seeks to destroy you.

Hot Dogs!

I never thought I would live to see the day when people would die for lack of water and food in the good old U.S.A. When we got news of Hurricane Katrina's predicted impact, ACTS's fleet of semitrucks and mobile kitchens were stocked and loaded, ready to roll. First of all, we distributed about one million dollars of donated emergency supplies in Fort Lauderdale, in southern Florida, where Katrina left damages from a Category 2 effect. Then we reloaded and camped out with a seventeen-truck caravan in High Springs, in northern Florida, at Camp Kulaqua, a private Christian camp, where they offered us free housing. Katrina was gaining strength in the Gulf, and we had to wait until it came ashore again.

As soon as the hurricane passed, we were back on the road again. The extreme heat (one hundred degrees and above) and heavy loads were a lethal combination. This caused quite a few blowouts on the semis, even though many of the tires were brand new. We learned a hard lesson that day—traveling in such a large convoy was not wise, as it slowed us down considerably.

We drove about two hundred miles, which took us six hours, before we came to a police barricade. They had closed the highway. "Will you provide our caravan an escort for emergency relief?" I asked.

After making a few calls to various police departments farther ahead, they told us, "We are understaffed and wish we could, but we are not able to provide an escort into the area where you are going because there are so many accidents." However, they allowed us to take a different route. I believed this was because our logo, which read in big letters "ACTS Disaster Response," was on the sides of the trucks.

Driving became unusually difficult. It was starting to get dark. Vehicles and trees littered the highway. It appeared as if some of the drivers had been in a hurry and were caught unaware. They were not expecting to find debris in the middle of the interstate and were forced to leave their cars. Fallen tree limbs had totaled many of the abandoned vehicles. It gave us an eerie feeling to see where a major disaster had taken place, but it was as if no one remained. One flatbed semi had tried going around one such tree and had fallen over an embankment. The truck had rolled several times, crushing the cab. Thankfully, we heard the driver survived.

"It took us about five hours to go about eight miles," CBS quoted me in their documentary on ACTS.[3] As we traveled, a group of men walked in front of the caravan clearing trees. Another crew was on the top of the lead semi, clearing tree limbs that were hanging down sideways into the highway. In some places, we had to have two individuals on the top of our semitrucks and trailers to hold up power lines with poles, allowing us to pass underneath. Various pieces of equipment got snagged and ultimately broke off. Gashes were cut into the sides of our semitrailers and kitchens, grotesquely marring our new logos on them. The good news is that sixteen hours after leaving Florida (it should have taken us eight), we finally made it to our destination in Purvis, Mississippi, where Bass Academy had sustained a category 3 tornado. Most of the time tornados spin off around the outskirts of hurricanes, causing more damage than the hurricane itself!

The faculty at Bass Academy, a private boarding school in Mississippi, offered us a place to stay while we helped their devastated community. There was no electricity or water for miles around, but we were very grateful. Upon our arrival about one o'clock in the morning, Ginger, the girls' dean, gave us a big hug and simply said, "We knew you would come to help us, so we left the candles burning." Now, she had spoken in faith!

The next day, after visiting several Emergency Operation Centers and speaking with the police, we were designated the responsibility of providing hot meals for five surrounding counties. Neither the Red Cross nor other support agencies had arrived yet due to the extreme conditions and having too few organizations to cover the hundreds of miles of complete devastation.

Within three days of being there, it was evident that without restocking capabilities at our various mobile kitchen and distribution sites we would need not just one but a series of miracles to keep going. We would need enough water for about forty-five of us to bathe. We found that there was a pool at the Academy, however it had turned green because the pump was broken. Thankfully, we had a small generator, which we used to keep the water running for purification purposes. We then hooked up our large generators on our semitrailers to the power fuse boxes in the men's and women's dormitories in order to provide emergency power for lights and basic AC units used for combating the unbearable heat inside for sleeping. Because it was much cooler outside, I had been sleeping outside on the sidewalk, despite the buzzing and biting mosquitoes. Now we could walk into the bathrooms without flashlights. We could actually see where to flush the toilets after using them with five gallon buckets of water.

The city's water officials came to our site and asked if there was a chance of us bringing both of our 80,000-watt generators, which we were using for the dormitories, to the city municipality, where they might be able to power the city water pump to provide city water. This would also make the whole community's toilets functional. We quickly realized that if we could bless the city with our power supply, this would end up blessing thousands, rather than just ourselves. We moved these two generators to the city municipality but discovered they were not large enough. (Later, we were blessed with a larger 165,000-watt generator, which solved this particular need for future situations like this.) It had only taken six days before we could flush the toilets once again. What a beautiful thing! The water was still condemned for drinking, but at least we had some to boil and flush toilets with. It would be months until those farther away on the coast would experience the luxury of water.

Jim Ingersoll (an associate Director of Education), came to our site. After looking over the situation he asked, "Could you use some great youth energy to help with your distribution and feeding? If so, how many could you use effectively?"

"About one hundred and fifty per day," I responded.

Next Jim asked, "Can you feed and house them if I send them with their school leaders to supervise?"

"Absolutely," I responded.

Within two days students were on site. The rest is history. Every student left having had the life-changing experience of being the hands and feet of Jesus. Over the years Jim has helped deploy thousands of trained students to aid victims of hurricanes, tornados, and floods across the U.S. with ACTS World Relief. *Youth will rally to a vision of responsible leadership when given the opportunity to succeed and feel needed!*

Miracle of Multiplying Hot Dogs

At one kitchen, the student volunteers were feeding an average of fifty-five hundred people per meal. Before one meal, one leader told me, "We've only got about fifteen hundred hot dogs. Everything else has been used."

For me, in any seemingly impossible situation my first reaction is to turn to my Dad. The One with an unlimited supply of everything and anything, the One who owns all the gold and all the silver, would supply our needs! "Call your team together to claim God's Word," I simply replied.

In just a few minutes a group of youths had gathered, and with their hands outstretched, they thanked God that He would supply all the needs of the hungry, hurting community according to His riches in glory. When they opened their eyes, it appeared that the same number of hot dogs seemed to still be there. Faith without works is dead faith, and faith without action actually equals unbelief, so the next step of faith was to begin feeding. As the people lined up once again, we kept feeding and feeding and feeding until the last person was served. Our final count revealed that God had multiplied fifteen hundred hot dogs to feed fifty-five hundred people for His honor and glory! He turned each hot dog into three-and-a-half hot dogs!

For every meal and at each kitchen we followed the same process. We would pray for God to multiply the food, and He would either provide just enough for that day through donated food or multiply it so it became enough.

Later on the same trip we were requested to deploy along the coast to Waveland, Mississippi. By the second week of feeding there, restocking supplies were arriving, and we were abundantly blessed. In fact, at one point we had so much spaghetti that we gave away two pallets and still had six left over, enough for 150,000 meals.

Lesson Learned

Always believe God's Word that He will supply all of your needs according to His riches in heaven! Your greatest impossibility becomes God's reality! Believe in those things that you can see through your eyes of faith!

PRAYER FOR TODAY:

1 Kings 18:36-37

O Lord, God of Abraham, Isaac, and Jacob, demonstrate today that You are God and that I am Your servant. Answer my prayer because I have followed You by faith, so that everyone may know that You are God.

Chapter 4

GET DIRTY—HELPING OTHERS BRINGS HEALING

ARE YOU ONE who is tempted to preach and talk about how people need to demonstrate acts of love but are not actually doing it? If so, it's time to get involved and make a difference in the lives of others (Matt. 9:37).

Ask, "Is there something I can pray with you for today?" When you understand what their needs are, be willing to help fulfill them. God has given you many resources, some of which may be unknown until you begin to give, helping others. Practicing what you preach will be the most positive gift you can ever give someone.

Spiritual Empowerment

If I think I am too important to help someone in need, I am only fooling myself. I am really a nobody.

—GALATIANS 6:3, AUTHOR'S PARAPHRASE

Helping others requires getting dirty. When we get dirty helping to clean up the messes of others, surprisingly, we are the ones it helps the most. It is so easy to allow bad habits or challenges to keep piling up all day long, week after week, month after month, year after year. If you take care of the little things, you won't ever have to deal with the big things.

Choose to get dirty by starting to release your hold on treasured trash, or it will continue to multiply. What is treasured trash, and why would someone want to hold on to it? It could be something as simple as unhealthy eating habits, such as eating three candy bars instead of one or eating until you are stuffed rather than being moderate. It can be work-related, such as working fourteen to sixteen hours rather than eight to ten, or taking on too many projects and becoming overwhelmed. Allowing a job to consume the majority of your time and energy can lead to stress-related diseases and create problems within your family. Treasured trash can even be what you watch on T.V. Most of us know there are certain types of programs that are not suitable for viewing, even for adults, but it's the subtle devices of the enemy that can create havoc in our lives. One example is to watch adultery or fornication being romanticized, thereby desensitizing us to the spiritual ramifications of those actions. Ungodly messages have infiltrated not only adult sitcoms and movies but cartoons and even Disney movies targeted at our children. Things that seem harmless on the surface can contain demonic or immoral messages in visual images seen on the screen.

In Philippians 4:8 Paul tells us exactly what we should meditate on:

> Whatever is true, whatever is worthy of reverence and is honorable and seemly, whatever is just, whatever is pure, whatever is lovely and lovable, whatever is kind and winsome and gracious, if there is any virtue and excellence, if there is anything worthy of praise, think on and weigh and take account of these things [fix your minds on them].

A Parable

Firemen get their fire trucks, equipment, and bodies dirty with ash, mud, and debris when fighting fire. During 9/11 they were covered in soot both on the outside and the in their lungs, but in spite of this were thankful to play a part in saving others lives.

Garbage begins to stink and grow unless you get rid of it. When you do, the reward is great. It is refreshing when things get clean. We must manage what we do every day, or it will begin to overwhelm and control us. Many have become overwhelmed with issues that either they have created themselves or that are beyond their control.

There is a price to pay for working hard to clean up the garbage in your life and getting dirty in the process. Some of the dirt will stain your clothes, eat holes in them permanently, or make them smell and even wear them out. The good news is, getting dirty is worth it! The sooner you work on your messes, the sooner your wardrobe or personality will become transformed into a new and more likeable you! Healing comes through using these four keys:

1. Ask
2. Resource

3. Give
4. Practice what you preach

Spiritual Empowerment

Because I ask, I shall receive.

—John 16:24, author's paraphrase

---

1. Ask

"Wait a minute! Ask someone to help me with challenges I'm facing? Aren't I supposed to have it all together before helping someone else?"

A point of discussion amongst psychologists and counselors for years has been whether individuals should only help others if they have it all together themselves first. Based on years of experience, I am convinced that *healing comes quickly through helping others* when you do not have it all together first. Most of us try to be too independent. We think we should be able to solve most of our own problems. Many Christians mistakenly think we should appear strong and perfect. However, we can be blessed by allowing those who have firsthand knowledge in our area of weakness to help us. Many would love to help us if we would only ask. Read chapter 16, "Hope for Helpers," for more insight on this topic.

I strongly urge you to find someone who may be struggling with something in which you have had personal experience. If not, just find someone willing to struggle with you—period. God created us to help one another. By becoming accountable to each other, we are blessed. Some of us have a hard time hiding the results of our bad habits or inabilities after years of abuse. Sometimes our abuse comes at the hands of others, but how much more frequently are we the abusers of ourselves? The hardest person to forgive is our self. We just feel guilty. We want to pay penance. We want to earn our forgiveness, but it doesn't work that way. There's nothing we can do but confess our sins before God; He will take them away. Guilt will do its best to keep you from seeking the help you need to receive and the help you need to give. There is great fulfillment and release of guilt by asking someone else if they can help you. The world becomes a cleaner place when we get serious about working as a team. Get dirty! Get involved! Make a difference!

Because I confess my faults and pray with others, I am healed.

—James 5:16, author's paraphrase

Sometimes confession to a pastor or Christian counselor can be helpful: "I have a challenge with (name your specific challenge, e.g., overworking, overeating, pornography, managing time, managing finances, not being able to solve something, etc.), and I need your help." Accountability to others is essential.

> *When firemen enter a dark or smoke filled room, they like to ask or call out, "If you can hear the sound of my voice, come to me."*

The following stories are of real people who got dirty helping others. They learned how to meet the needs of others by asking, being a resource, giving, and practicing what they preached. In return, they not only gained healing but helped others gain their healing as well. They showed love in action.

What Sex?

Samantha came unexpectedly to my church office one day. She knocked on my door and asked quietly, "I need help. May I come in?" Brushing away my initial shock, I looked at the lovely six-foot two-inch tall blonde with long, flowing hair standing in the doorway awaiting my answer. Her low-cut dress brazenly revealed far more cleavage than I was comfortable seeing, and her perfume was so strong it made my eyes water.

With as much warmth as I could muster despite the shock of what I saw, I answered, "Yes, please do!"

Stepping a foot inside, she hesitated briefly, not sure what to do. "Should I close the door?" she asked timidly.

"Oh no," I gestured with my hand. "Its OK to leave it open." It has always been my practice to do this when being alone with females.

As part of my master of divinity degree, the required counseling courses taught us to listen first and ask questions second. Instinctively my training kicked into gear. I listened intently while deliberately focusing on her eyes, determined not to be distracted by her constant bending forward toward me, displaying what appeared to be her pride and joy bulging from the fragile confines of her blouse. Tears spilled down her cheeks as if she'd been holding them in for such a time as this and now they flowed freely. "I was molested as a child by my father and am still hurting as a result. I am so filled up with anger! Now I'm caught up in prostituting myself because I enjoy the sense of accepting companionship, but it's become a trap because the love is not real. But I also need someone with whom I can trust to pour out my heart and soul."

At last, a real storybook way in which I could be used. There was no doubt in my mind that God had providentially brought her here to just the right place, and I quickly assured her that I was glad she had come. Then, continuing, I asked if she would allow me to pray a blessing on her life. She responded with a cautious, "Yes."

I gave her a warm smile and prayed, "Lord, thank You for drawing Samantha here today. You have promised that You will never leave or forsake Samantha and that You are always with her, even to the end."

The stress on her face began to disappear as she noticeably relaxed. We began dialoging about theology, and I found her to be unusually articulate. Her head knowledge of the Bible was profound. "I really enjoyed attending the seminary," she continued with her story, "but things just didn't connect." I wondered what she meant regarding the seminary but remained the listener. "Does your church provide a nonjudgmental environment where I might be accepted and loved?" she asked, and then went on to say, "I really want to experience a heart knowledge of God and develop a relationship with Him as a loving Father. The problem is, I've only had a head knowledge of serving an angry God."

"What do you mean by that?" I asked gently.

"Well, it seems like God will love me only if I obey all the Ten Commandments," she answered. "A list of *dos* and *don'ts*." Her frustration at having a mental picture of God that didn't line up with the loving God she read about in the Bible and her anger at all she had endured at her father's hand seemed to collide with the force of a collapsing dam. It came out in her tone, although it was evident she was desperately trying to keep her emotions in check. "Then there's another whole other list of things—another list of *dos* and *don'ts*—clearly pointed out from my denominational upbringing. I was raised in a very strict church-attending family, where I learned there is only one true church. My father, who has since passed away, was a deacon and threatened me with bodily harm if I ever told anyone of his sexual abuse toward me. He knew if I did it would ruin his position and standing in the church. My father was worried that others would think badly of him and his church!"

Righteous indignation erupted within me as I wondered silently how a father could have willingly and knowingly destroyed his own child's life! It was incomprehensible to me. A child is the most blessed gift with which God could have ever entrusted to him. Tears of compassion had already begun to flow in my spirit for what Samantha, the child, had endured. It was downright criminal.

"My mother came from a Victorian mindset," she continued, "and is a very faithful Christian who only believed in sex for procreation." Although the various sexual details Samantha was sharing made me uncomfortable and ready to ask for a time-out, I knew she needed to talk about it, so I allowed myself to be drawn out of my comfort zone to be a help for her. Samantha continued by saying, "I served in the army and was deployed in the Middle East. The army thought they would make a real man out of me."

"A real man?" I thought to myself, my brain not quite connecting the dots between the words I heard and the image I saw. "That's strange," I thought.

Samantha continued, "I am also a master mechanic." Taking a deep breath, Samantha hurriedly plunged forward with her next statement, "I have an overwhelming desire to complete my sex change."

Whoa! The seminary never prepared me for a situation like this! That's when I began to realize I was in over my head. "No wonder she looks like a football player," I thought. Desperately, I hoped my shock hadn't registered on my face where she could see it as I breathed a prayer requesting wisdom.

"My original name was Sam," she explained as she wiped tears from her eyes. By this time her mascara had smeared her meticulous makeup. Her eyes were puffy, her cheeks mottled from the stress of describing her trauma.

I was so overwhelmed with her story I didn't really know what to say next. It was certain that I must have had this "deer in the headlights" kind of blank stare on my face. After my mouth caught up with my rapidly pounding heart, I blurted, "God loves you so much that He came to die for you and me, because He knows how much we need Him!"

Later, I told the person to whom I was accountable in ministry of my encounter with Samantha, I was unsure which name or gender to use. He only added to the complexity of the matter by asking, "Are you going to have any more counseling sessions with your newfound liability?"

"Liability?" I thought. "This is a human being, a person, a child of God who is hurting beyond anything you or I can even comprehend. But a *liability*?" His choice of words seemed uncharacteristically callous.

"You need to exercise caution regarding making him feel comfortable in attending our church," he warned. "We don't want him thinking we approve of his/her actions. What kind of influence might this have on the young, impressionable minds of our own teenagers?" He paused a moment, sensing the inner battle going on behind my eyes, then asked impatiently, "So what *do* you have to say?"

Tell me, what would you say? My job was kind of on the line. The only question to this newfound moral dilemma that kept ringing in my mind was, What would Jesus do? I could:

1. Disassociate from her—She was an image liability.
2. Point out that when she "cleaned up her act" the church would accept her back.
3. Refer her to a long-term professional counselor, hoping she would not return.
4. Make a decision as to how much time I could willingly invest in such a deeply emotionally damaged individual. (The time, if invested in healthy individuals, might produce more converts with less liability.)
5. Protect the youth from being exposed to perversions like this, lest they too fall.
6. Welcome her with unconditional love and let God change her. Choose to see her not for who she was but who she could become in Christ.

Which of these choices would you have chosen?

Unofficially, our church adopted Samantha into our fellowship. She was the best volleyball player on our league. Every time she scored a point, we expected a manly yell to come from her linebacker stature, but instead we heard this dainty, distinctly feminine, "Ooh!" We invited her to help teach an automotive and auto-body restoration class for our youth department. She was an excellent welder and instructor. Invariably, we could find her on the front row of one of our most intellectual adult Bible classes, taught by one of the physicians in our church. If the teacher could not remember where a particular Bible text was found, Samantha knew it and was quick to help him out.

Was it worth the scandal, all the stress and trauma created at our church by having her there? Yes. Was it a risky adventure? Absolutely. Did our retired church community spend far too many hours discussing their displeasure at her attendance? Without a doubt. Were our youth exposed to the challenges and consequences of choices, albeit in a healthy environment? Yes, they were. Did we learn to accept others for who they were and to treat them the way we would like to be treated? Well, not all of us, but many did. Did we learn that you can sound good on the outside and impress others with biblical knowledge, while God is working on everyone's hearts? Well, once again, not all of us, but many did. And praise God, yes, I did survive not being fired for taking the risk, despite my senior pastor's cautions!

Samantha's desperation drove her to ask for help, and by doing so, healing was a by-product. By Samantha asking for our help, we experienced the biggest change. Our church never would have had such a dramatic change had we not helped someone in such drastic need. If we had gone to her and condemned her for her actions, thinking we were witnessing, no one would have learned. Since she grew up in a legalistic church, she was desperate to ask us to accept and love her. In the process, we ended up benefiting the most. We learned to love her in a new way of extending unconditional love.

Many of us in the church came to see ourselves as hypocritical. We became more relevant and intentional in demonstrating a redemptive love to others by addressing the needs around us. This is what Samantha needed to see more than anything. She was unconditionally loved by most, and by sharing her talents with others, she also gained healing in many ways. Over time I noticed that she no longer spoke of suicide and death. Many years later, some of the youth told me that this experience taught them to think carefully about their choices, for clearly choices could bring about serious consequences. They were also appreciative that I was willing to risk exposing them to someone like Samantha. This had allowed them to understand what was happening in the real world around them and to look to God for solutions to their hurts.

Lesson Learned

Every day you can choose to see the redemptive potential of what you and others can become by faith. Your challenges are His opportunities. You can choose to either chastise yourself for the mistakes and wrong choices you have made, building upon a mountain of trash or bad investments, or you can choose to see your mountain of experience as building on solid ground. Jesus has forgiven you and sees you as His child. He sees only the good in you and what you can become in Him. You are His masterpiece!

Jesus says, "All have sinned, and the wages of sin is death, but the gift of My life promises a little peace on Earth as well as eternal life" (Rom. 6:23, author's paraphrase).

2. Resource

You have the ability to provide a resource that someone else needs. This important key is to let others know they can call on you to receive what they need.

Spiritual Empowerment

Thank you, Lord, for inviting me to bring all my challenges to you, because You have promised to turn them into opportunities.

—Matthew 11:28, author's paraphrase

A Parable

Firemen are wonderful examples of being a great resource of both knowledge and networking well with others. They understand that in order to be "First Responders," their success is dependent on uniting the resources of both personnel and equipment.

Not Beaten Down

John wept as he described to us how his wife, Sally, and their dog had drowned in a wave that had washed over their house during Hurricane Katrina. Three times he had left a local shelter to return to their home, begging his wife in every way imaginable to leave with him. He showed me a picture of Sally, whose last words to him were, "Don't worry; I'll be fine." She was swept away, along with their cherished Irish setter. Every material possession he owned and the love of his life was lost in a moment. Yet he was able to say, "I am so blessed to be alive!"

Then as the reality of facing an uncertain future seeped in, he asked incredulously, "But how am I ever going to start over again? I did not buy flood insurance because my house was seven miles away from the ocean."

He had come to the ACTS World Relief distribution site, where twelve hundred cars daily passed through our lines to receive food, personal care kits, water, and ice. They were also offered a hot meal cooked in one of our mobile kitchens. "Don't let me take anything that someone else could use more than me," John said, concerned for those around him who had also suffered loss. Then he asked, "Why do you come to help us, when you could just stay at home where it is comfortable?"

One of the volunteers answered, "Because we care."

Taking just a moment to process that in his mind, John then asked, "Would it be OK for me to come back tomorrow and help distribute donated items to my neighbors?"

We never seemed to have quite enough volunteers, so with a tired smile and the foresight to recognize a God-moment in the midst of it all, I assured him heartily, "John, we would love to have you! We sure need your help, and bring some other neighbors if you want as well."

The next day he was there bright and early with a special glow on his face. He had brought two of his neighbors with him as well. In spite of all his challenges, he saw beyond his needs to the needs of others. He had a burden on his heart to help someone else, knowing they had suffered the same as he had, though specific losses may have varied. As he and his neighbors were helping those in the distribution line, I overheard them greeting those they recognized as they handed out boxes of emergency supplies, "Hello Sister Jones, it is good to see you survived," or, "Hey, haven't you already been through line once today?" and "How else can we help you?"

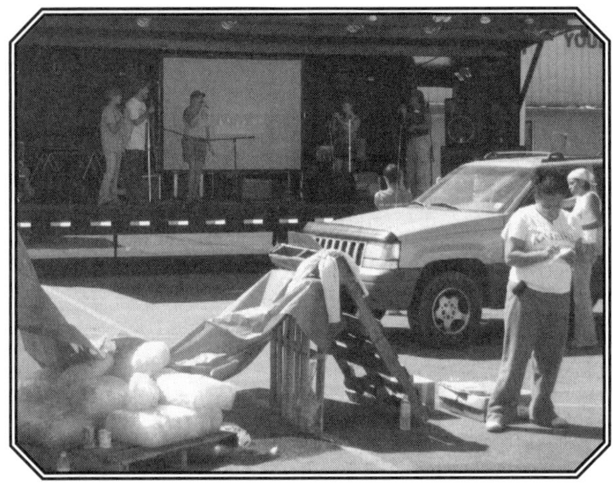

Something that made a huge impact on the motorists as they drove through the line was the ACTS mobile sound stage, where youth were singing words of hope with energetic worship music. Their music and uplifting lyrics were acutely appreciated. This provided an environment for emotional healing. Praise changes a negative atmosphere to one of healing, and the Bible says that God inhabits the praises of His people (Ps. 22:3, KJV). Many would pull out of line to listen to them and literally weep, as they still had no electricity to watch T.V. or listen to the radio. Other youths would surround these individuals and wrap their arms around them, comforting them as they sang and prayed together. This helped bring healing.

After several days of helping, John told us, "You'll never know how much healing I've experienced by getting my mind off myself and helping others. I've been encouraged by my neighbors, who have even bigger needs than mine." I offered to pray for continued blessings in John's life, and he gratefully accepted. I began, "Lord, we thank you that you have come to give John life and to give it to him more abundantly. Satan has tried to steal, kill, and destroy everything good out of his life, but You have promised to supply all his needs according to Your riches in glory" (John 10:10).

Lesson Learned

John became a resource by providing needed emergency supplies to his neighbors. By providing these resources, he then gained his own healing from deep loss. You too have resources God has blessed you with. Share these with others, and gain healing from your past.

God knows that we must get dirty helping other people in order to gain healing ourselves. There is a new generation of people who are committed to being involved in becoming an army of people ready to show unconditional love! We need each other. It is only by risking getting dirty that we can truly begin to understand each other's pain. In the process of helping others, we experience the greatest blessing. It is time to realize that the entire universe owes us nothing. We are created to bless others. "You're blessed when you care. At the moment of being 'care-full,' you find yourselves cared for" (Matt. 5:7, The Message).

3. Give

When you give away something you love, you will gain your greatest blessing. Love grows in proportion to how much you are willing to give away!

Spiritual Empowerment

I am more blessed when I give than when I receive.

—Acts 20:35, author's paraphrase

A Parable

Firemen are very used to giving away a tremendous amount of compassion, which is why they find fire fighting very fulfilling in spite of lower pay.

Something Small but Something Great

I had heard of people giving their personal Bibles away, and I thought, "Ahh, there's nothing to it! It's not hard to giving my Bible to someone who needs it," but boy, was I wrong when the time came to it.

Apart from the sweatiness and blistering heat of the sun's powerful rays, it was a gorgeous spring day in Haiti. You could smell the perfume of the luscious fruit in the faint breeze. Mangos. And lots of them. The island was bountiful in producing these sweet, succulent fruits. One could hardly even notice the devastation that was waiting around the next corner...We had been stationed in Haiti for a week and a half, but every time we saw another home laying in ruins or [an area] once known as a plaza center vacant because of the rubble that had crowded the walkways, the reality of the scene...brought you to...tears. It had been a successful day at the small medical clinic located near the local hospital in Port-Au-Prince. The medium-sized home was almost the ideal setting to allow between eight hundred and fifteen hundred patients to come in daily and be attended to in an efficient manner. But with piles of boxes filled with meds and treatments, it was a bit challenging to move around and retrieve for the doctor what was needed. So my job was to make things a little easier by organizing everything and making a designated place for it. Even though the work seemed endless for me, for the doctors, and any other volunteers (good-hearted people), we knew that we had come to help in any way our talents or degrees permitted us to.

After bringing the cleaning fiesta to a close for the afternoon, I headed toward the hospital to grab a snack that mom had so thoughtfully packed in the suitcase "just in case." As I made my way down the small pathway leading to the little bridge that crossed over, to my imagination, a once-clean stream now filled with garbage, I saw a man casually sitting next to the wall as if waiting for something or someone. I noticed as I walked closer he had a collection of paintings for sale to any of the passers-by, who almost always seemed to be volunteers from the ACTS disaster response team. He timidly but with pleading in his eyes asked me if I had anything I could give him.

With an attempt to speak the English he did know, he said earnestly, "I have nothing. I have not even a pair of shoes because of the earthquake. Is there something you have to give me?"

Touched by his situation and simple request, I thought, "What on Earth could I give him? All I have is my clothes, which are a little too feminine than I think he is wanting, and shoes that won't even come close to his shoe size." I sadly told him no and continued walking toward the hospital. Then the thought suddenly came to me: "Autumn, this is your chance to give someone something that you have never given before. How many times have you heard others sharing their stories of giving their Bibles to someone who needed one? Now it's your turn." Confused by the mixed feelings of selfishness but yet feeling the compassion to respond to the need of this gentleman, I prayed, "Lord, the moment has now come to me where I can decide to give this man my Bible or stick with what I had originally told him and 'forget' about it. Why do I feel this way? I should not even be battling the question of whether to give or to withhold my Bible." Slowly walking up the steps to the entrance of the hospital, I knew I needed to do what I needed to do. However, I said to more myself than God, knowing it would probably happen, "If this man is still in the same place tomorrow and asks me again if I have anything to give him, I will come back and get the Bible for him."

> Sure enough, as I headed to the clinic the next morning for group debriefing time and worship, there he sat. And to my surprise, I felt joy and excitement in place of the selfish thoughts from the day before. Somehow God had given me the peace and assurance that this Bible would help him, in whatever way it may be. As I turned around to go back to the room that inside held my most precious possession, I thought of what I could write [to] him. It would be something simple, because inside those pages I knew read wisdom, power, and grace. As I held the small black Bible in my hands for the last time, I kissed it and held it to my chest as if saying good-bye to a dear friend, which it indeed had become.
>
> As I approached the man again, this time with something in my hand and a happier smile, I waited for the question. He could barely even finish his sentence before I got closer to him and told him I had something for him. I felt the liberating power and hand of the Holy Spirit as I offered him my Bible. He looked at me with surprise, which turned into a big smile of gratitude, and said, "Thank you. I know it is something very personal, and I know it will bless me." More than the words and appreciation, I cherished the look on his face and will always remember the small but great gift I gave that morning. I had received the greatest blessing through giving my best gift!

The narrative above was written by Autumn Canther, age twenty, during her trip to Haiti after the earthquake.

My Cherished M30

One of my most memorable vehicle purchases was a beautiful gold Infinity M30 two-door sports car. Production for the M30 lasted only three years with only five thousand models—half coupes, half convertibles—having been produced, making the M30 a rare car. The previous owner had taken exceptional care of this particular M30. It had a premium sound system and power everything, including a retractable sunroof. After driving it for a few years, it needed the topside of the engine rebuilt and a new timing chain. I asked my son, Andrew, to help with the project. We both got dirty while gaining new mechanical knowledge and experience in the journey of restoration, and before long, we were happily driving it again.

About this same time I hired a new marketing director for ACTS World

Relief. Larry and his pregnant wife had just moved to the area with only one vehicle. Though they had tried sharing their one vehicle, in reality it had become apparent that his wife needed another vehicle for her job.

Sympathizing with their plight, I approached him one day. "Larry," I asked, "Would you like to drive the Infinity until you can save up a little money to buy another vehicle?"

Quickly he responded, "Yes, I would really appreciate that."

After he drove it for a while, I volunteered, "If you like the car, I would be willing to sell it to you." For a split second, I couldn't believe my own ears! I loved this car! But before it got the best of me, I continued even further, "...for below book value."

Immediately his eyes lit up with excitement, then faded almost as quickly as he asked tentatively, "How much would that be?"

Later that week during family supper, I spoke with my family about the great need of this family. My son, Andrew, couldn't quite process this whole situation of giving a car away and angrily accused, "Dad, are you crazy?" He was somewhat resentful down deep inside, as he had loved this car too. "Why would you give away a good car like that?"

Ah, another teaching opportunity between father and son. I explained, "Son, sometimes the best way we can help ourselves is by not allowing ourselves to get too attached to material things."

We decided not to just help them a little bit, but to so radically help that they would recognize God in it. Their need was so great, so far beyond their own capabilities; yet God had seen fit to bless me, then provide me the opportunity to be a blessing. I approached Larry again. "Larry, if you like the Infinity, we would like to give it to you as a gift."

He was shocked. The desire to accept, the integrity to refuse, and his great need for a car that he couldn't provide caused swirls of emotion clearly seen in his eyes. "No," he replied, "I want to pay for it or give you something in return." I've found that oftentimes people who have such dire need are the most reluctant to accept the fulfillment of that need unless they've earned it. Some find it difficult to just accept that God took care of their need completely, without any type of repayment necessary. Sure, God needs you and me to be the delivery mechanisms of those moments, but then we also get to share in the blessing.

In the process of helping to fill Larry and his wife's need for another car, we actually gained the greatest blessing. And while blessing Larry and his wife, we sowed seed for another car. God promises to give seed to the sower (2 Cor. 9:10), and whatever we sow, we reap. The best time to help others is while you are alive. You can't take any of it with you when you die. The most revolutionary concept is that when we give first, we are releasing heaven's miraculous opportunities to receive from the One who owns the "cattle on a thousand hills" (Ps. 50:10). Not only is this a kingdom principle, but it also makes good business sense. As I learn self-control in material things, I save more money by not buying things needlessly.

Lesson Learned

When you help others by giving something away you love, you are the one who is blessed the most! When you begin giving away or releasing things, your greatest dreams come true. If you really want to experience character growth, give away something for which you've worked hard to obtain. Give something away that hurts a little to part with.

The Day My Dad Died

Joy comes in the morning.

—Psalm 30:5, nkjv

My mother and father both had a love for mission work. Utila, part of the Bay Islands in Honduras, had especially captured their hearts. Twenty years earlier, with great joy, they established a medical clinic, school, and dormitories there. In 2008 we had planned another trip to Utila, where I would be leading a disaster-preparedness training seminar. My father, who had been struggling with Alzheimer's for ten years, had not been able to go to his favorite island paradise for five years.

One day, I received an email from Mom that simply read, "Dad is not well." I called her, only to find out his condition had taken a critical turn for the worse, but there was no clear way of knowing how much longer his struggle might last. She appreciated my offer to fly there and be with them in Arizona, but instead she encouraged me to stay in Tennessee. She implored, "Let's continue with our plans to go together to the Bay Islands next week. It's where I would love to help."

About four o'clock the next Friday morning, my cell phone rang, and I noticed Mom's name on my caller ID. I knew the news would not be good. Mom told me that Dad had just passed away. As a minister, I have performed many memorial services and have sat and prayed with many individuals as their loved ones breathed their last. No matter how many times one has done that sort of thing, it does not necessarily prepare you for when your own father is gone. Since I was no longer a pastor over a congregation, it was the first time I had ever experienced such a personal loss without the support of a church team, which had always been like a big, extended family. It helped me to better understand how others feel when they are not closely attached to others in their time of need.

By faith I reached out in the best way to gain healing and proceeded to call a good friend of mine, Jim Ingersoll, whose mother was terminally ill. He has led with me in many disaster responses by scheduling high school groups from around the nation to respond with ACTS. "Jim," I asked, "How is your mother doing today?"

Sadly he replied, "The nurse just informed me she probably only has forty-eight hours left."

"Would you like for me to come and be with you?" I asked, reaching out to share the burden of watching his mother slip away.

"Yes, I sure would," he replied. "You've always been there for me, and I really appreciate it."

With a heavy heart of my own and a lump in my throat caused by the pressure of unshed tears, I offered, "Let me pray with you right now. 'Lord, You have promised to supply all of Jim's and his family's needs according to Your riches in glory, and we give You thanks for this promise in Jesus' name. Amen.'" Just the year before, his father had passed away, compounding his intense loss and exposing our mortality.

Though presently in the middle of a hurricane deployment in Texas, I got into my truck and drove to North Carolina to be with him, praying that by reaching out to him, it would help us both in the grieving process. This is what I had always taught others. I had not yet shared with Jim that my father had just passed away. After arriving I claimed Bible promises as his brother, his wife, and I held his mother's hands. She opened her eyes as if to say, "Yes and amen," even though she could no longer speak due to the stroke she had the week before.

As I was ready to leave, I finally shared with Jim the news of my own father's passing. He followed me to my car and said, "I need to pray for you in your time of need. I know what you're going through." I thanked him and together we encouraged one another with a big hug, as we both fought back tears of sorrow and understanding.

The next week, Mom and I arrived in Honduras. Not only were we able to lead out in training an ACTS World Relief first response team from Union College, located in Lincoln, Nebraska, but we were also able to have a beautiful memorial service for Dad. Later his ashes were placed in the beautiful island paradise where he ministered so greatly. His heart is buried where he felt the most loved and needed.

Lesson Learned

Is your world changing too rapidly and falling apart, and no one seems to care or understand? Reach out and help someone else in spite of your pain. God's Word is true: We are more blessed when we give help to someone else (Acts 20:35). This takes our mind off ourselves and causes us to feel like a blessing too.

Some say, "God helps those who help themselves," but that is not in the Bible. In fact, God helps those who *can't* help themselves. We couldn't save ourselves, so He sent us Jesus.

Victims of disasters are usually unable to help themselves, so He sends us as His ambassadors. Jesus encourages us to help those who are hurting and don't deserve it: "While we were still sinners, Christ died for us" (Rom. 5:8, NKJV). The gospel is summed up by understanding how much God loves to free us, to forgive us and liberate us in order to love others unconditionally. The question is, Can you forgive yourself? Ask yourself, Do I live so that God will accept me, or do I live because God has accepted me in Christ?

4. Practice What You Preach

Is God's Word contradicted by your lifestyle or traditions? Are you able to recognize this contradiction? In order to help others gain healing, you must be willing to release those obstacles or even traditions that prevent your life from being an example of a living Jesus to others.

Spiritual Empowerment

I have been called to live in freedom, not to satisfy my sinful nature, but freedom to serve others in love. For the whole law can be summed up in one command: "Love my neighbor as myself."

—Galatians 5:13–14, author's paraphrase

Today, there is a powerful movement to help those in need. This brings us miraculous mental and spiritual healing. If someone wants to know what the essence of the gospel is, do you begin by explaining your denominational doctrines or by demonstrating a loving Jesus to them? The first approach creates knowledge of Jesus; the second creates a loyalty to Him.

> ***A Parable***
>
> *Firemen must practice what they are taught. If they do not, their lives, the lives of their team and the lives of others will be in jeopardy.*

The Perfect Pastor?

The first church I pastored was in Lake City, in northern Florida. One day as I pulled into our driveway after the worship service for that week, I waved at our neighbor, who was out in her front yard. She was about thirty years old and had two children. One was a newborn, who she had in a baby buggy close by. It was obvious that she was having a problem starting her lawnmower. Pulling the cord over and over, she tried to get the stubborn mower to start, but it wouldn't. I walked into the house mumbling to myself, "Stupid mower; she needs to trade that one in." I promptly went into my office, which overlooked her house. Peering out the window I watched as she gulped down a glass of water, trying not to faint from heat exhaustion, and continued to pull on the cord. She stood under a large pine tree that offered minimal shade at that time of day in the nearly one hundred–degree heat.

"Why doesn't she just give up, quit, and go inside?" I wondered.

"Why don't you go out and help her?" was the question that came to mind.

"Ha. Yeah, now that's a radical thought," I mused. After all, it was the Sabbath day, and I had grown up attending church regularly. I knew the Ten Commandments, one of which is, "Thou shalt not do any work on the Sabbath." God Himself had forbidden me to help my neighbor at that time, because to do so would cause me to disobey His rule regarding the Sabbath. I had read my Bible through many times and had preached many a sermon on the topic of Jesus' statement in John 14:15, "If you love Me, keep My commandments" (NKJV). In fact, that had been the topic of this morning's sermon as well.

Jerking down the window shade so as not to be distracted from my day of rest, I went into the bedroom and took off my church suit, then reached for my sleepwear in order to get ready for what some jokingly refer to as "lay activities," which means taking a nap. I was well aware of the many unwritten rules pertaining to what one could or couldn't do on the Sabbath. An important tradition with which I was raised was not to do anything that caused you to break a sweat on the Lord's Day. A biblical definition of *sabbath* is "to honor God in worship and rest from normal work routines for personal gain" (Exod. 20:8–11, author's paraphrase). My conscience kept pricking me, though. In college, I used to repair a fleet of lawnmowers and knew very well that I might be able to diagnose the problem. "I'd help her any other day," I argued with myself. "I've tried to let her know what day is holy, but she refuses to come to church with us."

It was at that point that God spoke to me: "Love your neighbor as yourself." If I were in the same situation, would I want someone to help me out? I didn't need to judge her for her actions. That's God's job! Jesus also said, "If your ox is in the ditch on the Sabbath day, help get it out" (Luke 14:5). It is a day when you *can* take time to help others in need (Matt. 12:12)! I paused, then went back to the drawer and pulled out my jeans. "All right, Lord," I breathed and hurried across the street. All the while I was praying that Joe, one of our church members who lived right down the street, wouldn't see me. I knew he would have to pass right by my house to get home from church. He could be coming any minute! The fear of getting caught breaking the rules by man rose up within me, even as I was obedient to what God impressed me to do. It was bad enough to be breaking the Sabbath, let alone for me to be the pastor and break the Sabbath! All my life I had fought these same insecurities and feelings of guilt. I often wondered who was watching me, judging me, and talking about me. I wanted to be perceived as being the perfect pastor. God knew I needed to break a little holy sweat, and as I made it across my lawn to hers, my attitude changed.

Stopping by her lawnmower, I asked, "Can I help you?" Beth's face lit up with joy. I began the diagnosis. It took about five minutes to see that because she had left the choke on, the spark plug was fouled. After cleaning the spark plug, it fired right up and was good to go. I couldn't help but imagine that surely the ox that had gotten caught in the ditch on Sabbath in biblical times would have enjoyed a drink of cool, clear water and maybe some fresh oats and even a cooling bath after being stuck in a muddy ditch. Allowing myself to become further liberated from my state of legalism, I offered to push the lawnmower and mowed her front yard. It actually felt kind of good to sweat. Even on the Sabbath!

The next day, I went back over and mowed her backyard, which was only an acre large. Now, I could understand more clearly what the Bible means by saying that "God made the Sabbath for man, and not man for the Sabbath" (Mark 2:27). The Sabbath was designed to be a blessing for us, a rest from having to think we have to make an income seven days a week in order to survive the oppression that comes from buying too many material things. God blessed the Sabbath day at Creation, and He invites you to receive your blessing by entering into it by faith. Otherwise it is nothing more than legalism. That was a turning point in my life in understanding the spirit of the law of liberty. Jesus came to set free those who were held captive to sin and the condemning nature of the law.

Several months later it was on another Sabbath that my neighbor was loading a U-Haul truck because they needed to move. When I saw them struggling with a few large items, I went over and broke a little more sweat. They were so appreciative of my brief help. I believe this is what Jesus would have done. The following day we finished the project.

I have tried to make it a practice to help move many church members as well. I have found that if there is ever a time in your life when you learn who your true friends are it's when you ask if they would help you move. I've never seen so many faces pale at the thought or heard so many stuttered excuses as to why they can't seem to make it as when I've asked for that kind of help. The ones who have helped me move are still my best friends!

Lesson Learned

Live the gospel to your neighbors first, and then they will ask you what you believe second.

PRAYER FOR TODAY:

Matthew 6:6-9

Father, You alone are my majestic, holy and loving God. I want to experience Your power today, and may Your miraculous, perfect purpose spread throughout all the world, as it is in heaven. Because You are My provider and sustainer, You have promised to supply all my needs according to Your riches in heaven. Today, I forgive ______, who has intentionally or unintentionally hurt me, and now I thank You for forgiving my intentional or unintentional sins. When I am tested and tempted today, I thank You in advance that Your promises will give me strength to overcome all the power of the enemy!

I will glorify Your name forever, for You are an awesome God!

Chapter 5

FAITH, FOCUS, AND FOLLOWING THROUGH

THESE THREE INGREDIENTS—FAITH, focus, and following through—are all essential for sorting and prioritizing what is important in your life. They are attributes God loves. If you desire to live a fulfilled life, leaving off even one of these ingredients will prevent you from accomplishing what God has called you to do. I have known of many who had great faith, but were not focused enough in following through with the vision God had given them. God has a plan for you!

Spiritual Empowerment

Faith is the victory that causes me to finish the race.

—2 TIMOTHY 4:7, AUTHOR'S PARAPHRASE

A Parable

Firemen use a tremendous amount of faith in dealing with each of their team members and their equipment. They learn to have a clear focus on saving the perishing from destruction. Most importantly, they refuse to give up while fighting fires and are committed to following through when called into action. Many times they are called to accomplish the impossible, which many would say was is risking their lives foolishly.

Faith

What is your definition of faith?

The *American Heritage Dictionary* defines *faith* as:

1. Confident belief in the truth, value, or trustworthiness of a person, idea, or thing.
2. Belief that does not rest on logical proof or material evidence.[1]

Miriam-Webster's Dictionary of Law defines *faith* in legal terms as:

1. Allegiance or loyalty to a duty or a person, sincerity or honesty of intentions.
2. Fidelity to one's promises and obligations.[2]

The Torah describes faith, as "steadiness and steadfastness in the commands of God," which comes from the Hebrew word *emunah*.[3] His promises are also His commands. The primary idea of faith is trust.

Living by faith has changed my life. I have learned faith is total dependence upon God and His Word, which becomes supernatural in its working. People with faith develop a second kind of sight. They see more than just circumstances; they see God right in them. Can they prove it? No, but by faith they know that He's there nonetheless. Faith and love grow bigger and bigger when combined.

Many Christians think it is presumptuous or demanding to boldly claim Bible promises for every situation in life. Remember, it is not demanding if it's concerning something God has already promised.

If you promised your child a trip to the zoo on Tuesday next week, would you think it demanding for your child to keep reminding you of your promise in their excitement?

"Daddy, remember you promised we were going to the zoo on Tuesday!"

"Yes, we're going to the zoo on Tuesday."

Then finally Monday dawns. "Daddy, tomorrow we're going to the zoo right?"

"Yes, we're going tomorrow."

Tuesday arrives, and you are greeted with, "Today's the day, Daddy! We're going to the zoo!"

Do you get irritated or angry at the constant reminder of your promise? Do you view it as a demand from your child? Of course not. This is something *you* promised!

> Come into the presence of God with a holy boldness or confidence in God, not ourselves. We can have confidence and boldness based on the merits of Christ. Plead the promises of God without the fear of

being presumptuous. Present your requests to God in faith, asking for the very things you know you need."[4]

As a believer, you can even demand Satan to stop his work by the authority of God's Word! Most Christians think it is only appropriate to claim promises when praying for forgiveness of sin or salvation, but God's promises extend even beyond those lavish gifts.

Focus

Are you keeping a focus on what God is calling you to do?

It is very easy to lose your focus in daily living. We are living in a time when distractions with TV, novels, movies, and other forms of entertainment can easily create an imbalance in our priorities. The reason for this difficulty is that we have a hard time determining what is normal or acceptable for our lives. When God comes first apologies are freely given, forgiveness is modeled, and family time comes before TV—and we can experience happier lives! In order to maintain spiritual, emotional, and physical health in our daily lives, balance includes:*God*, so He helps us keep everything in a positive perspective.

- *Relationships*, so we maintain love and loyalty.
- *Recreation*, so we don't burn out.
- *Rest*, so we stay as healthy as possible.
- *Service*—love in action.

Too little of these elements, or too much of the last four, will destroy us. Only you can determine how much should be invested in each area, depending on the situation you are currently going through in life.

Following through

You can practice faith and focus while serving others, but follow-through develops spiritual maturity! Only those who finish what they have begun experience the true rewards of commitment.

I love to find solutions to keeping the positive blessings of life from dripping away. Years ago, I cultivated the discipline of writing in a special book every time I had an idea to make something better from current inventions. Then with the help of a patent attorney, I prioritized the ones I thought were the best. He agreed with my choices and gave me two directives that needed to be done before coming to see him again. They were:

1. Go to the library or Internet and research any patent that looked similar to mine.
2. Write a narrative based on how my idea was different from all others.

This process saved me thousands of dollars over the years. A patent attorney can research this for you, but you will spend about four times as much to get your finished product into production. The first patent cost me about five thousand dollars. Thereafter, because the patent attorney trained me how to do my homework, the next five patents cost only about fifteen hundred dollars each. Statistically, only about 1 percent of submitted patents make it to approval. Of those who get approved, only about 1 percent make it to the market. This process taught me a lot of self-discipline.

Raising my two children was very rewarding, but certain items in baby care frustrated me at the same time. Two basic items that needed improvements were pacifiers and baby bottles. Both of our children had chronic problems with colic or gas. I remember rocking Andrew, my firstborn, especially late into the night. Just as he fell asleep, *boop*; his "binky," what we called his pacifier, would pop out of his mouth, waking him up. Not wanting to turn on the light and wake him up completely, I would scramble around on the floor on my hands and knees, groping in the dark for his binky, which often seemed to be as elusive as that pot of gold at the end of the rainbow. Finally grasping the inexpensive combination of rubber and plastic that was as valuable as that pot of gold, I would say to myself triumphantly, "Ah ha! I found you, you little rascal," and proudly place it back into his mouth. Waiting until he was fast asleep once more, I would lay him down in his crib with a certain amount of satisfaction that dads could do it too! (As a father, it was sometimes a bit threatening that my children's first instinct was to usually want their mom and the food she could provide over anything I could possibly offer.)

Then I got an idea! Why not come up with a binky that glowed in the dark after the lights were turned off, came in different flavors, and could be made with FDA-approved materials? Sure enough, research proved that no one currently held this type of patent. I spoke with chemists, did additional research, and was making progress. It took about six months to carefully chart out the solution to this problem, but I was certain that this would be my first patent. (The second patent I was going to file was to solve another area of great consternation concerning baby bottles.)

Building a House in Record Time

When you are told, "It can't be done," do you become more determined to prove that it *can* be done? Evaluating others' counsel of caution or telling you what can't be done is sometimes very important because of the price you may have to pay physically, mentally, emotionally, or spiritually.

My wife and I were living in Naples, Florida, expecting our second child. We were excited but also a bit anxious. We were building a house and wished to complete it in time for the arrival of our first daughter, according to the ultrasound readings. This was the second house I had built, filing the permit as an owner-builder. Together my wife and I had drawn up the house plans with the help of Bob, my father-in law, who had a very successful career as an architect and custom home builder. I looked up to and respected him a great deal. In fact, while in college during the summer, he had hired me to do grunt work and rough carpentry. It was intimidating working with someone of such great experience and skill as he was, plus I was trying to impress him enough to win his satisfaction as a potential son-in-law, for I wanted to marry his daughter!

It was important to me that this house be finished quickly, as I wanted to complete it as a gift to my pregnant wife, who was about ready to give birth. Based on his years of experience, Bob advised that our house could be built for around ninety to one hundred dollars per square foot, but I wanted to prove to myself that it could be done for sixty dollars per square foot. Of course, that meant that I would need to do most of the grunt work by digging footers, helping with the carpentry, and doing all of the painting and landscaping. He also said it would be impossible to complete the project in the time frame I had stated. But much to my delight, we finished building it in record time, well ahead of my self-imposed deadline. When the final bills were tallied, the total cost came in at fifty-six dollars a square foot! Not only had we built it in record time, but also under budget!

We had built our new home in a new phase of an established community. From beginning to end, without land power or running water, it took two and a half months. It took me a little longer than anticipated to put the finishing touches on our customized house, which included fourteen-foot-tall flat ceilings in the center section, vaulted ceilings in the master bedroom, and round pillars throughout the house, suspending a plant shelf that wrapped around rounded walls.

Miraculously, it was ready for us to move in before Sherri gave birth to our daughter Autumn. We had finished it so quickly that the city had not yet given the final certificate of occupancy to the new phase zoning department. Without it, the fire department refused to turn on the water lines into the new section, which also meant that I had to remain on temporary power, a step up from the generators used for most of the construction. We were given special permission to move into the first house of this new phase without water or permanent power! I hooked up a pump for pumping water out of the lake about 150 feet away so we would be able to flush the toilets, but praise God, within one week of moving in, we officially had permanent power and fresh running water! Moving into that house was a special gift to our new family.

Being a pastor and a builder at the same time required a strong commitment to the three ingredients of faith, focus, and following through. You might be going through the challenge of working two jobs or going to work and school at the same time—or juggling raising children, work, and school together. If one of these is the case for you, remember that God is your refuge and strength to help you in your needs (Ps. 46:1).

A Second Patent

We had installed a beautiful light grey carpet throughout our new house, which looked very pretty, new and clean! After all of the time, energy, sweat, and money we had poured into this wonderful home, what irritated me considerably was to see any spots or stains on the carpet, especially from a baby bottle. My biggest pet peeve was for Andrew, who was three years older than Autumn; Sherri; or me to be holding a baby bottle, have it slip out of our hands, and hit the new beautiful carpet. I often watched as Autumn happily tossed her bottle on purpose for sport, cooing and giggling with delight as she watched me try to grab for it in mid-air, only to have it hit our beautiful new carpet and leave a stain or dirty spot after wiping it up. As Autumn got older, sometimes she'd toss her bottle out of her crib or on the floor, and it would lay there for who knows how long before someone would find it, the majority of the contents no longer in the bottle but having drained out one drop at a time on the new, beautiful carpet! It seemed I was forever going around wiping up spots, though the remnants of these stains glared at me from a distance when I entered a room.

"Surely there must be a solution for this problem!" I thought. Purchasing every imaginable bottle design on the market, I began cutting them all apart in order to design a new bottle that would automatically right itself no matter how much fluid was in the bottle, eliminating stains on the carpet.

At last, both baby inventions were ready for final submission. It had taken nine months from the beginning to having two finished prototypes that actually worked! Next came a stretching curve of growth in my character. Imagine my huge disappointment in finding that from the time I had begun work on these two inventions until my completed project, both already had new applications on file by two other individuals, and they were too similar for me to succeed in receiving a patent. The binky was patented by some lady in the Philippines and the up-righting bottle by someone in the U.S.

Lesson Learned

Have you followed through with what you believed God was calling you to do, only to have it self-destruct around you? What may appear to be a failure to you now, is merely preparing you for greater things to come!

I may have lost the battle in not getting these two baby care patents, but I had won the war in proving to myself that if you persevere long and hard enough, you can learn from each experience in order to accomplish your goals quicker and more efficiently the next time.

Refuse to give up on life or look at it through the eyes of failures, obstacles, or bad decisions, but instead choose rather to see them as opportunities to learn how to jump over them quicker in your next opportunity for success!

Dedication Pays Off

There were six inventions for which I did receive patents. One was a golf table board game consisting of real pictures I had taken of some of the most beautiful golf courses around the country. This was played strategically with dice and cards. Players tried to be the first one to make it around sand traps and into the hole. Another was a sock rack designed to hang in your closet with little removable plastic devices to keep them sorted, and at a glance one was visually aware of the various colors that were available. This prevented the need for pawing through a sock drawer trying to locate the right color, then having to find the right mate. The remaining four patents had to do with pool applications. Two of the pool inventions had to do with the mechanical side of how they functioned, or utility patents, and the other two had to do with design patents to protect how they looked. I purchased every kind of pool strainer and chlorinator lid and began modifying them to look like what was envisioned in my mind. These became prototypes, which I then took to a graphic design artist, who not only drew it for others to see but showed the exact measurements as well. Next, I researched the best materials for mold manufacturers, getting bids on making the end product.

In my designs, the lids had handles of varying sizes on them, which allowed the consumer to remove them easily without the need for tools. The choice needed to be made of whether to have the molds made of aluminum, which were good for about one hundred thousand presses or to have the molds made of stainless steel. The stainless steel cost about three times as much as the aluminum but lasted longer, pressing over a million copies of your invention.

I then took my prototypes and drawings to several manufacturing plants. I chose to have four stainless steel molds made. Each had interchangeable inserts for the different lid sizes that weighed about six thousand pounds. These cost about thirty thousand dollars each.

It was exciting to see my product coming down the assembly line after a few modifications. The next challenge was to attend world trade shows and market the product. The real satisfaction was to see that in one year every main distributor of pool products, such as Gorman, Pinch A Penny, Home Depot, and many others, were carrying and selling my invention. Wal-Mart was willing to carry my products if I were willing to pay for the cost of supplying them up front; then they would send me a check after the products were sold. This is a technique used by many corporate giants to keep them from fronting money on products, thereby putting the burden on the supplier. This is where an inventor usually needs a financier or partner. The other, simpler option is to find a buyer to produce your invention.

The only thing I did not anticipate was overseas competitors, who were also observing my product and ultimately were able to produce my line of easy to remove chlorinator and filtration lids for about half the price. My attorney reminded me that the real purpose of a patent is not to prevent others from copying your product but to give you the right to sue them for doing so. Large distributors know that most small inventors cannot afford to fight them in court, where one could be tied up for years.

It was very rewarding financially to recoup my initial investment in the first year, and I gained a tremendous amount of experience on follow-through. I realized that you can succeed in accomplishing just about anything you set your mind to by using that which with God has blessed you.

Lesson Learned

You can choose to look at challenges as a waste of time, or you can choose never to let Satan have the last word on situations. These experiences can either defeat you or make you stronger. When someone is making things difficult for me, I now choose to praise God for them, because they are causing me to be more determined to overcome everything they do to destroy me!

Miracle Pump!

Two weeks after Hurricane Katrina, Joan still had mud caked in her ears and other crevices after a twenty-foot wave washed over her house, which was two miles inland. It was a blessing that she did not live closer to the beach, where the wave came at thirty feet high. Up to one mile inland, it wiped everything off the face of the earth. Up to seven miles inland, the wave finally splashed onto Interstate 10, leaving a line of seaweed on its thirty-foot bank. Any houses in its path were covered with water, mud, seaweed, the occasional snakes, alligators, and especially eels.

Joan was fortunate to have survived at all, but now two weeks later she craved a freshwater shower with the intensity of a junkie looking for a fix. Joan had been drenched from head to toe with seawater from the tidal wave, and the salt was embedded in her clothes and her skin, causing her to scratch until she was raw. "Is there any chance that ACTS can make a shower for our community, since you have blessed us with food, emergency supplies, and cleaning kits?" she asked.

A group began to exercise faith and talk about how God could help make that miracle happen. "Let's focus on making a list of needed items," one fireman suggested. It was concluded that the following items were necessary:

- Plastic roofing material: We had a few rolls left from the three hundred rolls we had brought on our flatbed semitrucks from Florida, some six hundred miles away.
- Wood to make the structure: There were piles of wood all over from the rubble of once-beautiful wooden structure houses and businesses.
- PVC plumbing and shower heads: These were available if you searched for them from destroyed homes.
- Cardboard to make signs for "In Use" and "Open" shower stalls.
- A pump to create pressure for the water held in a thick rubber bladder.

The pump was the biggest problem, because no one knew where we could get one. After a season of prayer, the group decided to put their plan into action by following through, believing a pump would show up from somewhere, because they had seen God work many previous miracles. Many would never have activated such a plan until they had the pump in hand. But our group acted according to the promises of God. The Bible tells us about Gideon, who actually did not exercise much faith by demanding that God show him several miracles before he would take action in leading Israel into battle to conquer its enemies. But God was faithful to Gideon, and we knew that He would be faithful to us because we had faith and had seen him work.

As what often happens when we pray, God goes to work on our behalf, but we don't necessarily see what He is doing. Our shower construction group did not know that nine hundred miles away a school group from Avon Park, Florida, had just finished packing their trailer to deploy with ACTS. All of a sudden a car pulled up and the driver came in and said, "We have a new pump we would like to donate for you to take to Waveland, Mississippi."

Tom, the leader said, "Oh, no. We have packed everything so tight we don't have room for it." But then he paused for a moment. Then as much to his own surprise as to everyone else's, he continued, "Well, I don't know what we would use that for, but it looks too good to leave behind." They unpacked some other donated supplies to make room for the unusual last-minute item and left to bring their treasures, including forty youth who could hardly wait to help someone in need.

Back in Mississippi, the showers were completed. Some bystanders began to murmur, "It was kind of dumb to go through all the work of making showers without a pump to make it work," but the shower construction group prayed for God to reward their faith for the showers, which would not work without a pump.

Just then a van pulling a trailer came into view. Tom jumped out and said, "We've come to help. We brought emergency supplies, chain saws, and a pump." *A pump!* One of our leaders, Dale Bass, pointed and asked him, "Do you see that group praying over there? Go tell them about the pump. It's their miracle you have brought with you!"

Within two hours the showers were up and running. People in the community got excited, including Joan, who came out of the shower and screamed with the relief of someone who had been dirty for two weeks and had yearned for a shower every day. "I'm finally clean!" Her clean hair and body sparkled with youthfulness once again. She felt like a real human being again. That shower had not only cleansed away the salt and grime, but her depression had been washed away too! Of course, many of our staff were thankful too, because they were smelling like little pigs from working for the ten days in one hundred–degree weather without a drop of rain in sight.

Lesson Learned

We began building the showers by faith. We focused on the needs of the hurting community—showers. What if we had not followed through in completing the shower project because there was no pump to be found?

Never give up believing for your greatest impossibility! Faith, focus, and following through are all essential for you to receive your breakthrough. If you leave off just one key ingredient, you will miss your miracle. Many apply the first two ingredients in life but have not learned to persevere long enough. World changers are those who finish the race of life by faith and get the prize of salvation.

PRAYER FOR TODAY:

Psalm 5:1-12

Help, Lord. I need You this morning and expectantly bring my requests to You! I ask forgiveness from sins, like lying, pride, deceiving, and whatever else You convict me of right now. [Take time to ask for forgiveness for other specific sins.] I refuse to be separated from Your presence, which brings healing to my life right now, in Jesus' name.

Because of Your unfailing love, I love to worship You!

Lead me in the right paths today, or my enemies and challenges will conquer me. Tell me clearly what to do and where to turn today.

May any potential enemies be caught in their own traps today. Some of them are trying to flatter me. Chase them away from me

today. I release any animosity or anger against them. I pray blessings on their lives instead.

I take refuge in Your presence, and I sing joyful praises to You forever!

Protect me today, all my loved ones, and those who love and don't love You yet.

Send someone across my path today who is hurting or does not yet know You, to whom I can be a living, loving Jesus.

Lord, bless me today with Your shield of love!

Chapter 6

LOOKING, LISTENING, AND LEARNING

IMPOSSIBILITIES BECOME POSSIBILITIES by using three keys of looking, listening, and learning in changing your world and developing relationships with others. In order to develop a relationship with God, these same keys are necessary. We look to God in order to understand what His will is for our lives. We listen to Him in quiet, reflective times. The ultimate test of learning is when your example and manifestation of love is consistent with your words.

Spiritual Empowerment

Thank You, Lord, for being there for me when I intentionally search for You.

—MATTHEW 7:8, AUTHOR'S PARAPHRASE

A Parable

Firemen are constantly looking for ways to improve their knowledge in saving lives more effectively. They are taught to stop, look, and listen to the sounds around them. The key to a fireman's success is to always have an attitude of learning and be willing to be taught.

Wreck or Renovation?

While driving on a country road to visit a friend, I was looking in people's open garages and behind their houses hoping to find that unloved, unique collector muscle car that needed a new owner. All at once I hit the brakes;

I had spotted an old, rusted Buick under a large oak tree. By definition, a muscle car has an engine with three hundred horse power or above and refers to vehicles produced before 1971. I pulled into the driveway and knocked on the door of the small ranch house. A retired gentleman opened the door, and I told him how I had noticed his car from the road and admired it.

The first rule of thumb is never to ask if they want to sell their old rusted vehicle, thinking to get a bargain. Some may consider it to be an insult. Many people would absolutely think you were insane for wanting to buy old, rusted out–looking vehicles. They would say, "You couldn't pay me to take that vehicle to the junkyard."

On the outside, this car truly looked like it was ready for the junkyard. After introductions were made, I asked, "Is this your vehicle?"

He answered, "Yes," and went on to share how he had bought the Buick brand new just before the military sent him to Vietnam. He had intended to restore it but had never gotten around to working on it. However, he still had a love for it. I was listening as he shared stories of how he and his wife had enjoyed going on many vacations in this car, as well as how he had raced some of the fastest cars of this muscle car era, such as Ford Mustangs and small block Camaros, and won.

"Would you be willing to show me your car?" I asked, understanding that this was no longer just any car but one with a colorful and memorable history that was personal. By my listening more than talking, we had established the beginnings of a relationship with each other.

"Do you happen to have any pictures of the car when it was new, Jim?"

His eyes lit up with nostalgic joy, "Oh, yes!" he replied, and off he went to find some. He showed me pictures of him and his wife, Tracy, standing together next to the car's hood with two big scoops on it as they embraced. Next we went outside and he showed me his pride and joy. It was a 1970 Buick GTX hardtop four speed with a 360 horsepower, 455-cubic-inch engine! There were only about 400 of these made with a 4 speed.

I was learning more about the car he loved. I asked, "Does this happen to be the original engine?"

Immediately he replied, "Oh, yes. I'm positive it is, but it needs to be rebuilt."

Wow, this car was highly collectible! It was also terribly rusted out, including the frame. Rarely will I investigate any further if there is extensive rust, because it makes restoration very costly. Rust is like a cancer, and even though the rusted areas can be cut out and covered with Bondo or fiberglass (which lasts about twice as long), rust hidden to the naked eye can blister out of a beautiful paint job in several months.

Yet this was a very special collector car. I asked if he might happen to have the original build sheet or bill of sale. (This adds about 35 percent more value to a collector car and substantiates original features, such as the four speed.) He did not remember keeping it. He invited me to look over his car as long as I wanted, and he returned inside his house. I removed the rear seat and looked for where the build sheet was usually fastened to the underside. There it was! The original, although faded and discolored in shades of brown, was still intact, fastened to the seat bottom. I did not pull it out at the time but waited, hoping to do so later. Next I verified that, sure enough, the stamped numbers on a small pad on the engine verified that this *was* the original engine! (This adds about 50 percent more value to a collectable car.) I then walked back up to his house.

"Jim, would you be interested in allowing your pride and joy to go to a new home where it would be restored into the beautiful car you remembered?" I asked, trying not to let my excitement with such a great find be detected.

After getting his phone number and calling him several times, he finally asked how much I might be willing to pay. "Let me come see you, and we'll talk about it," I said, then hurried over before he changed his mind. After arriving, I asked, "How much would you be willing to sell it for?"

As he paused a moment contemplating his answer, I could almost see him replay in fast forward and with great fondness all his favorite memories with that car. "About three thousand dollars," he said, weighing the value of his memories against the reality of the car just taking up space and being an eyesore in his yard.

"How about twenty-five hundred?" I counter-offered, holding out the cash.

His eyes locked on the money. That was a good sign! "OK, I'll take it."

After signing a bill of sale and getting his title, I asked, "Would it be possible for me to leave the Buick where it is for about two weeks?" He agreed.

Next I ran an ad in a car magazine as a car that needed total restoration with matching numbers from the original engine. The first day the advertisement ran, a collector bought the vehicle for my full price, knowing he would have to do a frame-off restoration. His goal was to restore this car to its original beauty. This was truly a situation where the greatness of the car was in the eyes of the beholder—and in the right hands. One man's trash is another man's treasure! I love seeing things not for what they are but what they can become!

Lesson Learned

Do you purchase a car only by the way it looks on the outside? Do you judge a person too quickly by observing only what you see on the outside, thinking you are a good judge of character? When looking for someone to love, look beyond what is on the outside. God loves to look at the inside first, knowing who we can become in Him.

I found this collectable car by using the three important keys of searching—which are looking, listening, and learning—all I could. After the sale, Jim shared with me that a number of people had offered to buy his car in the past, but I was the first one who cared enough to listen to the story of his history, which then created a relationship. The value of the car was not what was on the outside but in listening and learning what was under the hood and hidden under the rear seat. You will find out what someone has or who they are by looking, listening, and learning in order to discover the unusual hidden treasure.

God will reveal what He has in store only for those who pray to see others as God sees them. They may not appear to be desirable or acceptable on the outside, but God knows their heart's desires.

A Diamond in the Rough

Gwynne was a great musician in high school. She was the choir pianist and also played for several singing groups. She was known for being able to play and even sight read the most difficult arrangements. We had the opportunity of performing together on many occasions, mainly in church, community outreach settings, and choir trips. We also attended several classes together during our years at Adelphian Academy in Michigan.

After I became a pastor in Florida, Gwynne's mother had played the organ for me at several of our annual TV-broadcasted camp meetings, and she had shared with me her concerns for her daughter. Gwynne had not attended any church for many years, and a former classmate had told me that Gwynne had lived a hard life. It didn't matter that Gwynne was now a grown woman; her mother was like any other, desperately searching for someone, anyone who would help her daughter!

It was heart-breaking to hear of one more person from high school who had dropped out of church. The number was alarmingly high. It had been about twenty-five years since graduation, and I was pastoring in Mount Dora, Florida, near Orlando when I learned that Gwynne was also living in the area. After requesting her phone number, one day I called and in response to her hello I said, "How are you doing, Gwynne? This is David Canther." We exchanged generic pleasantries, and although she seemed friendly enough and genuinely pleased to hear from me, I detected a wariness in her voice.

"We need someone to play the piano at my church," I stated. The shock she felt at such a statement resounded loudly in the complete silence on her end. Even the sound of her breathing had disappeared, but I hurried on, "We've just lost our regular pianist and need someone like you. Your mom told me you that you were in the area, so I was wondering if you would be interested in playing for us." There was a long pause, so long in fact that I was just about to ask if she was still there, when I heard a soft sigh. In that sigh I could feel a vast array of emotions that words could not fully convey.

"You don't want me," she said softly. "You don't know who I am anymore." In that statement I heard the shame, guilt, and despair she felt at her life. She went on to tell me about her life. She'd become pregnant out of wedlock, and although she married the father of her unborn child, her church in Michigan demanded that she resign from the various leadership positions she held because she was not a good role model for the children in their church. Gwynne understood and meekly complied, but she missed very much being involved with music. Several years later she and her family moved to Florida, where they were welcomed into a local church, and once again Gwynne was actively involved in music ministry.

However, after nearly ten years enduring a very rocky marriage, she and her husband divorced (pregnancy does not necessarily make a good foundation for a lasting marriage), and once again her church demanded she resign from music ministry because she was not a good role model for the children in their church. Already emotionally worn down from everything that was wrong in her marriage, Gwynne decided she did not want to be responsible for corrupting the children in the church, so she walked out, never to return.

Gwynne went on to tell of how she had taken up with a man, and they had lived together for a number of years. During that time she had become addicted to drugs and alcohol and had spent some time in jail. At the time of my phone call, Gwynne had broken off her relationship with him but still retained some of the bad habits. Listening to her story, I could hear the desperation in her unspoken words. She was desperate for someone to find the value in her that she could no longer find in herself, desperate for someone to forgive what she could not forgive herself for, and desperate for someone to offer the hand of grace—and mercy—and help her stand up again.

"I must admit, though," she said with a smile that could be heard in her voice, "I do miss the music."

Ahh, there it was: my open door. She lived forty-five minutes from my church, and I already knew from her mother that Gwynne was having a tough time financially, so I offered, "Gwynne, what kind of financial package would make this attractive to you?"

We talked further, and in closing she gave me an ultimatum. Having admitted to her past, she reasoned, "David, you might as well tell the church board I'm a smoker. They'll smell it on me anyway. I know I should quit, but to be honest I don't have any plans to do so in the immediate future."

"Gwynne," I assured her, "we just want to love you. It's up to God to change you."

She almost laughed out loud, but it came out as, "Ha! If you can really do that, I'd be impressed!" She insisted on two guarantees before she'd agree to come play for us: 1) that I would be up front with the church board about her smoking, and 2) that no one would preach to her about the harmful effects of smoking; she already knew them. Having already been disciplined by two separate churches, she didn't think she could survive it happening a third time. We must agree to accept her just the way she was and not get impatient with her if God didn't change her the way the church board wanted. I agreed.

I met with my church board and appealed to their sense of compassion. "Gwynne is a good friend of mine and is going through some challenging times right now, and she needs an opportunity for God to do something big in her life in the right, loving environment. She doesn't believe that a church exists where she could be loved and accepted just as she is. She smokes and is in financial hardship, but if you are willing to show her your support, she said she would love to play the piano for us. I went out on a limb and told her that I believed we could help her with a stipend. After all, we already help many people out financially from our community that we hardly know and ask for nothing in return."

Each member cast their vote and the decision was made. Now it was time to let Gwynne know. "Gwynne," I exclaimed enthusiastically when she answered, "the church board has voted unanimously for you to come play the piano! Now, how soon can we schedule you to come?" I was already leafing through my datebook to get a confirmed start date for her.

Again, there was a long pause. It wasn't until much later I learned the reason for that long pause. She had gotten stuck on the word *unanimous* and hadn't heard the rest of what I'd said. In that one word she said we had conveyed unconditional love to her, something she needed desperately. In that one word we had collectively declared her valuable and needed. In that simple word, she understood it meant it to mean that no one said no. The walls of hurt, guilt, betrayal, and condemnation that had taken years to build began to crumble.

You would think that would be a nice ending to her story, but it wasn't the end. We had agreed upon a date, giving her time to practice, as she told me she hadn't played piano in about ten years. That day had finally arrived, and I looked forward to not only welcoming her to my church but working with her again musically.

On the first week that she was scheduled to come play for us, word got to me that I had a phone call in the office. "David, it's Gwynne." My heart began to sink at the sound of her voice, which was strained and tense. "My car won't start, and I can't get a ride. I won't be able to come today."

Somehow, I knew in my spirit that it was fear more than car problems keeping her away. One of our families lived near her, so I told her that I would call them to see if they could pick her up. Hanging up the phone without giving her the chance to argue with me, I called the Peters. Sure enough, they agreed to pick her up. When I called her back to tell her they were on their way, she was polite, but I could tell she wasn't very happy. Silently I sent up a prayer on her behalf, then, leaving the situation in God's hands, I went about my morning activities.

Gwynne arrived appearing brave on the outside, but if anyone had looked in her eyes they would have seen that she was terrified. She did a great job that day, and the service went smoothly. Afterward I overheard several people telling her how much they had enjoyed her music.

It was about eighteen months later, and Gwynne was just about to play special music when she surprised everyone by first going to the podium and asking for everyone on the church board to please stand. Those who were present did so, though they looked from one to the other trying to figure out what was going on. "I wanted to see who you were," Gwynne said with a big smile on her face. "When David first asked me to come play the piano here, I had a smoking habit of over a pack a day. You are the ones who voted unanimously to let me come play here anyway. I wanted to tell you thank you from the bottom of my heart. You gave me a second chance when no one else would." She paused just a moment as she made eye contact with everyone standing before continuing. "And I wanted to let you know your gamble on me paid off, for today makes nine weeks since I had a cigarette!" My church family, now her church family, jumped to their feet in a standing ovation for what God had done in her life.

A few years later, Gwynne stood at the podium once more as she declared to her family that although they may not have known, she was also now free from marijuana too. (She had been stoned that first week she came to play for us. In fact, I found out later that she had been so scared to face church people again that she had smoked three joints! For years she played stoned, while God worked to deliver her from the addiction and from the fear that kept her in bondage to it.) Once again, they rose to their feet in applause for God's miraculous power in her life. She went on to raise money for missions in Cuba, El Salvador, the Dominican Republic, Africa, and the Philippines.

Now here's the rest of the story: One Friday night when Gwynne was still living with her crack addict boyfriend, alienated from her family, she had gotten high. Getting high was a daily occurrence, but this time her boyfriend had laced the joints with additional drugs. Her heart began to race and thunder in her chest. She had trouble breathing, and her vision blurred. She was scared and thought she was going to die. Suddenly it was as if her eyes were finally opened and she saw the life she was living. "What am I doing here?" she asked herself. "I don't belong here!" She told me that the parable of the talents came to her mind, and she remembered that the unused talent was taken away. And she began to pray, "Lord, please don't take away my music. I promise to one day use it for you, although I don't know how or when. Please save my music!" Immediately peace washed over her soul, and she knew God had heard her prayer. Her heart rate slowed back down to normal, her breathing stabilized, and her vision cleared.

Although that particular Friday night occurred about three years before my phone call to her, when I asked if she would come play piano at my church, that long silence was because she recognized it was God calling her to hold up her end of that Friday night prayer. Little did I know at the time that to Gwynne I was the voice of God!

She first came to our church to play twelve years ago, and Gwynne is still at that same church. Not long after she began playing for us, her mother joined her, and for seven years we enjoyed their organ and piano duets, as only mother and daughter can do.

Lesson Learned

I went *looking* for Gwynne as God goes looking for you! I *listened* to Gwynne's need to feel needed. I went out on a limb and encouraged my church board to accept her—just the way she was, just like God does for us! She had given up on herself, but praise God, He hadn't given up on her! When Gwynne thought she was learning how to love and be loved once again, we as a congregation were learning the most!

Today, because of her past, Gwynne is able to encourage those who would stay away from God for fear they've gone too far. She tells them, "Hey! I went back to church because they *paid* me! How honorable is that?" But it got her in the environment to hear the Word of God and to be surrounded by people who were committed to loving others!

PRAYER FOR TODAY:

Ephesians 1:17-20

I ask that You, Father, may give me the spirit of wisdom and revelation of who Christ is and what He has done for me. I pray that my heart will be flooded with light to see the inheritance promised to me. I understand how incredibly great Your power is to me as a believer. It is the same mighty power that raised Christ from the dead and caused Him to sit at Your right hand in heaven.

Chapter 7

T.I.M.E.: TIMING, IMPACTING, MAXIMIZING, ELIMINATING

Do you recognize that *time* is the greatest gift God has given you? How you use your time and what you do with it determines your ultimate effectiveness in serving others. Many have good intentions but say, "I don't have time to help others." When you eliminate those things on which you spend negative, or wasted, energy, it is amazing how much time you really have to share love. Your weakest link or whatever sin is in your life will ultimately destroy you. You either need to deal with it and dispose of the distractions in your life, or it will consume you.

Timing is something we can't control in life. To be at the right place at the right time is when God provides an opportunity to bless you or help someone who is in need.

What you choose everyday is *impacting* your life and determines who you will become. *Maximizing* the time you have by using it to your best advantage is the key. *Eliminating* distractions and disappointments in your life will prevent you from becoming unproductive and burned out.

Spiritual Empowerment

> By faith I accept divine guidance. This gives me vision and establishes goals to accomplish vision.
>
> —Philippians 4:13 and Proverbs 29:18, author's paraphrase

Every day you make choices in what and how much you eat, watch, and say. The challenge in life is for you to align your life with God's Word and accept His ideal for your life. Because His Word is true, and it is His living Word, encapsulated within each promise is the power to bring it to pass in your life. It is important for you to have a correct belief system, despite however many negative experiences may have occurred in your life. God's teaching and instruction in His Word is the best roadmap for your life. By capitalizing on God's guidance in your life, you accept His timing, rather than yours, when it comes to the gospel of serving others.

A Parable

The timing of firemen in "First Response" is crucial to being ready at any time, 24 hours a day. How efficiently they respond is also crucial in impacting their task at hand. Their main career demands maximizing their time and eliminating distractions.

As I mentioned before, one of my favorite hobbies throughout the years has been to fix broken-down vehicles and to collect and restore classic cars. I love to see how something that has been rejected and viewed as useless by some can become something great.

Fixing broken things is extremely rewarding for me. I love the process of assessing an object and seeing it not for what it is—an item looking as if it's ready for the garbage dump—but how it can become something great once again in the eyes of a new owner.

I love to become involved with someone who the church or society or family has rejected and cast aside as useless or unimportant. By helping transform them into a valuable asset once again not only in the eyes of others but especially in their own, all through love and encouragement, is without a doubt one of life's greatest blessings.

A guideline for determining whether or not something no longer has value or is garbage, or if it is something of worthwhile greatness to purchase is this: nothing is impossible to fix. The question is, Are you willing to invest the time and resources needed to fix it at this time in your life? You must ask yourself:

- Is this the appropriate timing financially or emotionally in your life to make this decision?
- Will the decision have a positive effect in your life and the life of others? In other words, is it worth the price you will have to pay?
- Maximize things that create positive outcomes. Get rid of or stay away from things when your gut reaction is one of caution.

- If you don't plan to fix it and use it in the next year, try eliminating it from your possession!

Blessed With the Best!

I responded to a newspaper ad while on a vacation in Sarasota, Florida, for a gold Acura, which is a high-end, luxury Honda. Roger, a retired salesman in a large marketing firm, answered the phone. Even though I knew his price was below book value, even without factoring in that his vehicle was twenty thousand miles below normal driving mileage allotments, I asked, "How negotiable are you on the price?" That took some courage, because the wrong timing can hurt a purchase. But if you plant that thought in their mind ahead of time, it is very helpful. I couldn't sound overexcited in purchasing this vehicle for his asking price.

Roger paused, then said, "Well, come and look at it, and we'll talk."

We met about an hour later. Upon seeing the car in person, I clearly realized acquiring this vehicle would impact my daughter Autumn's life in a positive way, as it would allow her to be able to drive another vehicle while she was home for the summer. First, Roger and I talked about common interests. It was my goal to establish a relationship with him. I then asked to drive his beautiful, meticulously cared for car. He had kept it garaged, along with full documentation of all service records for the vehicle.

I asked him, "Is there anything that doesn't work?" That is always a good question to ask, but in this particular situation, I believed I would not be spending much in repairs.

"Not that I am aware of," he replied.

Once again I asked the big question: "How negotiable are you on the price?" Mentally I was prepared to offer him two hundred fifty dollars less, but I was ready to pay full price.

He answered, "How about five hundred dollars less?"

I smiled a huge grin and quickly exclaimed, "That would be great!"

Later, after we had consummated the transaction, Roger shared that there were about ten other messages on his answering machine from individuals wanting to purchase this vehicle. I recognized that I was *maximizing* on yet another opportunity. Even between private parties it is wise to get a bill of sale, so I then asked Roger to write one out stating the selling price, vehicle ID, and title numbers, including both of our names listed as "buyer" and "seller," and the date, *eliminating* reasons for legal questions in the future.

When I went to have the title transferred at the department of motor vehicles, the receptionist informed me, "I see that the purchase price listed on the back of the title is far less than what the National Automobile Dealers Association shows its value to be, so sales tax will be charged on the listed book value."

Showing her the paper I said, "I have a bill of sale showing the actual selling price." I had maximized on yet another opportunity, saving another three hundred dollars in taxes because of this valuable piece of paper!

Altogether, God blessed us, and we now enjoyed driving a vehicle that was actually worth just over twice what I paid. Because of its pristine condition, the Acura looks like a brand-new vehicle!

While removing his personal items so I could take possession of the car, Roger noticed that the plastic clip to the glass holder was broken. He informed me that he had called the Acura dealership and ordered a new retractable glass holder for me. Later that week when I stopped in to the dealership to pick up the part, I was amazed to find out that this holder cost him almost two hundred dollars. Blessed once again! Most importantly, he was happy, being that he felt in charge of receiving what he ultimately wanted out of his car. I was happy too. I had also made a new friend. We've talked several times since then, reminiscing over shared life experiences.

Your best blessing in life comes when you come to realize that the people who ride in your vehicle are more important than the vehicle you drive!

Lesson Learned

The key to building loving relationships is to be consistently compassionate in your business dealings and in your marriage and to your children, grandchildren, and those in your community in need. Sometimes you may become tempted to mistreat others in business dealings and love only those who you chose to love. Your reputation of what others think of you in all you do is essential to be effective in serving others.

These keys will also help you when purchasing items and working through challenges to maximize being a good steward of the money with which God has entrusted you, while maintaining loving relationships.

People often ask themselves after failed opportunities, "Was it God's will?" Some individuals may state that the reason they missed purchasing something of potential value was because it may not have been God's will anyway; however, they miss out on tremendous opportunities by not following these simple steps. To create a stronger sense of confidence before purchasing an object, offer to provide a cash deposit that will be refunded to you if after having the item inspected it reveals extensive repairs are needed.

These practical tools are opportunities of great blessings! I thanked God for blessing me with the Acura, because the day before I had called regarding a newspaper ad for a Toyota Camry that was also a good deal. A time was set for me to meet the seller, but about five minutes before arriving to look at his car he called to inform me that someone else had just purchased it. I could have gotten angry and chastised him, feeling miserable because I had lost out, but instead I chose to trust in God and claimed by faith, "OK, God, I'm ready to receive a bigger blessing!"

Keys to Effective Emergency Response Deployments

As incident commander or unit chief of a deployment, timing is everything in leading. Your main object is to motivate others with a clear incident action plan, making quick life-or-death decisions. Everything the incident commander says or does impacts the outcome of both the ACTS leadership team and helps others in need in the community. Maximizing using volunteers' passion, time, and talents encourages them to deploy again in the future, and eliminating unnecessary tasks brings fulfillment.

Many people ask, "How is it that ACTS can have such a high rate of successful, rapid deployment in emergency response?" The important principle of learning how to make decisions as a team using the principles of T.I.M.E. and building relationships with each other and with local, state, and federal leaders is the key.

ACTS has been responding to disasters since 2004. This has included twenty-seven deployments, most of them federal declarations, with seventy-one thousand trained volunteers. Disaster preparedness has been a huge learning curve for me, as in what to do or not to do. Due to my somewhat perfectionist nature, it was a challenge to stop chastising myself by thinking, "If only I could do or say that over again."

In 2008, there was a string of tornados that devastated Tennessee, the worst in thirty-five years. After making a few phone calls to our regional ACTS World Relief directors, within twenty-four hours, three teams of trained volunteers were on their way with two hundred ten youth and adults from four different schools.

Our protocol is for a first response team leader to develop a relationship with the local emergency operations director in the county where the storm has had the most damaging results. If for whatever reason this cannot be done, then most often we have one of our team firemen responders visit the local fire station where the storm has occurred and find out what their greatest needs are. This is necessary in order for ACTS to provide resources to them and establish relationships.

Surprisingly enough, we consistently hear from the media, "Volunteers are *not* needed," and that local resources are taking care of the needs. Why are the media trained to say this when in most cases the community is destroyed and the reality of the situation is far different? The underlying reason is that local emergency leaders do not want a bunch of well-meaning volunteers showing up who will need to be fed and housed, putting a further strain on local emergency food and housing services, which have already been hugely affected by the disaster. In addition, they don't want an influx of strangers coming into their community who may be tempted to loot a variety of valuable personal items. Furthermore strangers, and many well-wishers, cause a heavier load on local law enforcement personnel, as they also do not have the necessary personnel to oversee or train volunteers in what to do. This creates another disaster, because it is also a fact that more individuals are hurt or killed trying to save others than were originally affected. This is largely due to a lack in safety training and management. *Trained* volunteers are truly needed!

CBS interviewed me for about six hours for a four-minute national feature on disaster preparedness and response. It was evident that their underlying desire was for me to say negative things about FEMA and destroy the agency's reputation, for FEMA had been highly criticized for their lack of performance in Hurricane Katrina, in 2005. Long ago I learned that the moment you start criticizing others, watch out, because you are about to fall yourself. CBS chose to title the feature "Faster than FEMA." It was good that I did not criticize them, because I continue to build strong relationships with friends in FEMA, who are trying hard to improve their performance and collaborate especially with the best faith-based disaster response organizations in the world. Faith-based organizations have learned how to respond effectively with far less resources than big government, and they have discovered how to harness the vision of attracting volunteers.

Lessons Learned

In personal and emergency response, the principles of T.I.M.E. (timing, impacting, maximizing, and eliminating) are what make helping others in emergencies rewarding!

Eye-Watering Smell

Henry was someone you could smell coming long before you could see him. It was obvious how some people would avoid even shaking his hand for fear of contracting some kind of terminal virus. I was Henry's pastor. One day he informed me that he had been evicted from his double-wide mobile home and needed to get everything out by the next day.

"Wow," I exclaimed. "One day doesn't give us much time to rally helpers."

The next day the first call I made was to the bank where his mortgage was held. "Is there any way that we as a church could help keep Henry from losing his house?"

"No, it is too late," the loan officer replied. "We have tried repeatedly to get Henry to pay or work on a new payment structure, but to no avail. It has been six months since he has paid anything toward his mortgage."

Later that day my son Andrew, his friend Tom, his friend's father, Ted, and I showed up with a rental truck ready to work. We knocked on the front door.

"Henry, are you home?" we called out when there was no answer. After knocking and calling to him again, we opened the front door. The smell almost knocked me off my feet. My senses were assaulted by a myriad of undistinguishable odors, all of which were beyond unpleasant.

Henry was not home. We knew that his home would be taken over by the bank the next day, and by the look of things, we had two days' work that we needed to cram into an afternoon. But we had walked through the front door and into another world. We've all heard stories of hermits living in detestable conditions, but this one surely would have won a trophy for first place. We could not even see to the kitchen because piles of rotting garbage were lined up like a tunnel throughout the house. We had to walk in single file, because there was not enough room for us to walk two people wide. When we finally made it to the kitchen, all we could do was stare in horror and amazement at the countless piles of old, half-eaten containers of food lying everywhere. It appeared that when he opened cans of food, Henry would leave them where they were after eating some of the contents or simply toss them in any given direction. The ants and roaches were having a party. Rat and mice feces practically covered the floor. Looking at each other in utter dismay, we asked each other, "Where do we begin, and what do we do?"

In disaster response, the first thing first responders do is begin a general search-and-rescue for dead bodies. It certainly smelled like something had died. I began clearing a path to Henry's bedroom. He had black sheets draped over the windows, which made the room pretty dark. We removed them, allowing light to filter feebly through the dirt and grime on the windows.

As I passed by the hall bathroom, I almost retched. The bathtub had a thick, seemingly impenetrable layer of green slime, origin unknown, that appeared to have been there for an indeterminate length of time. We surmised that his water must have been shut off due to nonpayment of his water bill for some time. Not only did the toilet not work, but the sight and stench of human waste would have even gagged someone without a sense of smell! Dirty underwear was strewn about everywhere amidst other articles of clothing, practically stiff with dried sweat, dirt, and grime.

"How can a human being exist in a house of this condition?" I asked incredulously to no one in particular. It was something I couldn't even fathom.

Andrew was groaning with stomach pain from the fetid odors. "Open all the doors and windows!"

We first searched through piles of boxes for important papers, pictures, or possibly money. Sure enough, we found uncashed checks mixed in with countless notices of unpaid bills. It seemed that with every piece of mail that came in his mailbox, his *timing* to pay had long passed. He purchased many unneeded items, *impacting* his life with one wrong choice after the next, creating massive confusion in his life. Yet he would still send off for another chance to win another million-dollar prize, like from the Readers Digest lottery. Countless papers indicated that he was maximizing his chance for a bigger prize than before, but the only thing he was really *maximizing* was collecting everything, without releasing or *eliminating* a thing.

Henry definitely did not believe in, or contribute to, the recycling process. His life had come to a complete, inefficient stopping point. Rather than managing life, it now was managing him. Behind his bedroom door was a loaded double barrel shotgun for protection in the event of a burglary. His best defense, however, was to rely on the intruders' eyes watering to the point of blinding them with a river from their tear ducts. His terrible living conditions were his best defense.

After a full day of sorting and packing, we met Henry at his new residence, and he asked, "Did you find a picture of my mother and my Bible?"

I responded with a smile on my face, "Yes, Henry, we sure did!" All the rest of his earthly possessions were either taken to the dump or to a thrift store, and someone else was blessed in their journey of life of receiving, releasing, and activating recycling.

The following week we became even more determined to sort through the good and the garbage at our homes. Henry was thankful that he could begin anew at a nursing care center and arranged his few belongings on his table next to his bedside. Life was now manageable again for him.

Lesson Learned

Implementing the principles of T.I.M.E. would have prevented Henry from losing his house. Thankfully, these same principles helped us in disposing of his personal possessions.

Tossed in the Wind

Jerry, at seventy-three years old, lived a rather unusual lifestyle. He had worked hard all his life and, according to his children, was a multi-millionaire father who lived on top of a mountain in a simple single-wide mobile home. Jerry's wife had passed away fifteen years before. He lived alone with his dog, cat, and three registered quarter horses. His beautiful horses were valued at forty thousand dollars each. He took exceptional care of them on his rolling one hundred acres of fenced property in Tennessee. Whenever his daughter or son desired to come visit with his four grandchildren, they were welcome to ride horses or just relax.

After the sudden passing of his wife due to cancer, Jerry came to grips with how fragile life was and chose to live to love those whom he cherished. Some of his former business associates and banker friends had miscalculated the stock market *timing* while living in their big houses with a big mortgage when they retired, only to reap a huge amount of stress. Jerry's choice was *impacting* his children and grandchildren, leaving them with a cherished legacy of love. He was *maximizing* the time he could spend with each of them, rather than saying, "I wish I would have…."

His son, David, and daughter, Michelle, had often encouraged him to build a more substantial house if he wanted to remain living on top of the mountain, one that could weather the strong winds and tornados that were common to the area, but Jerry thought *eliminating* the payments of building a new house on top of the mountain would be a better decision.

One evening, conditions were such that weather reports claimed the high probability of tornados in the area. Although Jerry often watched the weather channel while he ate, this night he did not. Suddenly, a category 5 tornado came through his property. No sooner had the tornado—sounding like a freight train—alerted Jerry to danger than it had sucked his mobile home right off its foundation. It was now wrapped around a cluster of pine trees. The steel frame looked like something out of a sci-fi movie, the twisted pieces sticking out at odd angles about fifteen feet in the air. Just like that, Jerry's home was gone! He was found dead about forty feet from the site of impact, still sitting in his dining chair. Actually, he had died instantly from choking on his food, not from injuries sustained by the tornado. One horse had also perished after having been thrown through the air like a rag doll. The other two were virtually left unscathed. In an instant, the tornado had touched down, leaving complete devastation and death in its wake.

ACTS World Relief sent its first response team into the area despite the usual announcements on TV that volunteers were not needed.

When we meet with leaders of affected communities, it is standard protocol for us to share with them the following information regarding our deployment procedures:

- ACTS World Relief is National Incident Management Systems–compliant and has trained CERT (Community Emergency Response Teams) team volunteers who are experienced from having responded to many international emergencies who would love to be a resource with their CERT teams or fire department. Our experience comes from responding to seventeen federally declared disasters, both domestic and international.
- ACTS has memoranda of understanding (MOU) or statements of understanding (SOU) with many state agencies in their plans for comprehensive emergency management. We collaborate with local, state, and federal agencies. By providing these services to gather data, it helps to qualify each county for more and quicker federal emergency assistance. We use mission assignment FEMA incident action forms, which we submit daily.
- ACTS has certified and screened individuals who work with the Department of Health under ESF 8 (Emergency Support Functions) of Health and Medical who are qualified to be assigned a grid section of the map of any affected area and conduct a door-to-door special unmet needs assessment. We provide emotional, spiritual, and physical care by trained volunteers. We bring the results each evening, or whenever needed, on a spreadsheet showing where the needs are, including the addresses.
- ACTS has trained teams who sort and carry debris to the roadside if those affected desire assistance. We also provide emergency cleanup or de-mucking.
- ACTS has commercial mobile kitchens, which operate under ESF 6 (Mass Care), to help provide hot meals for both the volunteers and those affected in the community. By request, we can serve up to thirty-five thousand hot meals per day with our larger kitchens. We also have a statement of understanding to work in collaboration with the Red Cross.
- ACTS is totally self-sufficient in housing needs.

- ACTS can establish points of distribution for the community with our fleet of semitrucks, all-terrain forklifts, and large, circus-sized tents for instant warehousing and the distribution of in-kind donation goods. We have experience in managing state warehousing for Florida in 2004. Our resource inventory list will never incur a cost that we will not reimburse.
- Go to the ACTS website at www.actswr.org and view testimonies from governors and emergency management directors like Jeff Kelley, who ACTS has worked with in Bridge City, Texas. The CBS feature on ACTS World Relief is also available for viewing at that website.
- ACTS is a member of national VOAD (Voluntary Organizations Active in Disaster) and AERDO (Association of Evangelical Relief and Disaster Organizations), which shows how closely we work with other organizations.
- ACTS uses the CAN (Coordinated Assistance Network) case management software to record data of initial to long-term needs of individuals which is submitted weekly.

When we shared this with the emergency management director in Tennessee, he immediately introduced us to the mayor and fire chief. He then handed us a grid section of their county. Due to lack of personnel, they had not been able to complete thorough assessments of the unmet needs in these areas.

This is how we came to Jerry's property on top of the mountain, where we found his son and daughter in tears. "How can we help you?" we asked.

They responded, "Could you please try to help us find some of dad's personal papers and also the registration papers of his quarter horses? The horses are only worth a fraction of their value if we cannot locate these papers. They were placed in a dresser next to his bed." Not a piece of furniture had been found since the tornado, and we knew a miracle was needed. Calling together a specially trained search-and-rescue team for this specific assignment, I explained to them what we needed to find. Then we huddled in a circle with arms locked together in prayer.

"Lord, You know where these important papers are located. Thank You for using us as Your servants to find them for this devastated family. We anticipate that it is not by might, nor by power, but by Your spirit that these papers will be miraculously found." (Many of our youth in ACTS are well trained in claiming God's Word by faith. They have seen Him work with the impossibilities over and over again. Seeing and being a part of God's miracles is what keeps them committed to serving others.)

As we looked down the mountainside, we could see the unmistakable narrow path the tornado had taken across a road, over a pond, and up the other side of a mountain about two miles away. The trees left behind had been completely stripped, uprooted, or broken in half. We looked over at a pile of rubble about ten feet high by fifty feet long. In that pile was what was left of everything Jerry had owned. The challenge was coming up with the strategy of how to sort through the pile and effectively separate the good from the bad!

First, we began with the principles of sorting, discussed in chapter 5, "Faith, Focus, and Following Through." Next, we implemented the keys of searching from chapter 6, "Looking, Listening, and Learning." Then the principles of this chapter were needed for disposing the garbage into piles, because time—T.I.M.E., timing, impacting, maximizing, and eliminating—was working against us.

There is a team of at-risk adolescent youth from Advent Home in Tennessee who frequently respond with ACTS. They understand the chain of command better than any, and we assigned them in one direction. Another group of seven went to work on the large pile. Another team went down the hill, across the road searching in the pond, and up the other side of the mountain looking for valuable papers. As incident commander, I remained at the command post, the site where the mobile home had once stood. After about an hour, the teams began returning with their treasures, excited by what they had found.

As we began assembling the valuable personal papers, we found registration papers for two of the horses still totally intact. They had been found one mile away, up the other side of the mountain. Tim found the registration papers to one and Shellie found the papers to the other as they climbed trees, where miraculously the precious papers had been held, waiting for God's children to bring them safely home. Many other important papers were recovered, including insurance and banking documents. With great joy we handed them to the family members and praised God that we were able to play a small part in helping to reassemble their lives and give hope to the hurting.

Lesson Learned

Jerry had actually learned the principles of T.I.M.E. in his lifestyle. He just happened to be at the wrong place at the wrong time when the tornado hit his house. After his death, the principles of timing, impacting, maximizing, and eliminating were utilized by a special sorting team in performing search-and-rescue techniques.

On the day of the search those youth realized, once again, that they were the extended hands and feet of Jesus to a suffering world. Their lives were forever changed as they utilized another opportunity for living to love those whose lives had been shattered, giving them hope for just one more day!

PRAYER FOR TODAY: the Prayer of Aaron

Bless and protect me. Smile upon me and be gracious to me. Show me Your favor, and give me Your peace.

—Numbers 6:24–26, author's paraphrase

Chapter 8

TEAM WORK— MULTIPLYING, MOTIVATING, AND MOVEMENTS

Would you like to multiply the gifts God has given you in ACTS of Love? Are you effective in motivating others to serve effectively? Are the words you speak always positive and encouraging, attracting people who want to be in your presence, and join your team? You are about to discover more keys to unlock the power of the gospel!

Those who put down others will only have short-term relationships, because this ultimately creates division within a team. The ultimate goal is for you to create a movement for God's kingdom, which is unstoppable! God wants you to be effective in multiplying and motivating others around you to build a *team that becomes a movement* for God's kingdom! Your gifts will keep on multiplying the more you share them. Your influence for good will grow in motivating others to accomplish more and more, when they become inspired by what God is doing through you! You are creating a *team approach to life*, which becomes a movement in accomplishing miracles. Let's explore ways to develop unity and healthy teams!

The greatest miracle is having a healthy team in marriage. Approaching life too independently and mistakenly thinking you can do most everything on your own will ultimately create loneliness.

Spiritual Empowerment

Lord, I am one of Your positive speaking, faith-filled army. Thank You for rescuing me and giving me victory!

—Judges 7:7 and Galatians 3:13, author's paraphrase

> Lord, I choose life and not death! My words will give life and health to all those around me.
>
> —Deuteronomy 30:19 and Proverbs 4:20–24, author's paraphrase
>
> My tongue has the power of life and death to influence those around me.
>
> —Proverbs 18:21, author's paraphrase

Jesus sent the disciples out two by two. The reason for this was so they could encourage one another because He knew there would be challenging, discouraging times ahead.

Do not become discouraged if you seem to be overwhelmed in serving others. Find a partner to begin a team, and it will grow! Remember, it only takes one rotten apple or negative person, even if he or she is well-meaning, to destroy everything good you believe God will do through you! But God promises, "Where two or three of you are gathered together seeking Me, I will bless you" (Matt. 18:20, author's paraphrase).

Accomplishing the impossible is only possible when we are united together as a team! Satan knows this all too well and spends most of his time trying to keep us divided, or fighting amongst ourselves. Reaching out to other members of the team and meeting their needs will eliminate the majority of negative, wasted energy and multiplies exponentially the efforts to help others. "United we stand and divided we fall" is an important rule of life. The most powerful demonstration to convert others to Christianity is for believers to be a united a team!

Furthermore, the words you choose to speak will either bring life or destruction to you and to those around you. David says that "one who stirs up dissention" is one of the six things that God hates (Prov. 6:19)!

A team can be destroyed in a moment or over a period of time through hurtful, thoughtless, negative, or destructive words against individuals or organizations. This principle cannot be overstressed. I have personally learned from it and have watched it take place over and over again. Individuals turn against each other when this takes place.

Thankfully, love covers over all our wrongs and mistakes when we ask for each other's forgiveness (1 Pet. 4:8).

What can you say if some well-meaning individual thinks you should know about the latest challenge someone might be facing and speaks negatively about them? I like to say, "Why don't we just take a moment to lift __________ together up in prayer right now and pray for God to bless them?" It's amazing when you do that a few times how these individuals will no longer seek you out—or you might gain an encouraging prayer partner!

> ***A Parable***
>
> *Firemen are masters of multiplying the talents of their team into motivating others to accomplish great feats of historic proportion in saving lives. They are clearly known as creating a movement in exemplifying teamwork for lives of action!*

How to Become a United Team

I have used these essential ingredients of building a healthy united team for many years. They are listed below in a building order of importance:

- **Faith:** Begin everything you do with God.

  Faith pleases God.

  —Hebrews 11:6, author's paraphrase

  Faith gives victory!

  —1 John 5:4, author's paraphrase

- **Focus:** Understand how God has a calling on your life.

  God is calling you to serve others in love.

  —Galatians 5:13, author's paraphrase

- **Fear:** Recognize it is an opportunity to apply the promises of God for victory!

  Love removes fear.

  —1 John 4:18, author's paraphrase

  God has not given you a spirit of fear.

  —2 Timothy 1:7, author's paraphrase

- **Flexibility**: We live in an environment of constant change.

  God desires to change the way you think.

  —Romans 12:2

- **Failure**: See it as an opportunity to view each mistake as building for success.

  You are a failure until you find the answer is trusting in Jesus Christ.

  —Romans 7:24

- **Forgiveness**: Be quick to offer this key, because everyone makes mistakes.

  God is faithful to forgive you, so forgive one another.

  —1 John 1:9, author's paraphrase

- **Fun**: Take time to enjoy life!

  God's joy produces your strength!

  —Nehemiah 8:10, author's paraphrase

  Think positively!

  —Philippians 4:8, author's paraphrase

- **Fulfillment**: Experience the result of loving unconditionally.

  God wants you to live a life of fulfillment!

  —John 10:10, author's paraphrase

- **Friendships**: These are the greatest gift, one that will last throughout eternity.

  Now you can have sincere love for each other because you are forgiven.

  —1 Peter 1:22, author's paraphrase

Snap, Crackle, and Pop!

God taught me the important principle of why teamwork is essential, even if it is not with a person. I had just finished restoring a 1970 convertible GTO with a 455 cubic inch, ultimate 340 horsepower engine. After six months of having the car on jack stands, I finally let it down on its four new tires and started the radical rumbling engine. Anxious to see how it would perform, I took the car out for a neck-snapping, rubber-laying short drive and realized a quick adjustment of the transmission linkage was needed so that it would shift better.

Again I jacked the car up in the air. I briefly thought about putting it on jack stands once again but rationalized, "Ah, this will only take a minute."

As I slid under the car, all of a sudden I watched the jack fall over as if in slow motion, and the car fell down on top of me. The heavy car bounced several times from having suddenly plunged from the height of the jack. Stunned, I listened to the alarming sound of my ribs snapping, cracking, and popping with each bounce. The car finally settled. "I'm still alive!" I breathed to myself, amazed I was still conscious. "Sherri, come help me," I rasped.

"She's never going to hear me," I thought to myself. The weight of the car on my chest made it nearly impossible to breathe, let alone take a big enough breathe that it would enable me to yell loudly for my wife to hear from inside the house. Fighting panic and praying for wisdom, I waited a brief moment. God is always faithful! Immediately I knew what to do, and by the grace of God, I kicked the jack around with my feet, stood it back up and jacked it back up with my legs. Painfully, I pulled myself out from under the car, using one of the frame rails.

Standing up was excruciating! My body felt like it had suddenly aged about thirty years. Trying not to groan with each step, I made it into the house, where I described my newest adventure to my wife. She immediately insisted that she take me to the emergency room, but I let her know that I would be fine and drove myself in to have X-rays.

The X-rays revealed that I had sustained four cracked ribs, but thankfully, none had punctured my lungs. That's when I thanked God for being so skinny, because the lack of space under the car prevented me from being able to inhale enough oxygen into my lungs, and had I been a larger person, I would have died. They cautioned me not to lift anything over ten pounds or do anything too strenuous for about six weeks. During my recovery, the worst challenge I experienced was when too many parishioners kept unknowingly hugging my broken ribs while leaving the church.

Lesson Learned

I have overcome the fear of being under vehicles by making sure that additional jack stands are present, working together as a team. Always have a plan in place for teamwork with backup jacks and other people present to help carry the load with you. Have you ever been tempted to think that you must take on all your problems alone? Our safety and survival in life physically and spiritually are dependent on working together in love, especially when your wife was in the house and could have helped had she only known.

How to Build a Marriage Team

Do you have a support team to help you in time of need?

You are only as strong in your life as the support team with which you surround yourself. We all need a team that would risk their life and reputation for us, a team whose members are supportive of each other. Sooner or later, you will come to need or appreciate more than words can say how much this kind of individual, person, or team means to you.

The very foundation of our society is being attacked through the destruction of one of God's first institutions: marriage. Many people no longer get married with the mindset that divorce is not an option, but instead our society has come to accept far too many justifications as to why people should get divorced. It may be easier to throw in the towel and not remain committed to marital principles, especially when you don't like or agree with what your spouse is doing. But there are serious consequences that pass down from generation to generation.

Are you someone who warns, "Don't do what I did," or "Don't make the same mistakes I did"? Unfortunately, those mistakes have a very high chance of being repeated. Families fall into behavioral patterns, modeled behavior, and circumstances, which become as strong as genetics and are nearly impossible to change on our own strength. God can provide the strength you need to break destructive cycles and turn your life's legacy into one that will glorify Him.

A friend of mine has experienced thirteen divorces touching her family in just two generations. If you have ever been the victim of divorce or come from parents who have divorced, then you well know how it can affect those involved for years afterward in every aspect of their lives. I'll say it again because this is important: the very foundation of our society is being attacked through the destruction of one of God's first institutions, marriage.

> Often after people divorce, it becomes all too evident that one cannot run from his or her problems. They are always with us until we face them and conquer them. Is it a temptation of yours to hide from challenges with drugs, alcohol, uncommitted, lonely sexual relationships, or pornography? In contrast, when serving and loving are inseparably woven together in ACTS of love, it creates a movement for God's

> kingdom! Love is patient and kind. Love is not jealous or boastful or proud or rude. Love does not demand its own way. Love is not irritable, and it keeps no record of when it has been wronged. It is never glad about injustice, but rejoices whenever the truth wins out. Love never gives up, never loses faith, is always hopeful, and endures through every circumstance. Love will last forever.
>
> —1 Corinthians 13:4–8, author's paraphrase

Thankfully, broken relationships are not the unpardonable sin, even though some think it is, and God can bring healing and restoration if we live a life of faith committed to Him. It is important to have a good support team as we journey through life. Every day we need to ask God to let the Holy Spirit change us to become more willing to love unselfishly.

The Five Miracles of Breast Cancer

My wife, Sherri, and I were in a state of shock when her mammogram revealed that she had a calcification that was later diagnosed as breast cancer. Through this experience, rather than create division, we came to realize how close you can grow as a support team in times of intense need; we became a stronger team. God provided multiple miracles throughout this time. God must have smiled, because when Satan wanted to bring hurt and pain, healing was taking place in our lives in many additional and unique ways.

We first began the battle by uniting with two of the most anointed faith-prayer partners we knew in ministry, my former associate pastor, Mike, and his wife, Vicky. We also invited their daughter, Rebecca. My daughter, Autumn, who had just graduated from college with a degree in journalism, and Rebecca, who is several years older and in medical school, used to be the closest of friends. When that relationship became broken, it had deeply hurt Autumn. It used to be that when the two of them got together, they would laugh, make crazy sounds together, and just plain enjoy life. But as they each tried to discover their own identities at a critical time during adolescence, and because of the age difference, they had grown apart. Due to the hurt that Autumn had experienced, she had developed a certain amount of resentment and unforgiveness toward Rebecca that needed healing. The healing began with Autumn and Rebecca becoming close friends again and discovering how much they still had in common, even after several years of not being in contact with each other. Later Rebecca invited Autumn to go with her and her family to Greece on vacation the following month. (Our families had gone to Greece together nine years previously).

James 5:16 says healing takes place when we:

1. confess our sins to others and
2. pray for forgiveness with others.

I have often shared with others that if they want God to do His part, they must be willing to do theirs first by forgiving any animosity in their heart toward others.

Miracle 1—Emotional Healing

Sherri had gone through a soul searching and cleansing process, routing out any animosity or unforgiveness she had in her heart. Finally, she knew she had done all that God had asked her to do by faith in putting Him first in her life. Now she felt confident trusting in God and His promises. She claimed these promises daily in her pray life (and still does).

Sherri experienced her first miracle by watching Autumn and Rebecca reunite as they quickly let go of all animosity. This began the healing process. Stress causes many symptoms physically that can drain positive healing energy, but reconciliation encourages wellness.

Miracle 2—Early Detection

Sherri's second miracle came when her physician miraculously re-ordered a second test from another company with a newer, stronger machine. Early detection is a key for a higher percentage of cancer survival. Newer MRI or CT scan machines have more powerful magnets, which reveal more clearly what is taking place.

This new test revealed that the calcification was actually a rapidly growing cancer that was still encapsulated in the duct on her left breast. The cancer was not visible to the surgeon during the original biopsy. The additional lymph nodes he removed were later proved to be benign. What a blessing! If this cancer had remained, it would have become invasive.

Miracle 3—Cancer Removed

They were able to remove all of the cancerous cells during the mastectomy. That was Sherri's third miracle. After the surgery, she experienced many nights of excruciating pain, which made it difficult to sleep. I think I was the most blessed to feel needed as I tried every way possible to help relieve her pain and to help her find a comfortable position. This shared experience of suffering together drew us miraculously closer together.

Miracle 4—Blessing Others

Sharing love always brings the most healing to those involved. The night after Sherri's surgery, my cell phone rang while I was sitting with her in the hospital. Caller ID identified it was my friend, Daniel. Quickly I made the decision to answer the phone, although many calls had been screened during this critical time of family commitment.

For a number of months, we had been praying together concerning healing to take place in Daniel's broken marriage relationship and for God to bring encouragement to him with his challenges. Earlier, I had left him a message asking him to call me so that I could encourage him once again. When I asked how he was doing, he began sharing how God was working in his life to teach him once again how to be a spiritual leader by placing God first. God was teaching him patience in love now, as he had neglected spending intentional time with his wife and God.

Then I asked Daniel a risky question: "Sherri has just come back from surgery for cancer, and she had a mastectomy. She is quite drugged, but would you please pray a blessing for her right now?" Holding the phone up to Sherri's ear, I explained, "Daniel would like to pray a blessing over you." There was a long silence on the other end.

Finally, stumbling at best, Daniel prayed a beautiful prayer for her: "Lord, please bless Sherri in her great time of need. Thank you, in Jesus' name, amen."

"I feel absolutely dumbfounded, embarrassed, and at a lack for words," Daniel said. "I didn't even know you were going through this challenge. How come you didn't share this with me?"

"You never asked about my challenges," I simply stated.

He apologized and said, "Thank you for taking this phone call. You just provided the greatest help I needed, to quit thinking of myself."

A few days later when we talked again, he expressed his thankfulness that I had believed in him enough to ask him to pray for my wife in her great time of need. He felt privileged, though shocked and speechless, because it had been years since he had been able to minister by helping others spiritually. My simple request had left him feeling blessed. He had left the ministry when he and his wife he had separated to avoid being an embarrassment to the church in his leadership role. It had been very awkward for him to attend his denominational church, because people with good intentions were asking where his wife was. Now, he was being nurtured by another church denomination, who knew nothing of his background. He asked me, "How come no one from my home church ever called to pray with me or ask if they could help in my time of great loneliness and need, when so many of them knew what was happening?" He continued, "You have helped me to realize that miraculously God can still use me, even when I've made mistakes."

Miracle 5—Debt Reduction

After one of Sherri's doctor visits the nurse told her, "Please go to the next counter, where they want you to see your account balance." Sherri looked at me with a look of apprehension. We were wondering how much we needed to pay in addition to the amount insurance would cover. The bill was fast approaching one hundred thousand dollars, and Sherri had a long way to go before all the required plastic surgery was completed. Typically, a good insurance policy will cover about 80 percent of all the expenses, if they decide to accept most of the doctor's and hospital's charges. We knew the amount could be higher, though. We both looked down at the paper the secretary was sliding toward us. It read "paid in full."

"What? Is this correct?" Sherri asked.

"Yes," the secretary responded. "Your doctor only charged for what your insurance would cover."

The next two blessings came when we received letters from the hospital surgeon and surgery room with zero-dollar balances! "Praise God!" we said simultaneously, especially since Sherri was off work for nearly two months because of the surgery and recovery. Autumn needed money to continue in medical school, and Andrew needed help with his construction management degree; we knew the remaining bill could be about twenty thousand dollars or more.

Remember, God has entrusted you with money, giftedness, and time for serving others. When you put God first in your life, He promises to open the windows of heaven and pour blessing on you, and you won't have room enough to receive them (Mal. 3:10, author's paraphrase). Your blessings may not come in the forgiveness of debts, or your blessing may come later than sooner. Just keep trusting God and your breakthrough will come! Praise God—"You forgive *all* my sins, heal *all* my diseases, and fill my life with good things!" (Ps. 103:2–5, author's paraphrase). "If anyone has enough money to live well and sees someone in need and refuses to help—how can the love of God be in that person?" (1 John 3:17, author's paraphrase). "Because we love others, God lives in us, and His love is brought to full expression through us!" (1 John 4:12, author's paraphrase).

God wants you to know today that your salvation is secure! Your debt is cancelled, and you are forgiven of your past sins. You have a zero balance. As you walk with God by faith, the only thing recorded in the judgment books is the word *forgiven*! "Because I confess my sins, You are faithful and righteous to forgive and cleanse me of my sins from every wrong." (1 John 1:9, author's paraphrase). "I can know that I have eternal life!" (1 John 5:13, author's paraphrase).

Perhaps you might be experiencing great feelings of loneliness, pain, or anger in your life right now. If so, begin praying God's promises, and ask God to reveal to you someone who might be suffering more than you with whom you can talk, write an email or letter to, or go to visit. This will be your greatest blessing come true!

Miraculous Marriage

My wife and I can agree that we have had many disagreements throughout our thirty-one years of marriage. We are about as opposite as two people can be in personality, adventure, and metabolism. Love has a way of becoming stronger through adversity, and we are blessed to love each other more now than when we were first married. It has been both a challenge and a blessing, as we have learned to respect each other's differences. Our greatest blessing throughout life has been to remain committed to God's source of unending, unselfish love as our strength.

Four Do's In a Healthy Relationship

Four golden rules have built an inseparable team in our commitment to serving each other in love:

1. Communicating your desires and needs before you *do* most things will avoid frustrating situations. (Desires constantly change.)

2. Show that you *do* love each other. (Men need this as much as women.)
3. *Do* make time for intimacy. (Let each other's desires direct what you do and how often you do it.)
4. Focus on the good, rather than the bad in everything you *do.* (Happy relationships focus on the positive, and it outweighs the negative.)

How to Build a Worship Team

Some individuals try to divert positive energy away from becoming teams in serving others by spending too much time and energy over matters such as diet issues, worship music styles, dress, the color of the carpet or the walls, etc. The important point in order to become a dynamic movement is to remain united while respecting each other's differences.

Music is one of the most powerful tools either for positive good to bring us into the presence of God, or it can be one of the most divisive topics. This issue divides churches in worship and as individuals and fragments a team spirit. It is important to try to discover ways to positively resolve this challenge, rather than expend endless negative energy. Some treat this topic as if it were equivalent to salvation. In one generation, the organ is of the devil because it was used primarily in the bar setting. For another generation, the organ is the only sanctioned instrument in church. Sound tracks with drums are generally accepted by conservative churches; just don't let the drums be seen. In other churches, a percussion drum set is unacceptable but an electric drum set is permitted. Some try to keep their churches united by only using an electric keyboard to add percussion.

At one church, we decided to design a service for the unchurched as a means of reaching out to the community. We knew that in order to reach them, we would need to speak their language so as not to be so different that they couldn't relate. Music is a universal language, so we decided to start there. We would then work with those who were positive and committed to outreach, even if it required some getting out of their comfort zones. We openly shared with the congregation that some of our members would not like the new service and that it was designed for the unchurched. It was designed for people who were not used to a high church or classical orientation. We would be providing a traditional service earlier in the morning for those who loved high church with beautiful organ and piano duets.

There isn't anything more controversial to some than percussion drums.

Although this service was not designed for traditional church members, some still attended this service and then complained bitterly about the drums. This was different from the way their traditions taught them church should be. We made sure to cover the drums for the other services, which helped considerably. Our efforts were blessed as we attracted many new unchurched individuals from the community, who later became members.

Autumn loves music. She grew up with a respect for a broad range of different styles in worship, because at Life-Changing Ministries we provided five different services. Each service was designed to meet different needs in our community. We offered: traditional, Jewish (Messianic), contemporary, and blended services. We also provided a service in an alternative environment, not in the sanctuary, with Christian contemporary music designed for youth who did not attend church at all. Because this service was conducted in the fellowship hall, we had special lighting, fog effects, free ice cream, and pizza. This service inspired our youth to invite non-member youths, who soon became committed to an experiential, contemporary, relevant godly environment.

In Psalm 150, David (the man after God's own heart) commands us to praise God in the sanctuary! Praise Him with tambourines and dancing! Praise him with cymbals (a standard element on any drum set)! Praise Him with clashing cymbals! That sounds like praising God in the sanctuary in the way David told us to praise Him would invariably result in worship that is more than quiet.

Worship music today is very experiential, and often lyrics are sung in first-person verbiage designed to help you connect your emotions to God. Previous generations were taught that showing emotions in worship was wrong. King David's wife mocked him for getting a little too emotional and excited about praising God. He had danced himself right out of his clothes! God struck David's wife barren for criticizing his worship. God created us to glorify Him through our praise and actions. The important point is just that emotions should not dictate true worship.

How to Create a Team Spirit of Worshiping through Music Many pastors think they are doing the right thing by trying to make everyone comfortable and not rocking the ship. The problem is they are only appeasing the intolerant minority. Here are some keys for creating a worship environment that is pleasing to God and edifying and unifying for the congregation:

- Always mix new songs with tried-and-true hymns to create a balance.
- Choose songs that have a clear melodic line for multiple singers to follow easily.
- Choose songs with an inspirational message.
- Choose worship leaders who are skilled enough to lead, knowing where they are going before they get there. (It can be embarrassing if you are left hanging while singing, when you should be silent.)
- Invite guests as an outreach and to increase participation.
- Practice should take place with an accompanist or band prior to leading the congregation in worship.
- Introduce new songs sparingly by teaching the congregation first how it sounds by instrumentation or by solo demonstration. This is important, since the congregation don't have access to music to read or follow.
- Drums should only be introduced if the drummer does not overpower the singers or other instruments. (Enclosing the drums in a Plexiglas drum cage is preferable in order to mix

sound levels.) Most individuals accept sound tracks with drums, because they are mixed professionally as background and do not drown out the singer. Electric drums or those on keyboard can be used in some settings which are less controversial.

- Words to the songs being sung should always be displayed clearly if hymnals are not used.
- It is best to have one worship leader lead with regularity, rather than rotating too often.
- It is best to have one worship leader stand in front of other worship team singers, in order for others to follow effectively.
- It is better to have one worship leader who inspires others with the way he or she looks, smiles, and communicates than to have a group who look like they don't believe what they are singing.
- Be willing to consider paying worship team leaders to create effective worship and continuity. This is as important as being willing to pay preachers who can be effective in attracting those who are willing to provide offerings.

These guidelines are based on my personal experience leading and designing many worship teams as a pastor, through training in worship seminars, and from my degree in music.

Messianic Jewish music, which still has its roots in the most biblical style, is highly interactive and emotional. Their worship is often peppered with impromptu dancing in the aisles. Their joy in worship is obvious. If you've ever observed a Messianic worship service in which people are dancing, freely worshiping as their hearts lead them, you can imagine the joy it must bring to the One the worship honors. Do you agree? If people were dancing with joy and delight and singing *your* praises, how would it make you feel?

Autumn was raised not only in a church family that worshiped in many ways, but she also enjoyed singing with my wife and me. Autumn is gifted with a four-octave range. Because of Autumn's gift, she has sung on various TV and satellite stations and in many countries. Both my wife and Autumn leave this world behind and enter the very throne room of God when they lead or sing in worship. It's because worship is very personal for them. When they sing praises to God in first person, it is as if there is no one else in the room but them and their Father.

Now that you understand the importance of worship in building a team, you are ready for additional team building principles based on worship.

How to Build a Ministry Team

1. Mentoring and Discipling

I began intentionally focus on mentoring and discipling leaders in community outreach. This focus attracted a new breed of fulfilled leaders. Some had only seen their leadership role as being responsible for the prayer during church service or taking up the offering. We began a biblical concept of discipling for multiplication. Over the course of three years, it was amazing to watch seventy different ministries get started, based on empowering them to lead a team.

2. Goal Setting

Next I challenged every leader to create a one- and three-year visionary goal that answered the question, How would your proposed ministry of serving others reach out to attract those from the community? A budget was also required so the finance committee could plan adequate support of the new ministries. Our chain of thrift stores tithed on their gross to our church. We designated that money for a special line item, "outreach ministry."

No longer did our board meetings consist of discussing leaking faucets or who was unhappy in the church and what could we do to make them feel comfortable or arguing over differences of opinion. Now, we were working and planning together as a team with the focus being outward on how to help our community's needs.

3. Small, Lean Teams

The more levels of bureaucracy and the larger the team, the more difficult it is to have a team spirit. A tremendous amount of time and money has been spent trying to justify jobs, and it is more difficult to understand to whom anyone is accountable. By working together as a team, personal differences are put aside and the power of Pentecost takes place. The fastest growing movements in the world emphasize loyalty to each other and unselfish love for all creeds, races, and nationalities, just as Jesus did.

Presidents know all too well that the best way to unite a country out of a depression or recession is to participate in a war. Inevitably the country rallies together, ultimately forgetting its current problems. Most countries would benefit greatly if party lines were eradicated and decisions were made based on uniting the country as a team, using solid principles and not just those that are not based on popularity.

How to Be a First Response Team

Governments have come to recognize the powerful force in faith-based organizations, which comes from their commitment to a team spirit. FEMA used to belittle faith-based organizations before Katrina but were humbled to realize that they could not rally enough troops as fast or as efficiently, no matter how much money they had, as faith-based groups could. Faith-based groups have a strong network of volunteers within their church structures who understand teamwork clearly. Most people do not really understand that FEMA and some popular non-profits are primarily management agencies, not implementers. They hire others to accomplish their purpose. The best relief organizations are implementers whose mission and goals are met without being overly dependent on government funding. This gives better accountability, less bureaucracy, and a larger amount of the money goes to the intended purpose. That is why World Vision, the Salvation Army, Operation Blessing, Convoy of Hope, and others like ACTS World Relief have grown so rapidly. ACTS World Relief can repeatedly take a donation of one hundred thousand dollars and multiply it into ten million dollars in value.

ACTS World Relief is based on the premise that we will only respond to help assist suffering communities when the local leadership agrees to unite to work together to bring healing to their community. In a deployment, usually the goal is for 50 percent of our help to come from the community in our feeding and emergency supply Point of Distribution sites (P.O.D.s). When doing unmet needs assessments, we request that local CERT leaders take us to areas of the community that need the greatest assistance. As of 2010, ACTS World Relief has utilized seventy-three thousand trained volunteers, the majority of them consisting of youths.

ACTS identifies active Christians that serve. It is built on the premise that the only way to be effective is to work together as a team, both internally and within the community, by using an incident command system. A big reason why people experience internal conflict and ineffectiveness in these types of situations is that they don't fully understand their roles. When professional emergency response leaders of devastated communities know that you have been trained to work together with them, speak the same lingo, and respect what they do, the power of unity is quickly realized.

It is common for the students of many different high schools and colleges to have a spirit of rivalry and competition among them. Countless times I have witnessed the miracle of seeing this totally disappear while they are living to love others in great need through disaster response. One boarding school that was close to where a tornado had devastated the community in Tennessee housed several groups who had come to help. As he surveyed the rundown condition and disrepair of the buildings, Mark, a visiting student, said, "Never again will I complain about how our dorm looks compared to this school's dormitories."

The leaders of several schools came to me and asked, "Could our teams volunteer to raise money and paint the inside of the dormitories after we finish cleaning up from the tornado?"

When asked if he would accept their assistance, the host principal answered, "Yes! That would be great, but only if our students can help as well." The visiting students gained a double blessing to help both those in the community and those who were their hosts. Many years later those students remembered the friendships gained by helping in the community.

Because ACTS works with many collaborating schools, we have the pleasure of observing as they come to see themselves as a part of a larger team when uniting together to accomplish the impossible. Uniting together becomes another strength in that we are able to provide continuity in completing larger tasks as groups rotate, becoming more effective than if they all worked independently. Disaster response requires teamwork, because once you start helping people, whether in cleanup, distribution, or mass feeding, it grows and grows in magnitude, like a snowball rolling.

Many well-intentioned people begin by feeding in a small way, like on a main street in town to those who are dependent on them for survival, only to leave because they ran out of time or resources. They go back home to tell their church or community what a great thing they had accomplished, when in actuality, they could have been much more effective if they had a bigger vision of filling others' needs by working with other leaders in the community. There is nothing more disheartening to suffering survivors than to let them know that you are leaving before their destroyed house is cleaned or searched through for cherished possessions. While serving others, we must not use the desperation of others in order to gratify our selfish agendas.

Abandoned Inmates

ACTS World Relief had begun its deployment for the first week of assistance after Hurricane Katrina in Purvis, Mississippi, at Bass Academy, about one and a half hours northwest of the coast.

As I mentioned earlier there we served about ninety thousand meals and distributed fourteen million dollars in donated emergency supplies to three surrounding counties, utilizing an army of youth from across the country. The police had told us that this area was not accessible to our seventeen-truck caravan because of extensive tornado damage, but we had a group with chainsaws walk in front of us and another that group stood on top of our semitrucks cutting trees and holding up dead power lines mile after mile. We were determined to reach those in need, even if we had to chainsaw our way into their community. When the residents saw what we were doing, they joined in to help us inch our way up the road. We remained inland until the water, which was loaded with a lot of toxic chemicals and sewage, had subsided on the coast before deploying volunteers to this hardest hit area.

The emergency operation center in Hancock County, Waveland, Mississippi, which had heard of our effectiveness in responding after the many hurricanes in Florida, requested that ACTS World Relief help assist them. We were asked to set up on a main road in Fred's Grocery Store parking lot, located in the middle of town. ACTS spent approximately the next year helping survivors who had experienced a thirty-foot tsunami wave, destroying their once beautiful, sleepy, historic town, along with many lovely, large oak trees. Robert King, a fire chief from Kissimmee, Florida, became the new incident commander of emergency management. At the Florida Governor's hurricane conference four years later, he thanked me for being one of the most professional, diversified emergency response agencies in the Katrina response.

Generally, the media tends to focus on areas the public can relate to, rather than on those areas hardest hit. New Orleans received a lot of media exposure because of the dikes breaking there, but ten miles to the east the devastation was more comparable to an atomic bomb explosion. Most structures within the first mile of the beach were stripped to kindling wood. For the next three miles, buildings were either moved or crushed. Fred's Grocery Store was in a strip mall about three miles inland. The wave had gone over the roof.

ACTS used Fred's parking lot to set up our work area. In this area, we distributed supplies, used our kitchens for mass feeding, and our tents became shelters for emergency health care. Across the street was the police station where a group of officers had linked arms with each other when the wave hit them with the force of a freight train. They said to me later, "We will never do that again!" All of them were spared, after spending what seemed like an endless three hours of gut-wrenching terror before the water began to subside.

The I-10 highway is about six miles inland from the beach. There the wave hit the embankment and left seaweed twenty feet up its slope, just below the highway. On the other side of I-10, the surge of water flooded the river system, where many homes on stilts ended up with boats on their rooftops or cars and trucks in their front yards. When the water receded in one second story bedroom they found an alligator, and in another house they found a cow when the water receded. Many snakes were found in attics months later.

Hours before the wave hit, it was rumored that the police went to the county jail and offered the prisoners a deal that a tidal wave was about to hit the county. They could either be dropped off in the middle of the water causeway bridge or remain in the jail without guard or staff to assist them until after the storm waters subside. The group that the police supposedly dropped off was never heard from again.

Most prisoners chose to remain with no food or water rations in their cell blocks. When the wave came ashore, power lines were demolished, and it was the next month before we saw any signs of restoration from the utility companies. They restored power to the grid areas closest to hospitals, jails, and businesses first. For several months, residents were without sewer or water, as the pipes had been broken and took longer to restore.

County leaders approached ACTS World Relief command center at Fred's asking for help from our healthcare team. This turned out to be one of the greatest adventures of faith our health team ever experienced. As ACTS volunteer nurses, EMTs, a physician, and a nurse practitioner listened, they explained how a group of inmates needed immediate care at the jail. These were the ones who had chosen to stay behind, but now officials didn't dare go in unless they had with them a health care team to provide for the prisoners' needs, since they had been abandoned for almost a week without care. We would be the first team going in to provide medications, new clothes, hygiene kits, food, and water to potentially very hostile inmates. They explained that although they would endeavor to provide security for our team, the potential of being taken as hostage and held ransom in protest of the conditions that they were left in was very high. We agreed to give the county leaders our answer in one hour.

First, I explained to this group of medically trained volunteers that there was no pressure from ACTS for anyone from this team to go to the jail, but that it might be a life-changing event to help those in need physically, emotionally, and spiritually. Then, we formed a large circle, placing our hands on each other's shoulders, and united once again. We asked God, "Lead us in our decision and that it might not be by might, nor by power, but by Your Spirit." Unanimously, the team decided to offer themselves up willingly to be a living instrument for Jesus, because He said, "When you have helped the most helpless in need, you have done it to Me. Your blessings flow through me because when You were hungry I fed You, when You were thirsty, I gave You a drink. You were a stranger, and I invited You into my home. You were naked, and I gave You clothing. You were sick, and I cared for You. You were in prison, and I visited You" (Matt. 25:45, author's paraphrase).

Lisa, the nurse practitioner, agreed to be the incident commander to lead the team going into the jail. When they arrived, with a lot of trepidation they began by telling the prisoners, "We are volunteers coming to help you!" They were hoping this might diffuse the prisoners' hostility, rather than a bunch of guards arriving with guns drawn, yelling, "Get in line or we'll shoot to kill." Our method worked! When you show love to others, in most cases love wins out. Give and you *shall* receive. That word *shall* is a guarantee.

God's favor was upon that team, just as He promised in Psalm 5:12, and rather than being hostile, some prisoners were so thankful that they hugged members of our team when they received water, medications, food, etc. Lisa's eyes teared up as she saw the inmates' living conditions. For almost a week, when the latrines no longer worked, the prisoners had to defecate in their cells. They now treasured the drinking water by gulping it down as if they had just discovered a bank full of gold for the taking. One inmate had a bad case of diarrhea, and he was quick to ask, "Does anyone have anything to plug me up please?" Lisa quickly asked Steve from the team to give the inmate some medicine.

Another inmate said, "I have never believed in God, but now that I see love being expressed through your Christianity, could you lead me to Christ so that I can know more of this kind of love?" There were many times when they had felt like they were going to perish, either from the hurricane or from the deep, lonely feelings of abandonment. A special inmate continued to encourage them by sharing the assurance from God's Word and having them repeat Jesus' promise, "I will never leave you or forsake you. I am with you always, even when it seems all hope is gone."

The medical team's lives were blessed more than the inmate's lives. It is more blessed to give than to receive. God had helped them overcome the spirit of fear, by sharing love with a clear mind and they were so glad. Perfect love casts out all fear.

If you ever want to experience the most character-stretching ministry, help those in prison. They read you like a book. If you are phony in your Christian walk and try to present some irrelevant Bible study, they won't give you the time of day and will tell you so as well. When you are genuine and have a personal experience with God to share, they will let you know by saying loudly, "Preach it brother!" or, "Yes and Hallelujah!"

Lesson Learned

When teams unite in vision, life-threatening situations are overcome.

Trains, Tragedies, and Triumph!

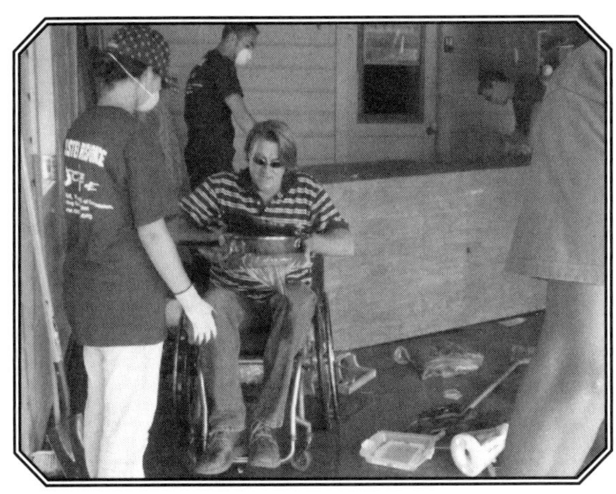

Fred had once worked for the railroad but was now wheelchair-bound as the result of an accident twenty years earlier. He had slipped and fallen while walking backward directing a train into the train yard.

He heard that Hurricane Ike was churning out in the Gulf of Mexico off the coast of Texas, heading for his community. Being a long-time resident, mandatory evacuations were all too common, and most residents had the belief, "It will miss us or die out in the last few hours." In the case of Katrina, they thought, "The government leaders are just trying to get our land. If we leave, we'll never get it back!"

Fred decided to stay, offering to watch over his mother's house just up the street. It was a major challenge to board up their houses and adequately prepare because of his accident from the train. His mother, Mildred, who was eighty-three, also needed a wheelchair. She had decided to leave just in time with a friend.

All of a sudden, Fred heard the sound of water sloshing through the trees and realized that he too should have evacuated under what was supposed to be a mandatory evacuation. Several times the police had driven up and down his street using their speakers to warn residents to leave, but usually about 80 percent choose to stay. In the Florida Keys they have so many mandatory evacuations that they literally have hurricane parties as an event at different people's houses.) Many people choose not to evacuate because doing so becomes a traffic-jam nightmare every time, because there are only two lanes for everyone to use. In most counties, it takes one day to get out and one to come back. Many get tired of this inconvenience, but after a major hurricane strikes, many survivors tell me, "I wish I would have listened and left."

As Fred watched out the window, he saw that the water was rising higher and higher throughout his neighborhood. Fortunately, his house was built on a hill, and he watched the water rise to the point of covering some of his neighbors' rooftops, which were in lower areas. He noticed familiar dogs and cats being swept away in the current, and a variety of eels and fish swam in to take their place. Hurricane Ike only brought in a fourteen-foot tidal surge, compared to Katrina's thirty-one-foot surge south of New Orleans. But Fred's community was caught completely off guard. Orange County, Texas, was fifteen miles from the coast, so they had never considered the possibility of a surge of this depth. The tidal wave caused all the once tranquil rivers throughout the neighborhood to become their worst enemy. After the water subsided, Fred got into his wheelchair lift van to go check on his mother's house. He was overwhelmed as he drove past the once beautiful homes, now ruined and filled with mud, seaweed, and stranded fish. A herd of eleven hundred cattle drowned in a nearby field, and a team was already loading up many of these carcasses into dump trucks and taking them to a large hole that had been dug to bury them before the carcasses could bring disease to the community.

Fred's worst nightmare had just come true. As he pulled into the driveway of his mother's house, his heart jumped into his throat, as he stared at the water line ten feet up the side of her house. His mother and her deceased husband, Art, had worked all their lives preparing for retirement, and just one year earlier they had finally paid off their mortgage. He knew that she did not have flood insurance. Fred didn't either. They didn't think it would be necessary, living so far from the ocean and several blocks away from the river. (A sad fact is that 75 percent of homeowners do not carry flood insurance. Many people mistakenly think that FEMA will pay for the cost of replacing their homes, but FEMA only pays a percentage of repair costs, from $1,400 to $29,900, depending on many variables.)

It was at this very same moment that I was riding in a van filled with youth trained in cleanup and demucking. "Stop!" I shouted, pointing in Fred's direction. "Look, there's someone in a wheelchair who looks like he needs our help." The van stopped, and I jumped out, introducing myself to Fred, and asked if he needed any help. The group of twelve trained youth volunteers could sort or take water soaked items to the curbside for him. After a long pause of silence Fred began to cry. Laying my hand on his shoulder, I explained that we had specifically asked for God to lead us to someone we could bless that day, which in turn could be a blessing to us. He quickly explained that he could not afford to pay us, but if we were willing, he and his returning mother would be so grateful for any help.

Just then his mother, Mildred, pulled into the driveway. Excitedly, they both explained how they had been praying, claiming God's promise to provide for all their needs. Though they certainly couldn't see how that provision would be possible now, they still believed for a miracle.

Turning to the van of anxiously waiting youth looking on with anticipation for the familiar wave that indicated they were cleared to get started, I waved and called to them, "Let's go!" Eagerly they jumped from the van, and we formed a circle of prayer around Fred and Mildred as Shara, one of the youth, prayed together with them for God's healing, "Bless them and enlarge their territory beyond what they can now see, that Your hand would be with them, and that You would keep them from evil. Thank You, Lord, in Jesus name amen." We all knew that sorting through what devastation remained inside those walls required a team, for it would overwhelm most people.

Mildred handed the keys to our team leader and apologized, "I can only imagine how everything inside is ruined, and neither my son nor I can help."

We reassured her that we understood, and it was OK; that's why we were here. Then I asked, "Where in the house did you keep your valuables, like money, jewelry, life insurance, or any other important papers?"

Mildred answered, "Most of those items were in the drawers to my bedside table and the roll top desk." Then she asked a bit more hesitantly, "Could you also please try to find my personal Bible, which was in the second bedroom on top of the dresser?"

I reassured her, "Our team will bring anything of possible value out to the both of you for you to determine what needs to be saved, or what needs to go to the curbside." FEMA has a policy that only those items that are placed at the curbside can be removed by the contracted trash haulers, who had trucks with big pinching claws to remove mountains of ruined treasure.

They both sat in their wheelchairs looking grateful. I knew that any items of value could be entrusted to any of these youth, who were used to helping assist those in need. It was only about two months earlier that some from this same team had helped a mother and her six-year-old daughter, who was having terrible allergy problems from the mildew caused by Tropical Storm Faye in Melbourne, Florida.

When the team opened the door, there was a unanimous groan, "Oh, what is that terrible smell?" They tried to muffle their complaints so as not to embarrass Mildred. There were two refrigerator/freezers that were still loaded with spoiled meat and other goodies, making it smell like something was dead inside. The youth began first searching for anything of value. They brought out watches, some of which still were running after being submerged. They found cash, antique coins, valuable papers, and bank checks.

The biggest miracle was when someone found Mildred's Bible, which had moved from the dresser to the top of her bedside commode. The toilet was filled with flood water, but the Bible was on top of the seat, remaining virtually dry on the inside. Julia screamed with joy as she handed this most valued treasure to Mildred. They embraced in a big hug. It only took two days of hard work for this team to have everything sorted and removed from Mildred's house, including the soaked carpet. It would have normally taken a couple of months to sort through everything and accomplish what we did.

Lesson Learned

Effective first response happens when teams unite in vision, and impossible challenges are resolved quickly.

Extreme Adventure Team!

ACTS loves to challenge and utilize college students who have specialized degrees in emergency management, rescue and relief, medicine, counseling, and chaplaincy, as well as EMT and paramedic training. One summer my daughter, Autumn, and I were invited to become certified in Rescue 3 training with a group from Union College in Lincoln, Nebraska, who teach international rescue and relief. (They have been one of our first response groups to set up logistics within the first twelve hours of major storms.) Each summer they go to a primitive area near Durango, Colorado, where there are excellent class-three to -four rapids, to receive practicum training in swift water rescue. They also receive training in technical high ropes, rappelling in a beautiful, snow-peaked mountainous setting.

Mike Lowe, president of Wilderness Way, and Dr. Michael Duehrssen, an emergency room physician, are specialists in this type of training. Teamwork is essential in surviving extreme conditions in the freezing forty-degree water and rappelling up and down three hundred–foot cliffs. Your life is dependent on each other's skills and confidence in performing rescue techniques. If one incorrectly tied knot slips while you are hanging several hundred feet in the air or hanging over rapids with huge boulders in the water, it could mean certain death. Both Mike Lowe and Dr. Michael Duehrssen have the technical knowledge and experience that comes with it, but each is a gifted mentor. They build inner confidence in those who have white-faced panic written across their face, saying, "Come on, you can do it," "Come on, we can do that together," or "I'll be right there with you." Frequently, you hear them encourage students and adults alike with a big smile of confidence.

The grand finale of the several weeks of training is to be graded on a night exercise or scenario, putting into practice what you have learned. The scenario is one of saving a group of nine drunken party goers who got into their raft for a thrill-ride down the rapids. It isn't long before the raft flips over and total chaos takes place when they all go shooting down the rapids. All forty of our rescue team were standing in a large circle for final instructions. Everyone was reminded how the team command structure—incident commander, liaison, safety officer, logistics, operations, and planning officers—would function together. In order for a team to work effectively together, everyone must know what each other's roles are.

We were all standing in our wet suits with glow sticks or waterproof lights fastened to our helmets, life jackets on, and gloves and booties on to keep our extremities from freezing. We were all divided into teams of six, which is an optimal size for accountability, then broken down into a buddy system of two. Your buddy was never to leave your side.

My adrenaline began kicking in, because even though I knew this was an exercise, I was keenly aware that I would be going down the roughest part of the river in the middle of the night! First, I would find survivors. Then, using whatever first aid techniques were required using professional straight boards, neck collars, bandage wraps, and stethoscopes as needed, I would check their vital signs and stabilize the survivors. When they were stabilized, I would load them onto our raft and take them down the rest of the river to the waiting ambulance, which would have its lights flashing, showing us where to exit the river.

My mind began replaying over and over the many times we went down the river in daylight. It was like a movie stuck on a loop as I tried to remember where all of those big boulders were. I remembered the techniques to eddy, or get behind, these boulders by rolling in behind them, where the water current will hold you if you fight hard enough. Just the day before I had passed the advanced certification by eddying behind five rocks out in the swiftest part of the river in the daylight, but this was a whole different ball game.

My daughter and I practiced over and over how to get under or over a "strainer." This is any object that has gotten wedged across the river, creating a tremendous force of water pushing against it. If you happen to get caught or stuck in the middle of it, you could easily drown or break bones by the force of the surging river holding you against the obstruction or under it. My thigh still looked and felt like I had been hit by a baseball bat, because of when I tried to prove to myself that I could intentionally get wedged onto the strainer and climb over the top. I'm still not sure that it was worth the thrill but do respect more now how the instructors were warning us about the force of the water on victims.

Just four days earlier my daughter and I had joined a smaller team of seven. We were asked by the county emergency rescue team and fire department to try to find a missing resident who had gone out in his canoe with a close friend on a bet to see if they could make it down another part of the river without flipping. The major problem was that they were both drunk. They only made it one hundred yards before the canoe capsized, and the missing resident was last seen heading toward a strainer.

We used all kinds of team techniques, including locking arms in a circle and turning as we walked while searching the shallower water. We held on to each other as we cut the strainer log, which was right in front of the island where the man was last seen. A rope gun was shot across an eighty-five-foot section of the river to wrap onto a large piece of the tree to help pull it loose and hopefully free the trapped victim. We used boogie boards to search the deeper water areas and used probing poles to feel where the man might be wedged. After searching for about four hours, his family was finally at peace that the river that he loved had become his final resting place.

Later that day my daughter, Autumn, met with the missing resident's friend and his son, who was seven, on the spot where the canoe had been launched. The man said, "I can hardly remember the foolishness we did, but will always remember and miss my close friend." It all happened because of the effects of alcohol.

Recalling this recent experience and after going over thorough instructions, I was asked to lead out in a spiritual thought before our final nighttime training exercise. I reminded them how the disciples were all pumped with adrenaline after Jesus had spent so much time with them teaching them how to depend on God for all kinds of miracles, healing people, multiplying food, raising the dead, and now ascending up into heaven by telling them, "Nothing is impossible with God" (Luke 1:37). "I have given you authority over all the power of the enemy" (Luke 10:19, author's paraphrase).

Some wanted to jump in the river immediately and be heroes by saving everyone they could find with the instruction they had learned. Some standing around the circle were large, muscular firemen; others were body builders; others, like me, were the slender type; and still others were the feminine, delicate type. All were about to combine their unique God-given strengths, abilities, and gifts to accomplish a mighty task of saving those who were in trouble. Would *you* be willing to risk your life, saving individuals while endangering your own life?

Most rescue teams refuse to try to save individuals for any reason in night rescue, because of the risk to each of the team members. But Jesus made the choice to rescue us while we were right in the middle of choosing the many consequences of sin. He rescued us from literally destroying ourselves!

Because we are all uniquely different, God can accomplish the most good in His army of everyone when we are combined in an unstoppable faith-driven team. Gideon did not need thousands to overcome the enemy, only three hundred faith-filled warriors. But Jesus did specifically tell the disciples to *stop* and *wait*, like we were doing before going on our "mission impossible." After we prayed, we were then ready to be used by God in building a loyalty to each other that is unstoppable.

Mission Impossible

We were driven upriver, where we began the search-and-rescue scenario. We all had large search lights and were scanning the banks of the river for possible survivors who had managed to swim to the river banks. Sure enough I saw some motion in the bushes and yelled, "Over here," to the others in our team. In a short while, we had Ginger's pulse and blood pressure checked and had gotten her stabilized on a stretcher and carried her upstream to where she was transported to the hospital.

Next we learned that a victim was located on the river bank right between two of the most difficult rapids on that stretch of water. We were asked to board our raft and head down river. Mike Lowe was the river raft guide, and once again he smiled and said encouragingly, "Let's go. We can do it!"

He expertly guided our raft around boulders and other obstacles. There was a particular look of concern on his face, though, showing he realized that he was responsible for all those involved in performing this rescue—a bunch of newly trained rookies in the middle of the night in what could turn out to be our own disaster in the making.

By the grace of God, we somehow managed to shoot the first big rapid, "Smelter," and then quickly turned the raft around a huge boulder into an eddy where we found Don, our victim. He was freezing in the Colorado night air, next to the river. He had been waiting for two hours for us to find him. After putting Don in a life jacket, covering him with a coat, and making sure he was stable, we carried him to the raft, trying not to slip and drop him as we were stepping over big rocks along the way. We had to lift together, walk in time together, and set him down onto the raft together. Don later told us, "There was no way I would have entrusted you to tie me to a board and shoot the rapids in the middle of the night unless I was convinced that you were working together as a team."

Mike then shouted to me, "Dave, go to the front of the raft and paddle as hard as you can when I ask you to, so we can safely navigate 'Corner Pocket.'" It was the other difficult rapid. This is where many rafts flip. You shoot five feet in the air, then come crashing down. This causes many to fly out of the raft. The current will hold you under for what seems like an eternity. We had practiced this section of the river many times without a raft and experienced what the strong current was like, holding you under, rolling you over and over. It was crucial that we didn't panic until it kicked us out.

"Paddle to the right. Now to the left," Mike directed. We had learned the commands for when to back-paddle and forward-paddle, depending which side of the raft we were on.

This had to be the most adrenaline packed time of my life! "Yahoo," I screamed as we plunged forward, zigzagging around one rock after another. It might have been just as good that we couldn't see many of them until we were past them.

Mike ordered, "Get rid of the glow sticks taped to your helmets, because they're preventing me from seeing the river." We quickly ripped them off as we made our way down the roller-coaster ride of our lives. We could hardly see, except for the full moon glistening off the water.

The four other teammates were ladies from the ages of nineteen to twenty-four years old. They were holding on for dear life to both the stretcher and the raft, with our victim Don still lying motionless. He was doing such a good job of acting, we were tempted to think that he had a massive heart attack and died of fear on the spot.

At last, we saw the lights of the ambulance on the bank to our left and paddled with all our strength to get out of the current before being swept past our place to exit. What an exciting, extreme adventure! After loading Don into the ambulance on his stretcher, we shook hands, hugged, and thanked each other for the greatest experience of our lives. It helped us to build loyalty and to realize how when working together, a team can overcome the worst situation and make an impossible mission possible!

Lesson Learned

Whenever you might be tempted to think that something seems impossible for you to accomplish on your own or it appears that you are divided in purpose, remember Jesus' specific command: always learn to work together in teams of two to three first. As a larger, united team grows, the power of Pentecost occurs in a multiplying movement. This is what I like to refer to as joining "the army of everyone." This movement consists of positive, faith-filled leaders who are committed to working together as a team!

PRAYER FOR TODAY:

John 17:20-22, Jesus' Prayer for Unity as a Team

As believers we are united in demonstrating Your perfect love. This will cause others to believe in You. Thank You for giving us Your glory now so that we are becoming perfect in unity. Thank You for promising to reveal Your full glory to us when we go to live with You forever!

Chapter 9
BUILDING LOYAL RELATIONSHIPS

Do you desire to develop deeper, more loyal relationships with others? When love is reciprocated through meeting each other's needs, loyal relationships are established. Loyal relationships do not occur through teaching alone but through crossing a valley together. Lasting relationships are stronger than politics and selfish agendas.

Spiritual Empowerment

I know what real love is because Christ gave up His life for me. And so I will give up my life for Christian brothers and sisters. I have stopped just saying, "I love you," and now I really show it by my actions!

—1 John 3:16–18, author's paraphrase

A Parable

Firemen develop loyal relationships with those they help in time of emergency. These individuals always remember who helped them in their time of need. Most firemen are well loved in their communities because of the compassion they exhibit.

Mentoring Youth, Changing the World through Loyal Relationships!

The greatest movement of change is created by you showing and demonstrating love to youth. There is no greater gift and joy than to be involved in mentoring the next generation by showing them how to love others. Adolescents and children love to be mentored in serving others! This is how they learn best. Youth love to remain faithful to God when we include them with the vision of serving others.

When you serve with them, you will develop life-long relationships with these youth, who will remember forever the time you take with them. Try to avoid placing the majority of time mentoring youth in just entertaining them. Once you have established a relationship with them, take them to the next level by teaching them how to creatively find opportunities of reaching out beyond themselves. After they have learned these principles, it will only be natural for them to do the same for the next generation! Children and young people will follow an example of role-modeling more than what anyone tells them to do.

Jesus loved to mentor children by inviting them to come to Him. While some thought that the children would distract from His mission of changing the world, He realized the importance of holding children in His lap. He taught them with illustrations. He also liked to use children to illustrate to the older generation how quickly they adapt to new ideas. The older we become, the harder it is to change. Jesus still wants to show us today that we must have the faith of a child to move our most challenging mountain and gain the victory!

Whether in disaster response or inner city ministry, ACTS World Relief's model in serving others is this: 1) adults mentoring youth, 2) combining volunteers with survivors from the community. Healing occurs by helping each other! When we move our training from sterile classrooms into environments in the community, lasting change and relationships are guaranteed! Serving becomes contagious.

Over the years, through multiple first response deployments of ACTS World Relief personnel and volunteers, I have had the privilege of witnessing the impact our model of adults mentoring youth and partnering volunteers with local survivors has had on the lives of many. This is an ideal combination for young people, and one that allows them the opportunity for maximum growth through observation and experience.

One high school senior from San Diego who volunteered with ACTS World Relief after Hurricane Ike reported, "I learned firsthand what the Bible verse means of not storing our treasures on Earth. I hope not to grow attached to worldly things but be prepared for Jesus' second coming instead." Another student wrote afterward that watching how hard another volunteer worked inspired her "to know that God does send help in troubled times."

Many students have commented to me that the victims' attitude and outlook impacted them pointedly. A high school student from California wrote after Hurricane Ike, "[The victims of the disaster] were so positive that they didn't say anything like, 'Why did God let this happen?' Instead, they would give thanks to God: 'We are still alive, and He sent you to help us'...This ACTS trip brought me a little bit closer to God." This student learned firsthand that when you show love by serving others, you are always blessed the most.

Some of the most exciting ways I have watched loyal mentoring relationships grow at home is when we united youth and adults together helping meet the needs in the community on Saturday mornings in what we called Life-Changing seminars. Included were the following courses:

- English literacy (one of the most popular seminars taught by Spanish fluent youth, using the King James Version of the Bible)
- Anger management
- Domestic violence
- Building strong marriages
- How to raise faith-filled children
- Plumbing

- How to miraculously balance your finances
- How to have parents understand youth (taught by youth)

These seminars were all lead by church members and guests who had a passion to share their gifts of expertise with others. Life-long, loyal relationships were gained by helping each other.

Loyalty through Grace and Forgiveness

My denomination rewarded church growth by providing an associate pastor to larger congregations that had demonstrated a sustained tithing record. (One hundred percent of the tithe was sent to the conference, or corporate office, which paid the pastors' salaries, and offerings were how our church paid its bills.) "We have selected an associate who will be coming from the seminary to assist your church," a representative from our church corporate office informed me.

I thanked the committee but made a very unusual request: "I would like to select my own associate pastor, if this would be possible." The committee decided that because of our rapid tithe gains, they would allow me to choose our new associate pastor.

I wanted to build on continuity and loyalty. The two qualifications I considered to be most important were:

- Spiritual passion for God
- Loyalty to the senior pastor

Several candidates really wanted the position, and after interviewing them, I called an individual by the name of Mike. His father had held a number of leadership positions in the denomination and was well known for having a high standard of integrity, compassion, and loyalty to those who worked and served under him. His son had graduated from the seminary, had been a pastor who had a head knowledge of the Bible, and was a successful traveling evangelist. Mike was about seven years older than me, which made it unusual to consider him as an associate. He had resigned from being a pastor and fifteen years later experienced God radically change his heart and lifestyle. He was now back in school completing his degree in hospital chaplaincy and was actively involved in a local church setting.

There were a few incidents from his background after being a pastor that made it a challenge for him to get the approval of my denomination's corporate office. For example, he had been divorced and had lived a pretty wild lifestyle.

In his favor:

- He had a radical conversion experience and now knew God through an intimate personal relationship of grace, rather than having only head knowledge, as he had previously.
- He was now married to a woman who shared his passion for God and also had a personal relationship with Him. She was a former Greek Orthodox who became a vibrant Christian through asking her husband too many questions about why he was no longer a practicing Christian. She had her doctorate in education, and together they made a remarkable team.
- He was a "now-faith" believer and stood on the Word of God as gospel truth. His current pastor had expressed great concern to me when he learned I was considering Mike for my associate. He told me, "Mike creates all kinds of challenges because people attend his Bible studies and ask for him to anoint them for God's healing, rather than realize God primarily uses doctors and hospitals today."
- Mike told me that if God and I would give him a second chance to serve God in full-time ministry, he would be faithful and loyal, no matter what happened.

Mike's wayward reputation preceded him, reaching some on the hiring committee where I presented his name. For what seemed to be an eternity, those decision-makers pondered my request with great hesitation. Finally someone from the committee asked with a puzzled look on his face, "Why him?"

I explained, "Because I desperately need someone who is loyal in a very unstable environment, and I believe God will use him in a powerful way!" As I said the words, I knew they were not only mere echoes of the belief in them in my heart but also prophetic. Mike would be used by God to care for me "for such a time as this." After the smallest hint of a pause, I continued, "Whoever has been forgiven most, loves God most."

Yes, it was a huge risk choosing Mike, who by human standards was considered a liability. But Mike was truly a blessing to have as an associate pastor. Even though we did not agree on everything, these differences remained personal and private. He always supported me 100 percent publicly. When well-meaning members ended up verbally tearing me to pieces, Mike was the one I wanted covering my back. Members who tried to create division between us pastors gave up in desperation and moved to another church. They couldn't get anywhere with Mike.

Finally a new era of history was being made in our church! A united pastoral team exemplified how two individuals can have differences and yet continue to love each other. By example we showed our respect for each other's differences and demonstrated how to still remain loyal to one another. What our church needed most was not just to hear from the pulpit how to build loyal relationships but to see it modeled to them in real life. Sadly, most churches waste their positive energy by being divided on petty, internal issues, which are not the life-and-death issues they might believe.

Seven years later Mike became the senior pastor when I began ACTS World Relief.

Loyalty Gained by Blessing the Beaten and Bruised

One day in February, Joyce's husband came home from work to find that supper was not ready. Unaware of the blind rage boiling within her mate, Joyce went about the kitchen with her food preparations. Her husband, John, watched, his wife's movements becoming slow motion in his temporarily insane mind. The voices of their two daughters, Jinny, age seven, and Jacqueline, age nine, became mere background noise, the words of their conversation unintelligible to him. His burly hands curled into fists as he stood there getting angrier by the second because Joyce had not recognized her error. Supper was not ready. It was unforgiveable! He made his way through the kitchen to where he was now standing, only a couple feet from her. The anger within him had become almost demonic; it was fueled by such overwhelming rage. Joyce turned to him with a bowl in her hand. The smile on her face quickly disappeared. She was just about to ask him if something was wrong, when without warning, she felt the force of his fist as he punched her in the face. Pain exploded within her nose, cheeks, lips and face. The impact temporarily blinded her.

"What is...?" she didn't even get to finish her question before the next blow landed on the side of her face. Her husband's powerful fist brought forth a new eruption of pain for Joyce, as the momentum of his fury threw her off balance so hard that she dropped the bowl and slammed into the table. The contents splashed on her dress, on the floor, and her husband's angry face. Hearing the loud commotion in the kitchen, the two girls ran to see what had happened. Frozen in horror, they saw their father pick up their mother and slam his fist into her once again as she tried to duck his next blow.

"Daddy! Daddy!" they cried. "Stop! Please stop!" Tears streamed down their cheeks, their hearts beating wildly at the horrible scene in front of them. It was something that belonged in a movie, not in their kitchen.

"Please stop!" pleaded Joyce, but the blows kept coming one after another. She could feel the bruises forming under the fragile skin of her face as his fists struck bone, cartilage, and soft tissue. As if in a tunnel and far away, she could hear her girls screaming for him to stop. She pled with them, "Please go to the other room." She wanted to protect them from this awful scene, but she couldn't even protect herself. How could she protect them?

Her husband kept screaming about her duty as his wife and the responsibilities she had as a mother. "And if I ever come home again and supper isn't ready, I'll kill you!" He shouted his final warning while at the same time delivering his final punch with his bloody fist. Her eyes were beginning to shut because of intense swelling. Her nose was bleeding and her lips and various places on her delicate face were lacerated.

As he left, Joyce knew that the time had come. She could no longer put off her decision to get her girls and herself to safety. She could barely move, barely even think straight. Lying on the floor, broken, battered and bruised, Joyce willed herself to get up, to finish fixing supper for the girls.

Suddenly she heard the tentative whisper of her girls. "Mama, are you OK?" She heard the terror in their voices. They had screamed so loud that their throats were sore and their voices hoarse. Joyce's attempts at reassurance were feeble but well intended. Her husband had beaten her almost beyond recognition. This wasn't the first time it had happened.

Finding a reserve of strength deep down within her that she didn't know she had, Joyce packed a few things for the three of them, and she hurried them into their car. It was quite a feat, considering Joyce's head was pounding so loud that it was deafening. She could barely see to drive through her swollen eyes. For those who don't know, when a mother is trying to protect her young, she is capable of doing the insurmountable in overwhelming circumstances.

Joyce went to the only place where she knew she would find help—our community center. She explained their situation to our store manager, Keith, and asked if there was a chance that he might be willing to help her furnish an apartment she had just found.

Joyce knew that if she did not find a secure environment for her girls, she might be forced to surrender them to be with her husband. Unfortunately, she had not reported this humiliation of physical abuse to the police.

Now, at the community center our policy had always been that if someone could not afford to pay for something they truly needed, we would give it to them instead. Keith was fairly new to his position as store manager. After Joyce picked out furnishings and clothes they needed, he called and asked, "Joyce is here and needs a washer and dryer, clothes for two girls, and furniture. The sofa she wants is one of the most beautiful Victorian sets we have ever had. It carries a price tag currently of eleven hundred dollars. What should I do?"

"Keith, there is an important principle you need to teach all the volunteers and employees," I answered gently. "It is not necessary to call me for approval in this sort of situation. Pray about it! Ask God to impress you what to do. That's the important thing, asking God. If in question, use the biblical model, 'give and it shall be given to you'" (Luke 6:38, author's paraphrase). We truly experienced that the more we gave away, the more furniture and donations we received (Acts 20:35).

Keith did just that. He prayed, "Lord, You know how much we need that sofa money to pay the rent this month. I will treat her how I would like to be treated. We will give her the best." Excitedly, the workers at the store loaded up a truck full of furniture, appliances, and clothes—all for free!

To Joyce and her two girls, this was the biggest emergency response one could ever imagine. As they left, the smiles on the girls' faces were like sunshine. Even Joyce, through her bruised and broken lips, couldn't help but smile, despite the pain it brought her. They hugged the staff at the community store, and then Joyce asked, "What church do you attend?" Joyce looked from one staff member to another, still overwhelmed with the generosity they'd received. "We want to learn more about why you would share so much love to people you hardly knew. We want to come to a church like that."

Later that month, Joyce and her two girls returned. (God had provided the store's rent through different means thant the Victorian sofa set we gave Joyce.) The bruises on Joyce's face had faded, and many of the cuts had healed. They were in high spirits and decided they wanted to help the community center that had helped them in such a big way. They were mentored by Sofie, who was wheelchair bound. Together they united to make a difference, helping those in need.

Many volunteers have discovered that though they come to help out, they in turn get blessed, for it is truly more blessed to give than to receive! Throughout the years, this team of volunteers has become so strong that they would do almost anything for each other. Building community is all about building loyal relationships through service to others.

Our church was blessed by a growing number of members. Those who were blessed invited others to attend our church. They had bonded in ministry by being willing to lay down their own interests for those who were hurting more than themselves.

Lesson Learned

The best way to establish long-lasting loyal relationships with others is when you first demonstrate unselfish, practical love. Are you willing to risk your reputation or self interest for a brother or a sister in need?

Sue, an ACTS volunteer, described it this way to me, "In just three days, I have come closer to those whom I have helped, those who have lost everything, than with many I have tried to become friends with over the last three years."

Loyalty through Giving Away Your Sleeping Bag

Andrew, my son, and two of his friends, Justin and Jason, left from college in Tennessee planning to spend a long weekend helping those whose lives had been destroyed by Hurricane Katrina in Waveland, Mississippi. They enjoyed camping and came prepared with their sleeping bags and gear for an adventure. They traveled there on a bus with forty others.

I hugged the three and asked Andrew, "Can you drive my pickup truck around to some of the remote areas where survivors have been hardest hit?" A thirty-foot wave had washed over those immediately on the beach. "Feel free to give them a tent, sleeping bag, an MRE (meal ready to eat), and some emergency supplies." A special donor had given money to purchase two hundred tents and sleeping bags, and we now wanted to distribute these in a personal way, rather than giving them out on the distribution line.

They hadn't been on the road long when Andrew said, "Look over there. There's hardly anything left of those homes on stilts." They jumped out of the truck when they saw Timmy, seven, and Julie, ten, trying to help their dad stretch a tarp over some poles to make a makeshift house for them to live in. They quickly noticed how the family was working together as a team. The children were unusually happy, as if nothing had happened to their house, which had been blown into the river.

"Would you like a tent with a bedroom in it?" Jason asked the family. The look on their faces was like asking a four year old if he wanted an ice cream cone. After helping them set up the tent, they hugged each other. The family rolled out the new sleeping bags inside their tent. This made them feel like they were now staying at the Sheraton. The memory of this encounter and the appreciation of the family would live in their minds forever.

A neighbor came running over and asked, "Is there a chance you have one more tent for a desperate family with two children? They have been living in their car for the past week."

Andrew and his friends looked at each other and said, "Well, we have one last tent, but we only have one sleeping bag, plus our own personal ones left." They instantly decided that it was time to give away their best, believing that God would provide later for their needs. The two children, Amy and Anthony, who were ages five and nine, began helping set up their beautiful new, temporary home. Mom, Dad, and the two children could actually visualize stretching out and laying down for a greatly needed good night's sleep. The two children were so excited when they received their own sleeping bags that they couldn't wait for the last pole to be in place before they were stretching them out inside their own little bedroom. Andrew then pulled out a new cooking stove that he had been saving for just the right family and set it up in front of their newly erected home. The wife burst into tears and said, "At last, I can cook a warm meal for my family! My son and his friend walked behind the tent to where their small white wooden house stood and looked inside. There was a foot of caked mud and seaweed inside every room. The refrigerator was laying on its side after floating around and coming to rest in the middle of the kitchen floor. "What a smell!" Jason said as they walked back toward the tent. As they turned to leave, the children clung to their legs thanking them. The three teenage boys climbed back into their truck and waved. They realized how God had used them to help encourage another family in need. They realized that day they were more blessed than the ones they endeavored to be a blessing to.

Lesson Learned

Join the unstoppable movement of volunteers whose lives have been changed forever by helping others in need. You in turn will develop life-long friendships with those who are tremendously loyal because of your kind deeds.

PRAYER FOR TODAY:

I praise You, Lord, for experiencing blessings today, for this is the day that You have made. I will rejoice and be glad in it. Holy Spirit, move in a mighty way in my heart today. "Now-faith" comes by hearing and submitting to Your Word. Faith rests on Your power, not men's wisdom. I am a believer, not a doubter. Your Word tells me that faith is speaking of those things that are not as though they were, those things invisible as though they were visible. I chose to put You first in my life, and I live in a relationship with You, Lord. I speak words of life and not death, faith and not doubt, encouragement and not criticism.

The weapons I use have divine power to demolish every stronghold of evil in my life. You have given me authority to overcome all the power of the enemy! You are my Deliverer. I walk in Your favor and in the power of the Holy Spirit. Abundant life comes to me now! You are my Shepherd; all my needs are met according to Your riches in glory. Because You have promised to never leave me or forsake me, I can be sure that You are here now, and because You are here, the power to heal is here.

I am a hearer and obey Your Word. I am more than a conqueror through Your love for me. I trust and depend upon You by casting all my cares on You. I praise You, Lord, that You have equipped me with all I need to stay strong in my day of adversity!

You will keep me from falling, because no weapon formed against me shall prosper. In Jesus' name, amen!

Chapter 10
BIG VISION AND BIG FAITH

THIS IS THE most exciting chapter, because it contains the results of living a life of service by loving unconditionally. It tells of actions taken in big faith that became miraculous manifestations! My personal motto is, Think big, start small, and *act now*!

Spiritual Empowerment

What is important? Faith expressing itself in love.

—GALATIANS 5:6, author's paraphrase

Big vision and big faith require your willingness to step outside the comfort zone of traditional business-as-usual thinking. Get out of the box! You are not fenced in with impossibilities. God sets you free to think big and pray for the very things you desire to accomplish! When you step out of the box and set out to do something radical for God, it may appear to others that you are not a team player because you are doing things differently than how they have always been done. But that is only because you are drawing others out of their comfort zones. The majority of individuals are not comfortable with this. Some may even view you as the enemy for a while. Take courage my friend, Jesus was well-known for constantly getting people out of their comfort zones, and He was definitely not known for being the best team player with religious leaders!

I like to say, "If you can control it, it isn't a miracle!" The encouraging news is that if you are faithful and patient, many of the visions and dreams God gives to you will come to fruition! Churches and individuals who are growing in miraculous ways are willing to use big faith and big vision by sharing love in their service to others. Churches, schools, and individuals who are able to change and adapt to a changing world will survive. We must build on the one God has established. Reach higher than you have ever dreamed possible!

A Parable

Firemen practice big Faith by climbing tall ladders and rushing into burning buildings with a water hose, hoping it won't let them down. Some of the greatest pictures of faith expressing itself in love are taken when firemen rescue children from near fatal experiences. They truly exemplify a model for big vision and big faith! There are some terrific Christian firemen who make great teachers.

Angel in a White Suit

On Tuesdays, at Life-Changing Ministry in Mount Dora, Florida, we held visionary meetings. The agenda was begun with prayer asking for the Holy Spirit to direct us and giving Him permission to change up our agenda and ministries, as He saw fit.

On this particular Tuesday, one of the agenda items was whether or not to purchase a limousine to be used in place of our bus to pick up guests from our community. Some months earlier, I had suggested "giving our guests the royal treatment" to the visionary committee. It could be used as a tax write-off. One had been found and inspected by a mechanic. The price had been reduced five thousand dollars. A special line item for "community outreach" had been created and funded from our thrift store and was in place to purchase items like this.

Nathaniel was driving by Life-Changing Christian Center on this same Tuesday. He was in one of his white limousines when he suddenly slammed on his brakes and for no apparent reason turned in to our drive. The Holy Spirit had impressed him to stop and go inside. "Lord, you know that I swore I would never set my foot inside another church after all the hurt I have been through with those so-called Christians," Nathaniel protested angrily, frustrated with God. But he obediently parked his limo and walked inside.

There was a small window in the door where the visionary committee was meeting, and after prayer, I noticed a gentleman dressed in a white suit who was unknown to me walking down the side hallway toward our room. Opening the door I asked with a smile, "May I help you?"

Nathaniel stopped, turned around and hesitantly answered, "I don't know." He paused a moment, almost as if he were confused at being there. "I was driving by your church, and something impressed me to stop in and offer my limousine service free of charge to help bring individuals from the community to church," he said quickly, then added as an after-thought, "if this might be of help. I have heard this place does good things to help those in need."

"Please, come in," I replied heartily with a "God, look what You've done again" kind of laugh. I invited Nathaniel to a seat in the room where the group of visionary leaders was gathered. With looks of complete amazement at the power and timing of God, the group shared how they were about to purchase a limousine to bring individuals to church who could not come otherwise.

Nathaniel assured us, "You don't need to do that. I have several limousines that I would be glad to use for this. The insurance, fuel, and maintenance costs will by my responsibility. I will even pay my drivers to come and sit in your service and let them observe what God is doing here."

What an awesome God we serve! Because of Him, we don't need to own it to enjoy it!

Remember Gwynne's story? She came back to church because we paid her to play the piano, and it got her into an environment where she was being spiritually fed. God changed her, and she is in active ministry today. Paying someone to attend church may not necessarily be the recommended or traditional mode of evangelism, but if God impresses you to do that, listen to Him, because you too may help change a life. I have known of public evangelists who, rather than spending thousands on advertising costs to send out flyers in the mail, paid one hundred dollars to each new person attending their meetings and had better results because they helped meet the new person's financial needs!

Nathaniel not only paid his employees to attend our services but had magnetic signs made that read "Life-Changing Ministries" to place on his limousines. He performed this service for many years. He even began attending himself and was able to resolve some anger issues rooted in a hurtful experience that he had many years ago at a previous church.

Later on another individual donated a black limousine to our church. According to the biblical principle of "give and you shall receive," we offered it to Nathaniel as a thank-you gift for all he'd done for us.

Entertaining Angels Unawares

In our community, there was a heavily wooded area that was home to a large group of homeless people. Some had tents, tattered and torn, while others just slept on the ground under the stars. We reached out to these people. We designated a special area up front for our special guests. Often they would be led in by a deacon, deaconess, or one of the youth. We made it a point to go over and welcome them, hug them, and let them know we were happy that they were there.

One-Stop Shop

Our church was a one-stop shop for many of our homeless guests. They would bring their dirty laundry in bags, and one of the church members would put them in the washer and dryer for them. They were able to bathe in one of our showers, which had previously only been used whenever there was a baptism. They would then be met with a fresh white towel and clean clothes. They would attend one of our morning seminars, participate in the worship service by sharing testimonies of how God was changing their lives, eat a nice hot meal in the fellowship hall, and then receive their clean laundry when the bus was ready to leave. When they had attended three times, we gifted them with a new tent stamped with a Life-Changing Ministry logo. You see, they had found a new home; they were not homeless!

As you might guess, not everyone in the church was as excited as I was about this ministry. There was always the fear that their presence might scare off some well-to-do members who contributed financially to the church and might not appreciate the smell that some of these individuals brought with them. It was my belief that individuals would be attracted to where the gospel of practical godliness in helping the hurting through serving was being exemplified and would freely lend their financial support to it. After all, church is a hospital for the hurting to get healed!

Ellen White writes:

> Angelic agencies, though invisible, are cooperating with visible human agencies, forming a relief association with men. Is there not something stimulating and inspiring in this thought…that the human agent stands as the visible instrument to confer the blessings of angelic agencies? As we are thus laborers together with God, the work bears the inscription of the divine. With what joy and delight all heaven looks upon these blended influences, influences which are acknowledged in the heavenly courts! Human agencies are the hands of heavenly instruments, for heavenly angels employ human hands in practical ministry. Their acts of unselfish ministry make them partakers in the success, which is the result of the relief offered. This is Heaven's way of administering saving power. The knowledge and actions of the heavenly workers, united with the knowledge and power which are imparted to human agencies, relieve the oppressed and distressed.[1]

Lesson Learned

The limo owner was made to feel needed, and he in turn was responsible for helping to bring many others to an environment where they were mentored to see a bigger vision of how God had a calling and purpose for their lives!

Big Vision: Short- and Long-Term Results of Serving Others

Do you want quick, positive results in both your life and the lives of others? Most positive results develop with time. Often the short-term results of serving others are going to be undesirable. The key to success is for you to remain faithful in the short-term results until you experience your breakthrough! Your long-term results will then bring tremendous fulfillment and develop big faith!

Short-term results of serving others are:

- Your commitment will cost you personal expense and time.
- You will be stretched beyond your comfort zones, which will give you temporary stress.
- Your religious views and legalistic tendencies will become threatened and challenged.
- Your perspective in values will radically change.
- Your personal relationships will change.
- Your prayer and meditation on God's Word will seem frustrating, empty, and routine at first.
- Your church attendance will begin by fulfilling only a form of godliness and entertainment.

Long-term results of serving others are:

- Your reward will be in proportion to the amount of unreimbursed expense and time invested.
- Your comfort zones will broaden, increasing your tolerance levels against stress.
- Your religious views will turn into true, practical Christianity.
- Your values will lead to your life becoming more fulfilling and needing to own less.
- Your personal relationships will become deeper, trustworthy, and loyal.

- Your prayer and meditation time will become deeper, richer, and faith-filled!
- Your corporate worship experience will become Spirit-filled, meaningful, personal and rich with testimonials of God changing lives.

Purpose-Driven, Fulfilled Lives

More than ever before, individuals are searching for true satisfaction, purpose, meaning, and fulfillment in their lives.

Warren Buffett and Bill Gates, the two wealthiest individuals alive today, understand the importance of serving others through great humanitarian accomplishments and relevancy. They united their amassed wealth to give most of it away in humanitarian service. This inspired others to join the fight against world hunger, disease, eliminate polio through immunization, and fight AIDS.

In every profession and whatever your income level, God is calling you to practice serving others in your attitude and lifestyle. Jesus came to serve others and not *be* served, setting the ultimate example for us. My wife and I are the happiest when we practice expecting or demanding nothing except for being thankful and appreciative for everything we give to help each other.

Andre, a pastor in Florida, once said to me, "Pastor Dave, I can't believe how much fun pastoring can be when the congregation starts getting involved in serving the needs of others! Your encouragement and the equipment you've provided to help us has been invaluable." ACTS loves to provide its resources of kitchen equipment and mobile medical units to be able to bless those churches and teams around the world who are committed to reaching out to serve their communities year-round.

Churches that meet the needs of their community will be sustainable into the future. When you meet the needs of your community first, additional buildings will follow to provide more services. Money follows ministry! If you think that your church's calling is to merely establish buildings and groups in every community and that they will automatically grow, you will be mistaken and ultimately waste billions of dollars donated by God's people. Many congregations find that their church buildings now stand empty, or they are constantly using all of their resources in time and money to maintain their mere existence. They are *not* growing because they have no time and money left to reach out to help their hurting communities. This should always be the *first* priority!

Schools that exemplify the value of serving others and demonstrate it through practical, related examples, will provide true education, grow and succeed. The schools where I have had the joy of helping create opportunities of serving, and are consistently growing!

By experiencing God's calling to serving others, you can testify how fulfilled you can become. God creates a passion within you to help others, which causes you to live in a state of constant revival. The challenge with intellectual revivals is that they create a spiritual high and then a state of emptiness if they are not accompanied with a manifestation of helping others in need.

God's Word Is Sure!

God will continue to demonstrate Himself in miraculous ways as you continue serving, but sometimes you will become discouraged. Remember the disciples' dilemma? For three years they were with Jesus every day, and He taught them to constantly show love by their actions. They healed the blind, those covered with leprosy, and made the lame walk. They helped Him turn water into the best wine, turned a small lunch into a feast feeding thousands, and raised people from the dead. They learned to speak by faith, and it was so! They knew who He was, yet after the big, miraculous resurrection, they were discouraged, moaning and groaning about feeling abandoned.

Elijah kind of felt that way, too. After performing the miracle of calling fire from heaven, which consumed the altar, sacrifice, water, and stones as a demonstration of just how big God was, Elijah ran into hiding when Jezebel threatened to have him killed. Come out of hiding today, and the power of God will grow in your life by serving others!

It is through our worst disappointments and biggest challenges that we become stronger. *A temporary failure only becomes a permanent failure when you quit gaining wisdom and strength from the failed experience.* There is a song my brother and I used to sing called "Never Give Up" that illustrates you must never give up when you feel you are at the end of your rope.

I Can Feel My Toes!

Donny Gates was six feet two inches tall, built like a football player, thirty-one years old and in great health when a construction accident changed his life forever. A crane operator where he worked accidentally hit Donny from behind with a big crusher ball. Seconds before impact, the crane operator yelled, "Look out!" It was too late. The impact sent Donny flying through the air, knocking him down so hard that when he hit the ground thirty feet away on his face, his legs literally folded over the back of his head, breaking his back in several places and severing his spinal cord. The jolt sent severe pain of indescribable proportions shooting throughout his body, which felt like razor blades. He was left motionless, crying out, "Please, someone help me! Help me. I can't move."

After multiple surgical procedures, Donny's doctor sadly told him, "You will never have feeling below your waist again. You will be bound to a wheelchair for the rest of your life." How could this be possible? His first wife had decided to divorce him, leaving him two children—a son, aged seven, and a daughter, five years old. Fortunately, Donny was naturally a positive individual, and he determined to make the most out of life. He was thankful just to be alive!

Donny did not have the opportunity to attend a Christian church while growing up, so he never learned some of the typical faithless sayings I have heard from many individuals, like, "Why don't you just curse God and die?" "God caused this accident for a reason!" or "Surely you don't believe that Jesus desires to heal you as He did in His day. Today He uses doctors, hospitals, and medicine." I have also heard people say, "It takes greater faith to simply accept whatever comes your way in life and be at peace with it."

The most common prayer that is prayed among well-meaning Christians when someone needs healing is, "If it be Your will, Lord, please, please hear my prayer to bring healing to sister so-and-so, who has done so many wonderful things for you, Lord." Let's look at this for a moment. Regarding healing, we pray, "If it be Your will, Lord." You mean, it's possible it may not be God's will for this person to be healed? Then how can we ask for healing? If we think that it may not be God's will for someone to be healed and that person goes to the doctor or the emergency room for help, are they being disobedient? Thankfully, God told us what His will is regarding healing, so we don't have to wonder (Isa. 53:5; Ps. 103:3; Matt. 6:10; 1 Pet. 2:24; 1 John 5:14). "Please, please hear my prayer," sounds as if we're begging God to do something He may really not want to do. Yet, He has given us authority over all the power of the enemy (Luke 10:19) and the right to use His name, the name that is above all names when we pray His Word by faith (Eph. 1:21; Phil. 2:9)! The only revelation we commit to God by faith is:

- How God chooses to bring healing (physically, emotionally or spiritually) and when
- God chooses to bring healing (instantly, gradually, or when we are made new in heaven) is up to Him.

God's desire is for His will to be done on Earth, as it is in heaven. His desire is for everyone to experience a taste of heaven on Earth, right now! God loves to give good gifts to His children, right now! The main reason you do not receive more gifts is because you do not ask more frequently by faith!

Somehow people think that if they beg God—as if He was a deity who doesn't seem to notice our challenges—and somehow if we can prove how good we have been, He might reward us. Healing is not a reward; it is a covenant right. Healing is part of salvation and was purchased for us when Jesus took those stripes upon His back before being hung on the cross. When we understand that without faith it is impossible to please God (Heb. 11:6) and that using God's Word by faith brings us victory despite great odds, He smiles and says, "Now they understand how to speak My power against defeat!"

One of our church members reached out to Donny. "You need to come to my church, where I have witnessed many miracles of God taking place. Come and hear some testimonies from those whose lives God is changing in miraculous ways."

He responded, "Sure, I'll be glad to!" Most people love to come to a church where God is moving.

He began attending week after week and hearing my associate pastor, Mike, and me share how faith comes by hearing, believing, and speaking God's Word. Romans 10:8–10 says, "By speaking or confessing God's word, it activates or unleashes His power within us" (author's paraphrase). God's will is for us to have life, to have it more abundantly (John 10:10), and to experience on Earth, some of the blessings that we will enjoy in heaven throughout all eternity.

"In the beginning…the earth was without form, and void; and darkness was on the face of the deep. And the Spirit of God moved upon the face of the waters" (Gen. 1:1–3, KJV). The Holy Spirit symbolizes power, yet the Spirit of God was hovering over the waters, and it was still dark. Nothing was happening. Why? Nothing could happen until God spoke His desired result (light) and not what already was (darkness). He didn't say, "Wow, it's really dark out here!" We were created in His image with dominion (Gen. 1:26). We are to imitate by faith what He does (Rom. 4:17), just as He asks us now to overcome all the power of the enemy by speaking His words of life!

The Word that Donny heard was a seed that began to grow within him the more he heard it. He heard that God's Word said by the stripes of Jesus he was healed. He never doubted God's Word but left God's method and timing up to Him. The doctors said he would never walk again unless a miracle took place. His spinal cord had been severed. Medically speaking, there is no surgery, medicine, or treatment that can cure or fix a severed spinal cord. It was an impossible situation. Yet again, God's Word says, "What the doctors say is impossible is possible with Me!" (Mark 10:27, author's paraphrase). The difference in Donny's life compared to that of a churchgoer was that he did not bring "traditional," faithless baggage to church. Such baggage can make the Word of God powerless (Mark 7:13), but Donny simply believed God's Word to be true. Every day, hourly, at home, he began speaking God's Word with the faith of a child. He asked God to fill his life to overflow with His presence. There were days when he valiantly fought back doubt and unworthiness, while claiming God's Word.

The Lord reminded Him, "I will produce good fruit in you of love, joy, peace, patience, kindness, goodness, faithfulness, gentleness and self-control in my time" (Gal. 5:22–23, author's paraphrase). But the battle between flesh and spirit warred within him.

Plenty of times Donny cried, "If you are up there, God, why don't you just heal me now?" Then realizing his impatience didn't exemplify faith, he poured his heart out to his heavenly Father, "Lord, legalistic, religious people who don't understand are persecuting me by making fun of me for claiming Your Word by faith that by Your stripes I am healed."

God reminded him, "Those who are born of the Holy Spirit are persecuted by those who only keep the law. Does the Holy Spirit work miracles in you because you obey the Law of Moses? Of course not! It is because you believe the message you heard about Me of the good news of how I rescued you from sin, forgiven you, and now am calling you to live in freedom to serve others in love. In the last days many will act religious but reject the power of God. Stay away from people like that" (Gal. 3:5; 5:13; 2 Tim. 3:5, author's paraphrase). These passages continually brought encouragement to Donny as he came to know that God's Word overcomes all the power of the enemy of doubt, discouragement, and despair! Donny realized that he could pray for anything, because he believed he could have it (Mark 11:24), or that anything is possible when a person believes (Mark 9:23).

During this time in Donny's life and by God's providence, I purchased two Dodge Challengers, a 1970 and 1971 model, which both needed restoring, in trade for a fully restored 1971 440-cubic-inch Challenger, which I had restored. Thinking of Donny in his wheelchair, along with this trade, I negotiated for a 1994 Ford 4 by 4 van with a 460 engine. It was dark grey with black custom iron bumpers, jacked up with oversize tires, and a heavy winch on the front to go along with it. The seller was a handicapped veteran who had his legs blown off by a hand grenade in Vietnam. He had installed an oversize power lift that could lift a wheelchair up to 750 pounds with ease! The van had hand controls, so the driver didn't need feet to drive at all. The van looked like something from a Batman movie, ready to take on the power of the enemy. We christened it the "God squad van."

My wife and I decided to let Donny use it for however long he needed it. His small minivan, although equipped for a handicapped driver, was constantly breaking down, straining to lift his 240-pound body. The day Donny lifted himself into this new monstrosity of a handicapped vehicle, no one could have had a bigger smile on his face then he did. He was ready to take on the world! He took great joy at being able to stop along the roadside to pull out people who were stuck in a ditch with the heavy winch. One day he laughed as he described pulling a tow truck out of a ditch. He was eager to pick up other handicapped people who wanted to come to church but couldn't due to transportation issues. One woman he knew weighed over 350 pounds and was embarrassed that she could rarely find a handicapped lift strong enough for her to go anywhere. Now, thanks to Donny sharing the gift he had been blessed with, she sat on the front row of our church every week with a special smile on her face. Donny used his blessing to bless others in greater need, and God's love continued to grow in his life.

Donny continued to feed on God's Word day after day. His faith for healing grew, even in what seemed to be an impossible situation. After three months of determined faith, Donny called me one day. "Pastor, I've got some great news!" he exclaimed excitedly. "God is beginning to give me sensations in my toes!" God's Word *is* true!

"Keep claiming God's promises," I encouraged. "Let's praise God together," I said, lifting my head while on the phone. "Lord, we give You thanks and praise for what You are beginning to do. Now bring it to completion, in Jesus' name, amen." Two weeks later, he began wiggling his toes and experiencing feeling in his legs.

Donny had a girlfriend he met after the accident. She had only known him to be a wheelchair-bound paraplegic. He wanted very much to marry her, but did not want to ask her to marry a cripple. Throughout his spiritual journey of meditating on God's Word and claiming His promise of healing, expecting a miracle, he was also acting in faith regarding his future as her husband, and he purchased an engagement ring. One night after spending time with the Lord, he felt that this was the moment! His girlfriend was out in the living room, and he was in the bedroom. He wheeled himself over by the wall, secured the brakes on his wheelchair and lifted himself out of the sitting position that he'd maintained the last nine years, pulling himself up to a standing position while leaning against the wall. Donny called over to her, trying to disguise his elation at anticipating the look on her face when she saw him standing for the first time.

With his eyes on the doorway, a huge smile on his face, and holding the ring box open in his hand, Donny waited for the woman who had stood by him for so long to come through the door. Seeing Donny standing on his own two feet was such an unexpected shock for her that she stopped in her tracks for a moment, struck speechless by the sight. Their eyes met as love flooded both their hearts. She ran to him without even noticing the diamond ring in his hand. At her embrace, they both fell down on the floor, laughing and crying tears of joy. Donny asked her to marry him, and she said yes!

The next day, he called me to tell me the news and to share his miracle story. "Donny, would you be willing to share what God has been doing in your life physically, emotionally, and spiritually next week at church?" I asked.

"Certainly. I would be glad to," he answered, anticipation in his voice. "Whenever you arrive in the handicapped van, I want you to walk in the front door on your crutches, and I will stop the sermon wherever I'm at so that we can glorify God as a congregation, because 'God loves to inhabit the praises of His people'" (Ps. 22:3, author's paraphrase). It is only when we believe with childlike faith, anticipating what God can do, that we activate anything miraculous. I like to say, "If it's so big it's out of your control to solve, then it's the birthplace of a miracle."

It was about 11:45 a.m. when I saw the God squad van pulling into the handicapped parking spot in front of the church parking lot, lined up with the glass doors in the lobby. All at once the deacons opened both doors, and there stood Donny on his crutches. I asked the congregation to stand, clap, and give glory to God, for they were witnessing a miracle from God. Donny slowly made his way up the aisle with deacons ready to assist on either side, should he fall off his crutches. When he got to the front, I asked, "Donny, please share with us how God has been changing you from the inside out."

"God first healed me spiritually, which was the greatest miracle, because He gave me peace from my past mistakes. Then He began bringing feeling to my toes and then my legs, which I have not been able to use for nine years," he said. "God could have healed me instantaneously, but then I would not have learned patience and persistence in the journey. The farthest I have walked in nine years since my accident, is this morning coming down this aisle."

"Donny, I'm going to ask you to do something radical for God. On the count of three, I want you to throw down your crutches and jump up and down in praise to God." It was certain that some who were present would say I was being presumptuous or that his legs were not really healed, that he was only holding up his weight and swinging his paralyzed legs with the aid of his crutches. He looked at me and without hesitation he nodded his assent. "One, two, three," I counted. At the end of three, he dropped his crutches, and the whole congregation was standing clapping, crying, hugging, and praising God. We were not a Pentecostal denomination, but the Spirit of Pentecost was present that morning!

As a matter of fact, my congregation, many of whom came from traditional backgrounds where the definition of *reverence* was only "extreme quietness in the sanctuary," learned that day that worship can be loud, boisterous, and enthusiastic. Worship can contain both silence and joyful celebration of God performing miracles amongst us. Worship wasn't meant to be a spectator sport but rather active participation of worshiping in "spirit and truth" (John 4:23). They now understood that *reverence* also means "to praise God"!

Donny only occasionally used his crutches again as he regained strength and has shared his miracle with thousands of people both personally, on cable TV, and in various camp meeting settings. He reminds the people he encounters that we never know how God may choose to work or how long it may be before we see a breakthrough; the only thing God asks us to do is to exercise our faith in Him by speaking and acting on those "things that are not as though they were" (Rom. 4:17, author's paraphrase). Donny had big faith, and he believed in the substance of what he hoped for—a miraculous healing—despite an impossible situation and the evidence of things not seen (Heb. 11:1) He kept the picture of him walking again, standing tall alive in his mind until it became more real to him than his present condition.

We read in James 4:3, "When you ask, many times you do not receive because your whole motive is wrong. You want only what will give you pleasure" (author's paraphrase), but Donny has a big heart filled with the joy of living to love others. He continues to share everything that he is blessed with by helping others in need, so God will be glorified. He also shared his favorite crutches with someone else in need! "When you say, 'Well, good-bye and God bless you; stay warm and eat well,' but then you don't give that person any food or clothing, what good does that do? Faith that doesn't show itself by good deeds is not faith at all. It is dead and useless" (James 2:15–17, author's paraphrase).

In most cases, God usually surprises us with an answer to our prayers that is different from what we were expecting. Jim Cymbala's definition of *biblical faith* is "total dependence upon God that becomes supernatural in its working."[2] People with faith develop a second kind of sight. They see more than just circumstances: they see God right *in* them. Can they prove it? No, but by faith they know He's there nonetheless. Faith and love grow bigger and bigger when combined together![3]

Do you want healing today in some miraculous way? Begin by forgiving others and stop speaking evil against them. "If you criticize and judge each other over what you are eating or doing or believing, you are criticizing and condemning God's Law" (James 4:11, author's paraphrase).

How to Conquer Faith-Destroying Animosity

The greatest power of the gospel comes by not letting animosity control you! Here are proven keys to overcoming animosity:

- Forgive the person who hates you.
- Quit talking about the person in a destructive way to others.
- Bless, praise God, and show mercy to those who hate and hurt you.

> Then the king said to the man of God, "Intercede with the LORD your God and pray for me that my hand may be restored." So the man of God interceded with the LORD, and the king's hand was restored and became as it was before.
>
> —1 KINGS 13:6

Overcoming animosity liberates you to be able to live to love others once again and will add years on to your stress-free life.

God's hands and feet in this hurting world belong to imperfect human beings. By focusing on them, we may become discouraged. It is easy to take your eyes off Jesus and begin focusing all your positive energy on other struggling, hurtful, angry, jealous, and bitter Christians around you. This tendency kind of sneaks up on you, and before you know it, the devil's got you sidetracked in a negative, self-destructive direction. I want to encourage you that you are not alone in your journey in the shark-infested waters of ongoing challenges.

Prayer for God to Open Your Eyes

> **And Elisha prayed, "O Lord, open his eyes so he may see." Then the Lord opened his servant's eyes, and he looked and saw the hills full of horses and chariots of fire all around Elisha. As the enemy came down toward him, Elisha prayed to the Lord, "Strike these people with blindness." So He struck them with blindness, as Elisha had prayed.**
>
> —2 KINGS 6:8–23,
> author's paraphrase

There may be times when you should pray as I have for God to open your eyes to see the bigger picture or the thirty-thousand-foot level, as I like to say, of what God is up to.

Lord, open my eyes so I can see how You are at work behind the scenes in the battles I am facing!

Many individuals who are visionaries don't live long enough to see their vision come to fruition. God blesses people with many gifts, but sometimes these gifts are not used to glorify God and lead to their ruin because of pride. They are idolized, and their shortcomings are overlooked. Examples of this include rock stars, movie superstars, sports heroes, as well as spiritual giants.

Fountain of Hope

I am blessed to see God's strong hand move in a rapid way in my life! While a pastor, I started taking a group of about twelve visionary leaders to the fastest growing churches across America. These churches were growing because they were successfully reaching out to the many needs of their hurting communities. This became a yearly event. A picture is definitely worth a thousand words, and invariably upon our return we would discuss how we could implement what we had seen in meeting the needs of our community.

The Dream Center in Los Angeles was one of our favorite places to go. By God's grace, they were able to take over a large vacated hospital and turn it into a campus where over one hundred ministries take place. They are helping those with drug addiction, prostitution, and AIDS and offer alternatives from court-ordered incarceration.

After several years of seeing what God was doing on the west coast and catching the vision, my team of visionaries asked if we might be interested in starting up a ministry similar to the Dream Center on the east coast. Yes, we were interested!

Right about that same time, a private hospital began announcing, "If any non-profit organization can fulfill three objectives, we will donate our existing facility to them after we move into our new facility." They were:

1. Win the confidence of the city's leaders by a majority vote in favor of your proposed usage, or the hospital, worth $3.5 million, would be demolished.
2. Submit a pro forma to the hospital of how this plan would work financially. If it could not sustain itself, the hospital would take back ownership of the property.
3. Have a 501(c)(3) non-profit status in order to transfer the deed from one non-profit to another.

Immediately I surrounded myself with a network of professionals: those who had their doctorates in economics, realtors, engineers, physicians, and health care professionals. I began taking our city's leadership to dinner to intensify my efforts at developing relationships so they would catch the vision and take ownership of the project. My wife and I donated ten thousand dollars for planning studies and expenses, and a Christian from the engineering firm Cuningham Group Architecture P.A. from the west coast who liked the vision donated an equal amount. That firm had converted many large, institutional projects for new usage, as well as helped design two prominent Florida theme parks. Furthermore, there were some asbestos issues in the old hospital building that needed to be addressed, so we had to show how the redesign of the facility for our intended purpose would prevent having to disturb some of the interior walls, which would have made the asbestos airborne.

We would call the ministry Fountain of Hope. It would include

1. A much-needed expanded daycare center for hospital and other local business employees. (Our church had experience in running a large day care outreach center.)
2. A hospice wing, due to a shortage of beds in the county. (This would provide revenue of about eleven hundred dollars per day per bed.)
3. A food bank, because there was none in the county.
4. An emergency care center for indigents. (Hospitals receive funds from grants for indigent care costs and money from the county that would be provided for this service. Because of health professionals volunteering, the money provided would go much further and help relieve the hospital of this drain.)
5. Low-cost housing, independent living, and mixed care for the elderly and handicapped on two separate floors. (This would stimulate the local small businesses, as the residents could frequent the restaurants and small shops.)
6. Short-term housing. The word *homeless* was a no-no, so we used the title short-term housing. We made it clear that the only way someone could stay at the facility was if they were drug free, were active in our rehabilitation program, and were willing to let us help them get work.

7. Volunteers from seminaries and colleges would serve for one semester or one quarter to train hands-on for their degrees in practical community outreach humanitarian services.

Fountain of Hope had many strategizing meetings. These meetings included the hospital attorneys, land developers, and our engineering firm and were productive in building confidence in the project. The architectural firm flew in repeatedly from California.

A big vision such as this approaching reality created great excitement! This was a new form of evangelism; this was meeting the needs of thousands, as Jesus would have done it. We felt that it was a vision inspired by God. This required big vision and big faith! The Community Ministerial Alliance (of which I was president) had caught the vision of what would be accomplished through Fountain of Hope, and they were very supportive, along with many others in the community.

I was about to learn that this idea was a challenge in the eyes of big institutions, because big ministry also threatens big business! There were many other, different organizations interested in taking over this facility for their cause. All presentations were to be made to the community leaders on a specific date. Our presenter had his doctorate in economics and had previously been a hospital administrator.

From the very first community meeting at which we were to make our presentations, I began to notice something strange. Many of the groups were not given much time to present their plans, especially our presenter. We tried to brush it off, thinking that maybe they just wanted an introduction to the various projects and that they would give each of us more time at later meetings. However, it was obvious that a lot of time was given to a firm hired by the hospital. That firm was studying the feasibility of developing the property into luxurious retirement condominiums. In their proposal, the hospital would lease the property to the developer, thereby retaining ownership. This seemed to be in direct conflict with the published set of goals in the newspaper set for the donation of the hospital.

After eight months of monthly community forums, the big city council meeting finally arrived. Just before the meeting where a vote would be taken, a final community meeting led by the hospital administration was held. It became painfully obvious that the desire not to donate the facility was becoming clearer when the hospital administrator said politely, "The hospital has reviewed all candidates and has decided to explore other options for the existing hospital."

The city council met and a vote was taken with a majority in favor of giving further conditional study to the Fountain of Hope proposal. They were impressed over the pro forma, which showed how financially viable the proposal was.

The challenge came when the president of my denomination (I was still a pastor), invited me to meet with the hospital president in his office. I had created a political liability because the hospital that wanted to tear down the old hospital was of the same denomination. He explained, "We are sorry that you have invested so much of your time in this, and if you want to retain your employment, I request that you immediately stop your work on this project. You can choose to continue if you so desire, but it will not be with the support of the leadership here today." It felt like I had been kicked in the gut and had all the wind knocked out of me. I felt betrayed by the very people who should have been supporting me. Some of you can relate to the feeling when you put your heart and soul into something, only to have it taken away. My stomach was so in knots I felt like throwing up!

Despite my feelings, I responded politely and quickly, "I would never proceed in such a large endeavor alone and will give you my word here today that from this moment forward, you will never hear of this project again. To go against your counsel and support and without the support of all parties concerned, working as a team, would not bring God's favor." For the next week or so, I was on an automatic diet plan, because while some eat more when they are stressed, I eat less or don't feel like eating at all. This was one of those times. I had to give it back to God, who knows all things best.

Lesson Learned

This is important: do not become bitter or resentful toward individuals when their perception of the situation is far different than yours or when politics plays a strong role. As clearly as you may be convicted that something may be the right thing to do, try to realize that sometimes those in positions of power make decision based on what has the least amount of political or financial risk, falsely thinking they can make everyone happy. Effective leaders realize you cannot please everyone, no matter how your popularity ratings may sag from time to time. *Failure is only when you quit trying.* Praise God through your pain!

As I was driving home, I was completely confused and felt totally betrayed by those who I thought loved me. "Lord, why did You open so many doors and cause us to overcome so many barriers together?" Some weeks later, in His still, small voice God told me, "David, *the best is yet to come!* Keep trusting in Me. I am preparing you. Just forgive them, as I have forgiven you. Now you can better understand how I was betrayed by those who I came to love." I was greatly encouraged by these words, and now I began to regain my appetite and felt like eating a good, hearty meal again!

For years afterward, I continued to offer support by volunteering as a chaplain at the new hospital.

Sixty-Four Million-Dollar Lottery Winner!

One day, Harry told me, "Do you know that my neighbor, Bill, just won the 64 million–dollar lottery? Why don't you go and see him? Maybe he will help with a contribution to ACTS!" Harry gave me directions to Bill's house, which was right across the road from where ACTS had its first office.

"Lord, how should I approach Bill?" I prayed as I headed to his house.

God said, "Just do what I would do and try to meet Bill's needs first."

I knocked on the door of his modest, ranch-style house, which his father had built years ago. Bill answered the door, and I introduced myself as a friend of his neighbor Harry. "Bill, I am not here to ask for any of your money," I quickly said. "Individuals who win the lottery need a real purpose for living!" I looked up at his six-foot three-inch tall frame and smiled.

"Come on in, Dave," he said, motioning for me to sit down.

"Bill, if you have not heard, the office and warehouse space for ACTS World Relief disaster response is located right across the street." I continued, "I have heard that you were in the special armed services and enjoyed serving others to bless your country. We could really use your knowledge of military skills and administration while working with local and state emergency response professionals. I'm asking if you would be willing to become a volunteer and a part of ACTS by helping to meet the needs of others in disaster response and joining me in deployments. We would really love to have you be part of our team."

There was a long silence as I waited for his response. "Would you please let me think about it? Come back next week and let's talk about this some more," he said with a smile.

The next week I knocked on the same door with a little more confidence. This time I had been invited. Bob opened the door more quickly this time. "Dave, come on in. I've been thinking about what you mentioned last week. Please tell me more of your vision."

I responded, "You and I both know how devastating the four hurricanes that hit Florida in 2004 were. One of my greatest frustrations was not having enough equipment to help others with. There is an army of youth who can inspire churches to serve others in desperate need throughout the year. They need training, kitchens, and equipment to help them in this ministry."

"You know something?" Bill said. "You are the only person who is not asking for money but offering to be a blessing to me."

Since I was not asking Bill for money, and since he continued to invite me to visit him, I did. We began to strategize how we could be more effective in disaster response. Bill asked me to provide a prioritized list of our greatest needs. He began by offering to purchase Joshua, one of our most beautiful semitrucks named after a great man of faith in the Bible. It had full sleeping quarters, a bathroom, and a pull-out extension on the side. Over the course of the next several years he continued to help purchase additional equipment, such as two sound stages or mobile churches. He has continued to share the vision of mobilizing thousands of youth in training them in worldwide relief. On a special national documentary about million-dollar lottery winners, Bill and I shared about his unselfish sponsoring of ACTS. Uniquely, his was one of the few documentaries to feature how he had blessed others with money that he could have kept all for himself. Bill became an example of how God called him to be a steward of the money he received and to live to love others by financially multiplying his seed. God blessed him with big faith and big vision!

ACTS has now given the vision of service to seventy-three thousand volunteers, provided fifty-four million dollars in donated emergency services worldwide, served close to one million hot meals, treated seventy-three thousand four hundred medical patients, cleaned five thousand homes, tarped twenty-five hundred roofs, and completed ten thousand needs assessments. Most importantly, ACTS has changed hundreds of thousands of lives by personally reaching out and touching them through the lives of empowered youth who could not serve unless the equipment Bill donated was made available.

The greatest thrill is to use the ACTS equipment and resources to empower churches to reach out to help their community's ongoing disaster needs. This creates revival in churches, just one church at a time, when we practice the gospel of serving!

God prepares the hearts of people in the most unusual, untraditional ways imaginable when they join together in unstoppable movements of service. Don't give up with the vision God is giving to you. Remember, He never asks you to do something for which He will not provide the resources. Sometimes it comes in strange and unusual ways.

God's Big Vision for You

God's plans for you are truly for big vision and big faith. He is calling you to unite and work together to meet the needs of His people in this method of end-time evangelism. He is saying, be blessed by meeting the needs of my suffering children.

At the time of the four 2004 hurricanes in Florida, I was having a fulfilling mountain-top experience pastoring in my local church. The church was truly reaching out effectively to meet the community's needs, and I spent very little time spending negative energy, which can consume a pastor's life. Innocently, I just prayed for God to give me a vision of helping the thousands who were suffering. Watch out for that kind of a prayer, because it can be a little dangerous. I naively thought that by rallying our church and youth volunteers to meet needs, I would be loved by all, including the institution by which I was employed.

God was preparing me for larger opportunities by turning challenges into victories. God reminded me that He has said, "I have plans for you!" (Jer. 29:11, author's paraphrase).

Prayer for God to Blind and Confuse Your Enemies: 2 Kings 6:8-23

After Elisha prayed for vision for himself, then he prayed the second prayer for God to blind the people, or confuse his enemies. This prayer is also very effective in blinding and confusing those who are seemingly always out to discourage and destroy your faith and vision.

> **Lord, I give You thanks in advance for blinding and confusing my enemies who act out of jealousy or incorrect perceptions to destroy Your kingdom!**

God will give you spiritual eyesight to understand things from His perspective. He will slow those who have a destructive spirit by causing confusion. When they finally realize how God is leading you in miraculous ways, they will give up exhausted, embarrassed, and humiliated.

ACTS stands for "Active Christians That Serve." Seeing Christians serve others has turned out to be our greatest blessing, as we now reach out to many inter-faith groups!

The three principles outlined in this chapter are:

1. Forgiving
2. Refusing to get even
3. Praying for God to bless others and praising God through your challenges

God had quite a sense of humor when He called me into personal and emergency response. I innocently thought that this calling would be as simple as growing a church. Little did I know that there were some serious church political forces which became a little insecure or jealous when ACTS rose up with lightning speed, appearing to threaten their organization. I became keenly aware that the principles of forgiving, refusing to counter false accusations, and most importantly, praying for blessings on those who tried valiantly to discourage you were most important!

ACTS was blessed again by being elected into the National VOAD (Volunteer Organizations Active in Disaster), an emergency response organization whose premise is to unite new organizations together to create a powerful synergy. Praise God! If I were filled with animosity, I would have not been able to smile through my tears in most of this ordeal as our new membership in NVOAD created perceived competition to some members who I used to volunteer with. They were learning how to collaborate with our new organization.

Jesus tried constantly to let leaders know in His day that politics and jealousy were crippling God's kingdom! Choose to see how challenges in life can be a blessing for those who have a vision of serving others in love.

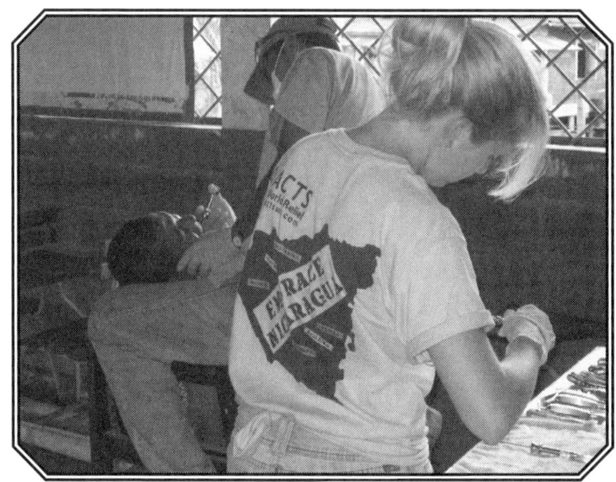

ACTS
World Relief

ACTS
World Relief
RESPUESTA RÁPIDA

I praise God that ACTS is now a worldwide faith-based organization. It includes many participants from my faith and many other faiths as well. Great advances are being made for ACTS to collaborate in a broadening, supportive relationship with thousands of youth from educational systems around the world. These institutions realize that we are living in a changing world where new ideas are greatly needed. ACTS now works in Africa, Mexico, Nicaragua, Jamaica, Honduras, and many other countries where God continues to rapidly open doors. ACTS World Relief adapts rapidly to a changing environment.

Wherever your big vision and faith is leading you right now, remember the faith-filled prayer of Jabez, who prayed, "Oh that you would bless me and extend my lands! Please be with me in all that I do, and keep me from all trouble and pain" (1 Chron. 4:10, author's paraphrase). And God granted him his request.

Successful *Big* Ideas

God truly desires to give you big vision and big faith as a result of reaching out to help those who are struggling and in need!

Faith is also expressed as people see many things in life before they actually exist. In obtaining a patent, only one in a thousand individuals who have an idea will succeed in getting it patented. Only one in ten thousand will ever have their idea produced in the market place. Becoming an inventor is only for those who refuse to give up. They believe 100 percent in their idea, they discipline themselves to stay focused on their idea, and they follow through on their great idea, even when many around them may not be supportive.

My vision of becoming an inventor was blessed by being granted six patents, three of which made it into production. Out of this experience, I learned this:

- *Insurmountable challenges:* One patent I filed was for a baby bottle that would turn itself upright. This would prevent it from dripping on the carpet or other areas. The only problem was, I was one week too slow in filing my patent. A lady in the Philippines filed something similar and got the patent instead. Don't delay in disciplining yourself in the pursuit of the desires of your heart.

  You will face many defeats, but keep refining and resubmitting your vision to God and others. There were many times when the new molds were not producing parts effectively, or the wrong material was being used and they would crack or not dry evenly, creating stress cracks. I was determined to press forward to a solution.

Remember, the main trick is to market your product after it first comes out in the fastest way possible, because a patent only means it gives you the legal right to sue someone who infringes on your idea.

- *Perfection grows with practice:* It became easier and easier to file applications for each new patent that I worked on. The first time, I needed to pay a patent attorney to learn the ropes and guidelines. By the second one, I learned how to go online or to the public libraries, where volumes of patents are on store, and begin to research any idea that resembled mine. By overcoming obstacles in your life, your character becomes stronger and stronger in the process until God says, "Now you're ready to do great things for My kingdom that will glorify Me!"
- *Don't give up:* If you find a similar invention, look at it as a challenge of how to prove that your idea is not like the ones you have researched. Establish how your idea is unique. Remember, you are unique to God! He wants to use You to reach someone no one else can reach. Don't give up, until God reveals that special person to you!

God has called you to be unique with His secret plan: "At the right time He will bring everything together under the authority of Christ in heaven and on Earth. You have received an inheritance from God. The Holy Spirit living in you is God's guarantee that He will give you everything He promised and that He has purchased you to be His own" (Eph. 1:9–14, author's paraphrase).

One day Autumn, my daughter, said she had been asked to give a devotional to her teachers in high school. She asked me what text might be good for her to share to bring encouragement to them so they could understand God's vision for their gifts. I suggested Romans 8:28:

> You can know that God causes everything to work together for the good of those who love God. You are called by God to His purpose in life. (author's paraphrase)

She looked her teachers in the eye and said, "Whenever you might be tempted to get discouraged, remember God is using you to change our lives forever. You are called by God to be teachers, and I just want to thank you for making a difference in my life."

There was hardly a dry eye in the room of sophisticated professional educators. "Thank you so much. We needed that encouragement for one more day of service. Not many take time to show or say thank you," the principal said.

Big Vision and Big Faith through Plastic Surgery

Dr. Brzezienski, my wife's plastic surgeon, had a big smile on his face as he looked at her two deeply scared, black and blue breasts. She was in his office following her mastectomy on one side and a reconstruction on the other. It was two weeks after surgery. He said some miraculous words to Sherri: "You look great!" For a person with faith in what he knew, Sherri could become in his hands a work of art! I kind of chuckled to myself and said, "That's visionary." Of course, my wife needed tremendous support from me to reassure her of the same conclusion as well. I quickly agreed with him. "Whew," Sherri sighed a deep breath of relief. The reassurance from the both of us helped encourage her in her long journey toward a new, different image of herself. Later when we were alone, she made a very strong statement: "I look like something that went through a meat slaughter house, being chopped up and spit out." I said with love, "Dear, you not only look beautiful now, but you will look more youthful than ever when the doctor is finished," while giving her a big hug. She cried as we embraced once again.

Every time we went back, the doctor would smile even bigger and reassure her, "You look great!" Before he would come into the small patient room, my wife would usually cry from the anticipation of the unknown next step. We would hug, and I would try to reassure her that she was more beautiful now than ever. This journey is a good exercise in developing the skill of speaking of those things that are not as though they were. They also cause us to realize that in reality, living to love goes much deeper than what we look like on the outside but who we are inside. Oh, by the way, my wife looks better now than ever!

Genetics is the largest contributor to cancer. There are certain things you can do to increase your chances of not getting cancer, like diet and exercise. I have known many close friends that developed cancer in spite of being either vegetarians or total vegans. They were actually mad at God when they died, because they thought they should be guaranteed good health. Life is a gift of God, not something you earn with a guarantee.

Plastic surgeons provide us with a wonderful example of how God looks at us. We are under constant reconstructive surgery emotionally, physically, and spiritually. He takes our scarred lives and says, "I love you, you are not condemned. You look great in my eyes." (Rom. 8:1, author's paraphrase).

The miracle of speaking words of encouragement to others that are genuine and come from the heart are invaluable in creating a positive vision of how they see themselves.

What Is True Success? Christianity Isn't Cool!

God says, "Keep your eyes focused on Me, because as you do, 'There is now no condemnation for those who belong to Me' (Rom. 8:1). My desire is to make you successful, to glorify Me! Those who sow in tears shall reap in joy. He who continually goes forth weeping shall doubtless come again, with rejoicing" (Ps. 126:5, 7, author's paraphrase).

Think about it. Jesus said some pretty unpopular statements:

- If you want to live, you must die. If you want to find your life, you must lose it.
- You must serve others instead of being served and bear crosses, suffering, and death!
- Riches are dangerous, but blessed are the poor in spirit. (Our culture looks down on those who aren't self-sufficient.)
- Blessed are those who mourn. (Our society says to be careful not to expose your lack of self-esteem or past sins.)
- Blessed are the meek. (We idolize those who are strong and influential.)
- Blessed are the merciful and the peacemakers. (Culture says revenge is strength.)
- Blessed are the pure in heart. (Society teaches you must be self-righteous, intolerant, or a bigot.)

Radical, sustainable Christianity is for you to experience the ultimate fulfillment of God's true gospel of serving through ACTS of unconditional love.

PRAYER FOR TODAY:

1 Chronicles 4:10, Jabez's Prayer of Big Faith

Oh that You would bless me and increase the possessions entrusted to me! Please be with me in all that I do, and keep me from all trouble and pain!

Chapter 11

PRAYER IS YOUR SOURCE OF POWER!

PRAYER IS YOUR greatest tool to keep your vision clear. I want to share some powerful prayers that help me tremendously. By making these prayers personal, I pray that they will help you, too, in overcoming any challenge you might face.

This is my personal prayer: "*Lord, thank You for blessing me to change Your world, through ACTS of unconditional love.*"

This is a short song I wrote. It is my prayer to you.

Acts of Love Song in Worship

Bless me with Your presence,
All the days of my life;
Serving You and others,
Glorifies Your name!

Lord, change Your world
Through my ACTS of love.
Giving and forgiving
Glorifies Your name!

(Repeat: Now I'm praising Your name!)

Prayer for God to Open Your Eyes

> And Elisha prayed, "O Lord, open his eyes so he may see." Then the Lord opened his servant's eyes, and he looked and saw the hills full of horses and chariots of fire all around Elisha. As the enemy came down toward him, Elisha prayed to the Lord, "Strike these people with blindness." So He struck them with blindness, as Elisha had prayed.
>
> —2 KINGS 6:17–20, AUTHOR'S PARAPHRASE

There may be times, when you too, should pray, as I have, for God to open your eyes to see the bigger picture of what God is up to.

> **Lord, open my eyes, so that I may see how You are at work behind the scenes in the battles I am facing!**

Prayer for God to Blind and Confuse Your Enemies

After Elisha prayed for vision for his servant, then he prayed the second prayer for God to blind the people or confuse his enemies. This prayer is also very effective in confusing those who are seemingly always out to discourage and destroy you.

> **Lord, I give You thanks in advance for blinding and confusing my enemies, who act out of jealousy or incorrect perceptions.**

God will give you spiritual eyesight to understand things from His perspective. He will slow those who have a destructive spirit against you by causing confusion. When they finally realize how God is leading you in miraculous ways, they will give up exhausted, embarrassed, and humiliated.

Prayers to Increase Your Vision: the Prayer of Aaron, Numbers 6:24-26

> **Bless and protect me. Smile upon me and be gracious to me. Show me Your favor, and give me Your peace.**

Prayers for Empowerment

> **I ask that You, Father, may give me the spirit of wisdom and revelation of who Christ is and what He has done for me. I pray that my heart will be flooded with light to see the inheritance promised to me. I understand how incredibly great Your power is to me as a believer. It is the same mighty power that raised Christ from the dead and caused Him to sit at Your right hand in heaven.**
>
> —Ephesians 1:17–20, author's paraphrase

> **I pray on my knees before You, because You are my Father. I pray that Your glorious, unlimited resources will cause me to grow strong by the power of the Holy Spirit. I pray that I may be rooted and grounded in Your love and to experience for myself**

how great Your love is for me. I want to be filled with Your fullness. Glory be to God, who, because of Your power at work within me, is able to do far more than I would ever dream of asking for or thinking of.

—Ephesians 3:14–20, author's paraphrase

Lord, I come into Your presence with:

1. A sincere heart
2. Full assurance of faith,
3. Freedom from guilt because of Your sacrifice.

I thank You that because of Calvary I am born again! I hold fast to the hope I profess because You are faithful, according to Your promises!

—Hebrews 10:22–23, author's paraphrase

Jesus' Personal Prayer of Faith, Praise, Serving, Needs, and Struggles: Matthew 6:9–13

Father, You alone are my majestic, holy and loving God. I want to experience Your power today, and may Your miraculous, perfect purpose spread throughout all the world, as it is in heaven. Because You are My provider and sustainer, You have promised to supply all my needs according to Your riches in heaven. Today, I forgive ______, who has intentionally or unintentionally hurt me, and now I thank You for forgiving my intentional or unintentional sins. When I am tested and tempted today, I thank You in advance that Your promises will give me strength to overcome all the power of the enemy!

I will glorify Your name forever, for You are an awesome God!

Morning Prayer: Psalm 5:1–12

Help, Lord. I need You this morning and expectantly bring my requests to You! I ask forgiveness from sins, like lying, pride, deceiving, and whatever else You convict me in right now. [Take time to ask for forgiveness for other specific sins.] I refuse to be separated from Your presence, which brings healing to my life right now, in Jesus' name.

Because of Your unfailing love, I love to worship You!

Lead me in the right paths today, or my enemies and challenges will conquer me. Tell me clearly what to do and where to turn today.

May any potential enemies be caught in their own traps today. Some of them are trying to flatter me. Chase them away from me today. I release any animosity or anger against them. I pray blessings on their lives instead.

I take refuge in Your presence, and I sing joyful praises to You forever!

Protect me today, all my loved ones, and those who love and don't love You yet.

Send someone across my path today who is hurting or does not yet know You, to whom I can be a living, loving Jesus.

Lord, bless me today with Your shield of love!

Personal or Congregational Prayer

I praise You, Lord, for experiencing blessings today, for this is the day that You have made. I will rejoice and be glad in it. Holy Spirit, move in a mighty way in my heart today. "Now-faith" comes by hearing and submitting to Your Word. Faith rests on Your power, not men's wisdom. I am a believer, not a doubter. Your Word tells me that faith is speaking of those things that are not as though they were, those things invisible as though they were visible. I chose to put You first in my life, and I live in a relationship with You, Lord. I speak words of life and not death, faith and not doubt, encouragement and not criticism.

The weapons I use have divine power to demolish every stronghold of evil in my life. You have given me authority to overcome all the power of the enemy! You are my Deliverer. I walk in Your favor and in the power of the Holy Spirit. Abundant life comes to me now! You are my Shepherd; all my needs are met according to Your riches in glory. Because You have promised to never leave me or forsake me, I can be sure that You are here now, and because You are here, the power to heal is here.

I am a hearer and obey Your Word. I am more than a conqueror through Your love for me. I trust and depend upon You by casting all my cares on You. I praise You, Lord, that You have equipped me with all I need to stay strong in my day of adversity!

You will keep me from falling, because no weapon formed against me shall prosper. In Jesus' name, amen!

Faith-Filled Memorial Prayer

We invite Your presence, for You are the Anointed One who heals the brokenhearted and sets the captives free.

Thank You for bringing spiritual healing to _______. (He/she) used to be blind to spiritual things, having a form of godliness or religion, but didn't know You. (He/she) experienced Your power, which changed (his/her) heart into a personal relationship of faith in You.

You blessed _______ with close friends who were filled with faith. (He/she) ran the race of life triumphantly, finished the course, and kept hold of faith. The victory, which overcame (his/her) world, was faith in You!

Today, we are thankful that _______ only had to die once. (He/she) died to trusting in self. When (he/she) wakes up, (his/her) body will be transformed into a perfect body, ready to live for eternity.

A great battle was being waged for (his/her) soul. Satan was trying to steal, kill, and destroy physically, spiritually, and emotionally, but You came and gave life more abundantly!

When some say it takes more faith to accept whatever comes their way, (he/she) fought the good fight of faith, choosing rather to stand on Your promises!

_______ was like Abraham, who spoke of those things that were not as though they were.

You died on Calvary for _______'s sins, so that (he/she) experienced peace and forgiveness.

Come, good and faithful servant _______. Enter into the joy of the Lord!

Prayer for Provision: 1 Kings 18:36–37

O Lord, God of Abraham, Isaac, and Jacob, demonstrate today that You are God and that I am Your servant. Answer my prayer because I have followed You by faith, so that everyone may know that You are God.

Jesus' Prayer to Glorify the Father: John 17:1-4

Glorify me today so that I can give glory back to You. You have given me authority over everyone and everything. Thank You for giving me eternal life, because I know how much You love me. In everything I do, I want to bring You glory.

Jesus' Prayer for Unity: John 17:20-22

As believers we are united in demonstrating Your perfect love. This will cause others to believe in You. Thank You for giving us Your glory now so that we are becoming perfect in unity. Thank You for promising to reveal Your full glory to us when we go to live with You forever!

Jesus' Prayer for His Suffering to End: Matthew 26:39

Father, if it is possible, let my suffering be taken away from me. I want Your will, not mine.

Chapter 12
HURRICANE KATRINA: ISN'T GOD GOOD!

THOUSANDS OF VOLUNTEERS arrived in Purvis, Mississippi, to help assist the struggling survivors from Hurricane Katrina. A husband and wife had called ahead to ask if there was any way they could assist thousands of students who were volunteering from all over the country.

While a group of us were unloading a semitruck of donated emergency supplies in one hundred–degree weather, sweat pouring down our bodies, I noticed a BMW pull into our site. Out stepped this married couple in their thirties. The lady, Gloria, was wearing high heels, a wrinkle-free dress, was well-manicured, and had a hairdo that looked like she was ready for a banquet. The man, Ben, was in designer jeans, a leather vest, and Italian loafers.

I had never met them before but immediately began to realize that this was about to be a life-changing event for them. As I approached them, lovely fragrances wafted from their direction. This was unusual for the situation and in direct contrast to the smell emanating from my presence. We had only recently been blessed with running water, and showers were still only something that dreams were made of.

I chuckled inside as I held out my hand and greeted them. "You are welcome to eat under the big tent with us. You can put your personal items in the gymnasium right over there." I pointed to a building whose front wall had a gaping hole in it from the storm. "We have just gotten our water running."

Ben looked at me with dismay. "Where is the closest hotel where we might be able to stay?"

I grinned and said, "Yeah, right. You and about one hundred thousand other displaced people! About three hours north you might find one." They had not considered this problem and didn't even have a sleeping bag! "Oh, this is going to be fun," I thought to myself.

They were very hungry, having missed supper the night before while trying in vain to find a place to stay. Gloria's face turned from happiness to green when a youth volunteer server put the first spoonful of applesauce on her plate—sprinkled with love bugs! The volunteer, surmising that this was a problem for her, quickly reached over and scooped off the unwanted guests!

"Welcome to the world of emergency response," I said to Gloria. "Why don't you both just spend some time here in the cafeteria tent?" The best way for victims to gain their healing is by mingling with each other, reviewing their journey and sharing encouraging experiences with each other. There in the tent, Gloria and Ben began to listen to stories of how ACTS volunteers had brought water and other emergency supplies to their houses when they could not find a ride to our distribution line.

Saved by an Angel

Ben listened to the story of one elderly couple in their eighties. Jim and Shelley shared with him how they had prayed, "Lord, please send an angel to our house with water so we can live just one more day." It was well over one hundred degrees in their house. They had no phones, power, or water. It was unbearable. They could not even get their car out because a big oak tree had fallen on it in their driveway and completely demolished it. No one even knew they were still at home or alive since they had no nearby neighbors.

Meanwhile, two ACTS student youth volunteers, Sandy and Jennifer, from a school in Pisgah, North Carolina, had prayed that morning, "Lord, please lead us to someone who is in great need today." In addition to individuals driving or car-pooling to our distribution line, we had vans and buses going out every day to take supplies to people in the community. Sandy and Jennifer knocked on the wooden door of Jim and Shelley's old white house. They had seen the smashed car in the driveway and hoped to find someone home alive. There was no X marking on the house indicating that a search and rescue team had been there before them. (Because of the thousands of miles that Hurricane Katrina had destroyed, the search and rescue teams had focused primarily on the larger cities.)

After knocking again, the door slowly opened. Shelley cried out as she looked back over her shoulder to her husband, who was still inside the front room. "Jim, God answered our prayer, and He did send us an angel today!" Sandy and Jennifer were standing there holding a case of water. After taking it inside, they all exchanged hugs, crying together and thanking God for bringing them together at just the right time.

Jim shared, "Shelley and I want you to know that we determined we probably only had one more day left before we were going to lay down and die, thankful for being married to each other for over sixty years." The volunteers connected them to another neighbor, who picked them up and brought them to the tent cafeteria to get more supplies.

Ben and Gloria thanked them for sharing their story. They embraced and exchanged more tears in the journey of growing to love each other through the gospel of serving.

Ben and Gloria wanted to work with the youth and help wherever needed, so they joined up with a vanload of students who were going door-to-door with rakes, shovels, and gloves. They were helping individuals with emergency supplies and cleaning houses that were full of mud. They planned to work in an area about two hours' drive from our base site and closer to the coast. It still was not safe to have the volunteers living where the toxic chemicals and sewage were still drying up. Gloria climbed into the van in designer pants and a color-coordinated pair of high heels.

The trip to Waveland was quite eerie. The team noticed semitrucks laying upside down, half driven through the side of gas stations and other buildings, commercial boats sitting in downtown residential neighborhoods, and a boat lodged in the drive-thru of a Burger King as if waiting to place its order. Finally, after two hours of driving, they arrived at the mud-covered pavement of Fred's Grocery Store, the Waveland parking lot that had been converted by ACTS into a massive emergency response community center.

The buzz of activity was far more organized than it seemed to the casual observer. FEMA trucks, ACTS semis, and the big all-terrain forklifts and operators were moving about, doing what they were meant to do as if remotely controlled and orchestrated from a centralized headquarters. Much needed fuel for our generators and volunteer transport vehicles was being delivered to our large one thousand–gallon fuel tanks, thanks to FEMA. Semis loaded with supplies were being emptied by volunteers and stacked on pallets according to whether they were food, bottled water, items for personal hygiene, diapers, or other items. Then the ACTS forklifts moved those pallets to their assigned places. One semi had been converted into a mobile ACTS kitchen. It was the place where volunteers prepared thousands of meals a day to feed a community that couldn't feed themselves. For the dining area, huge circus-size tents had been erected as a barrier from the blistering sun, offering welcome relief. It was here that the grateful Gulf Coast residents and volunteers ate three meals a day.

The most important feature was the distribution line. It was a work of art, snaking across the parking lot and disappearing into the horizon. Supplies had been organized into like groups and set up so that no one would need to leave their vehicle. As drivers came upon each supply station, three to four volunteers quickly loaded what they needed into their trunks, and then they drove on to the next station. Additional volunteers continued to restock supplies at each station. At both the entrance and the exit, police stood guard, helping to keep up a steady flow. This allowed thousands of vehicles to pass through daily, providing the most efficient way of helping the most people. It worked like a frictionless car engine. Its efficiency was so impressive that government officials requested ACTS's advice and expertise in organizing other emergency response distribution center. Two ACTS medical clinics made up from expandable semitrailers were located in one corner of the parking lot. It too was staffed entirely by volunteers. Doctors and nurses representing countries all over the world had come to give of their time and skills. Whether addressing cuts and abrasions, administering inoculations, diagnosing cases of dehydration, or setting broken bones, these medical personnel worked tirelessly to bring relief to a suffering community.

In a separate area were the showers, made by draping FEMA blue plastic roofing material over salvaged wood from once-standing homes.

As if this bustling center of activity wasn't enough, ACTS implemented a program that brought much-needed necessities to those who were unable to come to the distribution center or who had no transportation. Those who still had cars undamaged by the storm were few and far between. Those who had working cars *and* gas were a highly desired commodity and were quickly asked to help us help the community. Under the circumstances, to add an extra measure of security, volunteers were organized into teams rather than being sent out alone. Each team received its own set of essentials: water, ice, food, toilet paper, tents, bug spray, and more.

Surveying the scene, Ben and Gloria seemed somewhat overwhelmed with it all.

Just then I asked, "Gloria, would you be willing to team up with Carol?" I gestured to a young woman nearby. "She's a nurse. I thought she could give medical care, and you could give emotional and spiritual care. Does that sound OK?" Carol nodded her agreement, and it was fine with Gloria. Michelle, a photographer from a university in Tennessee, also joined their group. I introduced the three to the gentleman who would be driving them out into the community. He was a school principal and was accompanied by his wife and a group of students. They were ready to take off, since they had already loaded the van with supplies.

"Ben, could you help out by staying here at the distribution line as a safety officer to make sure no one gets hurt with all the moving vehicles, forklifts, and volunteers?"

"Yes," he responded, looking glad to have an assignment.

Before the driver put the van in gear, I made sure to explain to the group how crucial it was to stay together. It wasn't safe to be alone or in groups smaller than four. There is always safety in numbers. "Watch out for prisoners who either escaped or were turned loose," I warned. "No telling who is out there. And be sure to wear your paper masks when going into any of the homes. Toxicity levels from mold and decay are most likely off the charts. Also, be careful what you touch."

"Where do you want us to go first?" Gloria asked me.

"The area just up the road to the left, closest to the beach, has been hardest hit from the thirty-foot wave coming over them, but just let God lead you." Carol picked up two medical kits, and off they went.

The particular neighborhood I told them about was near the ocean. Before the hurricane, it must have offered quite an enchanting view of sunrises, sunsets, and pelicans diving for their food. However, the closer our team got to the neighborhood, the devastation grew worse. Although their eyes were seeing it, their brains couldn't comprehend it. *Devastation* was a word that couldn't even begin to fully describe what they were seeing! What they were seeing would make the pictures shown on TV seem normal. The ground was literally covered in sludge and dried mud. Houses looked like skeletons, broken and angled unnaturally. Windows, doors, and roofs were missing from most. The empty holes stared back with a look of the dead, the heart and soul of the house gone, having been swept out to sea or piled inland on someone else's yard. Trees were broken like straws and bare to the bone. Debris was everywhere. If their furniture and earthly possessions, now infested with mold, made it to the street curb, contractors would carry it away.

But wait, something was missing! The scene was like a vibrant watercolor mistakenly painted in sepia tones, no color anywhere. It was like stepping back in time before color photography, being only able to take pictures in black and white. Another thought struck: this was like a war zone after an atomic bomb! True, it hadn't come at the hands of invading soldiers, but the ocean had attacked this community with a vengeance! How had these people survived?

Layers of mud and sludge were so thick on the roads that you couldn't see the pavement underneath. If heavy equipment operators hadn't gone through the streets, forging a path through the debris, the team wouldn't have been able to drive through this area at all. At the first street, the driver pulled over and parked. Once again, the total devastation rocked them. The three ladies noticed some of the other students looking around wide-eyed. They divided up into small groups and approached what was left of the houses on one side of the street.

FEMA required that homeowners be present when their representatives came by, or the family would forfeit getting their assessment until a later time to determine if they were eligible for a FEMA trailer. The problem was, the homeowners knew FEMA was coming; they just didn't know when.

Our team made their way to the first makeshift house, constructed from blue plastic from FEMA made into a lean-to. Here they found a two-year-old baby named Julia who was covered with mosquito bites from head to toe. The mother, Carol, was trying frantically to breastfeed Julia, but to no avail. The ACTS nurse quickly gave Julia a shot to decrease her temperature. Carol thanked the ladies, and together they had prayer, thanking God that their lives had been spared from the thirty-foot wave that came over what used to be their house.

After saying their good-byes, the team went outside and looked for the van, but it wasn't there! They looked to the right and to the left, but the street was empty. "Maybe they went to the next street," suggested one of the ladies, but when they got there, the van was nowhere to be found!

Quickly they turned around and walked toward the street in the other direction. But again, no van! For hours they walked up first one street and then down another, but it seemed the van had disappeared into thin air! Where did the van go?

"Do you think they would leave us?" Carol asked.

"Of course not," Michelle assured her, conveying far more confidence than she felt.

It was so hot and humid that it was difficult to breathe. Sweat was running down their faces in streams, dripping off the ends of their hair and into their eyes. The three ladies' clothes stuck to them like they'd been glued on. Soaked with perspiration, Gloria's hairspray had turned into its own form of adhesive, plastering it to her face. The love bugs seemed drawn to the sticky substance. They must have swatted away at least a thousand!

As the three continued walking, they were becoming more miserable and more annoyed. Where was their van? They were extremely thirsty, but their water bottles were in the van. Their stomachs growled, reminding them that it was way past time for lunch. Gloria prayed out loud, "Lord, please help us get out of here!"

Just as they were passing the demolished remains of a house, a man came out from the back corner. "Hey, ladies it's not safe for you to be walking alone out there. What are you doing?" They stopped and asked if he had seen their blue van. He hadn't. "You need to get out of here as soon as you can," he warned. His concern for their safety was evident in his furrowed brow. "There are some pit bulls loose, and they've mauled several people. They were vicious, crazy dogs before the storm, but now they're psycho. It really isn't safe for you here. There are also escaped prisoners out here raping women," he explained. "You really need to get out of here!"

Almost as if on cue, they heard dogs barking in the distance. None doubted the validity of his words. They thanked him and prayed with him. Then, they hurried off in the direction where they were first dropped off. They'd been wandering the streets for hours. "Oh, why did I wear high heels?" Gloria cried out. Her feet throbbed and her legs ached. Her toes were cramped, and on top of it all, they all had to go to the bathroom—except, there was no place to go! As the sound of the barking dogs grew nearer, fear grew in their hearts. Despite their extreme discomfort, they hurried even faster!

Finally, they came to the street where they had started that morning. It seemed like a lifetime ago. They saw a truck parked on the corner and went over to it. A volunteer was giving out sandwiches and offered them some. A vision of food poisoning flashed through Carol's mind, and thinking of trying to keep the three healthy, she politely declined. They introduced themselves, and the volunteer told them he was with the Baptist church. He told them it wasn't safe for three women to be walking alone in this neighborhood, reinforcing what the other man had told them before. The ladies assured him that they were certain their ride would come for them.

The volunteer took matters into his own hands. He had seen various men come by and stare at the three ladies, who looked out of place in their community. He flagged down the next car and asked the driver if she would take them back to the ACTS distribution center at Fred's Grocery Store parking lot. Graciously, the woman agreed to drive them seven miles back to their destination. Never in all their lives had the ladies appreciated soft seats and air conditioning so much!

When they arrived back at the distribution line, they helped their chauffer find items that she needed and prayed with her. They thanked her profusely for her kindness in not only taking the time to drive them but in doing so when gas was such a precious commodity. It was a real sacrifice for her to go out of her way for them, but she had done so with a smile and a willing heart.

Waving good-bye to her, Carol and Michelle headed to the command center trailer to find out what happened to their van. Gloria was looking for Ben. Just as Gloria turned the corner and walked past the pallets stacked high with supplies, there was the blue van, and Ben as well! "I can't believe it!" Gloria exclaimed. They'd spent all morning looking for it. "They must be starting a search party," she thought. They must be scared they lost them. Gloria ran over to Ben and gave him a big hug.

"Have you seen the principal and his wife?" Michelle asked one of the volunteers walking by.

"Oh, yeah," he answered. "I just saw them in the main dining tent over there."

"You mean they were calmly eating their lunch in the nice, cool shade after they abandoned us?" Michelle asked. "They left us to fend for ourselves in the intense heat, in a dangerous area with no water, food, or a way to communicate?" Surely, they knew there was no cell phone coverage because of all the towers being blown over.

Gloria's frustration was building to a boiling point. When she and Ben both saw me, she unloaded. With heartfelt animation and dramatics, she relayed each detail of the atrocities they'd endured that morning. I listened intently, giving my undivided attention. When Gloria finished her story, she looked into my eyes expecting sympathy, but that's not what she got! Instead, I smiled broadly, my eyes dancing in delight, as I simply said, "Isn't God good!"

"Were you even really listening to me?" she asked. Ben was now watching on with growing interest.

Confusion was on Gloria's face. I quickly explained, "God enabled the three of you ladies to feel firsthand what these survivors are feeling. You didn't have any food, water, a place to go to the bathroom, or a feeling of security; neither do they. You felt abandoned; so do they! You have experienced exactly what these people are living with on a daily basis! Isn't God good! Now you can really relate with compassion to them. That's what Jesus did for you and I when He left heaven and came to this earth. He encouraged others by relating to their needs. He lost everything yet gave them hope!"

With tears in her eyes, Gloria nodded and said, "Yes, God is good."

You, too, will have a greater heart of compassion the more you reach out and serve others by loving them unconditionally.

Chapter 13
SERVING WITH UNCONDITIONAL LOVE

Mercy or Justice?

MERCY COMES WITH no strings attached; it is given freely and without a required response from the recipient. God does not need you to condemn hearts. God needs you as His hands and feet, dispensing mercy wherever you go, treating those you come in contact with the way Jesus did, with love, compassion, and forgiveness. Mercy is the opposite of our natural human tendency. Mercy treats another as if they never did wrong.

"How can that be right? How will people ever learn if we just keep giving them mercy?" some mistakenly ask.

God has commissioned you to be His agent to deliver mercy, to respond to others in ways opposite of what they are used to or expect. Showing mercy means we treat them as innocent. We give them the opposite of what they deserve.

The following story is told by Keith Rilea, who has been the ACTS and Life-Changing Community Outreach store manager for eight years. In it he illustrates living to love through service.

Dennis the Robber: an Experience in Mercy

> "We have been robbed!" were the first words I heard as I answered the phone just before leaving for work. This Thursday was not going to be typical. Someone had entered the thrift store, broken into the office, opened the locked drawer and taken everything—the petty cash, the deposit, and all the money set aside for assisting those in need. All of it was gone.
>
> The next thing I learned was that Dennis, one of our employees, had not been heard from since five o'clock the day before. As I drove to work I experienced a flood of emotions—disbelief, loss, hurt, anger,

and resentment, to name a few. I did not want to automatically blame Dennis, but it looked suspicious. Dennis had not been heard from all night, and he had access to the key for the locked drawer.

As I drove to work, the Holy Spirit was speaking to my heart. I realized my need to forgive whoever had done this. I had to make that choice. Next was the decision of whether or not to press charges. As Roy, the assistant manager, and I prayed about it, we became conscious of the Holy Spirit's prompting that we were not to press charges. But were we willing? Were we willing to treat who ever had done this as an innocent person?

At that point I did not think we were ready to treat them as innocent, but we did make the decision not to press charges. The police left, and we gathered for our regular morning worship. Roy picked up the devotional book and started reading. I was deep in thought and was not paying much attention to what he was reading when this thought came, "You are to pray blessings on who ever did this."

"Pardon me? Pray *blessings* on them? Let me see, I have forgiven them, we have not pressed charges, and now You are asking me to bless them? Isn't that going just a little bit too far?" As those thoughts swirled in my head, I surrendered and said, "God, if that is what You are asking us to do, then that is what we will do." As Roy finished reading, I shared what had taken place over the last fourteen hours and what God had just brought to me as we were having worship. As we prayed for forgiveness and blessing for whoever had done this, the presence and power of the Holy Spirit was evident. The whole atmosphere changed, as if a cloud of hurt and loss had been lifted from each of us.

Concern for Dennis grew as the day progressed with no word on his whereabouts. The last time he had been heard from was five o'clock the afternoon before when he called a friend and asked for a ride, saying, "I'm on Bates Street. There are two men with a gun chasing me. Come get me and I will give you fifty dollars." Dennis had called back a few minutes later and said, "Never mind, I got a cab."

History

About four months previously God had literally dropped Dennis off on our doorstep. Dennis had been traveling with a carnival and had been praying that somehow God would get him out of a bad situation.

The carnival he was working with had come to our town. In need of food, Dennis and a buddy borrowed a friend's van to come to our store to get food from our pantry. As Terry was serving Dennis in the pantry, the friend asked for the keys to get something out of the van. When Dennis came out, his friend and the van were gone.

Dennis used our phone to call around and see if there was a place that he could go as a homeless person, but to no avail. He spent most of the day sitting on our front walkway, and as the day progressed I had no indication from God that we were to help him further. I had to leave as soon as the store closed to attend a meeting. As I was getting in my car, God impressed me with this thought, "Put him up in a hotel for the night." I called Roy and asked him to give the guy on the porch enough money for a motel room.

The next day Dennis showed up again. We gently tried to tell him that he needed to be looking for a place to stay, but he said he knew this is where he was supposed to be. That evening he was still there. As we discussed what we should do, one of our volunteers felt that she was to offer him her spare bedroom. From then on Dennis was at the store every day, willing to help where needed. He was attending all three Bible study groups each week, even leading out on occasion when asked. Dennis felt that we were the answer to his prayer: God had not only removed him from a bad situation but had placed him where he needed to be to grow.

Confession Time

Four days later after Dennis disappeared, on Monday morning, July 9, as I answered the phone I was not prepared to hear his voice. "This is Dennis. I need to tell you that I did it; I took the money."

Using the stolen money, Dennis had gone on a binge of drugs and alcohol. He did not know how he wound up in Leesburg, about thirty minutes away, passed out behind a building. Someone found him there and took him to a men's shelter sponsored by the Leesburg First Baptist Church. They accepted him into their four-month program of intensive Bible study, instruction, and healing, where he could grow in his walk with God.

Watching God Work

The previous November, God sent us a gentleman to manage our growing food ministry. Tom had been confined to a wheel chair since 1972 as the result of a car accident. He had worked in a food bank in Indiana, had been in Florida for about a year, and was seeking to be where God wanted him. With his great sense of humor, his knowledge of running a food bank, and his willingness for God to use him, Tom perfectly filled a need at just the right time.

Tom knows his salvation is sure, and over the months we rejoiced together as we experienced God changing all of us. One day after lunch we struck up a conversation, and Tom began to share his thoughts. "I have seen how you handle different situations and especially how you handled Dennis stealing all that money. I have seen a difference in how you folks handle the circumstances of life. I have been around Christians, and I have worked where we were providing people with assistance, but I have never seen people respond to life with such peace, forgiveness, and mercy as I see from you folks."

Tom had been married for just over a year. His wife was a follower of Buddha and had let Tom know that she was not interested in discussing any of his Christian views. Tom went home that day and shared with his wife the same things he had told me. At the end of their conversation, Jene said, "Would you mind if I went with you to church?"

Tom and Jene found themselves together at church the next week, where she took copious notes. When they got home after church, Jene took a Bible down off the shelf and asked Tom if she could have it. Of course, he was delighted to give it to her.

Was it worth the money stolen to see Tom and Jene in church? Only God knows what the outcome will be, as we see Him drawing Tom and Jene closer to His truth.

The Rest of the Story

Realizing the money was gone, we made the choice to again acknowledge that God is our source for all things and that He would see to it that our needs were met as we trusted our blessings to Him. We prayed, "God, we give this stolen money freely; it belongs to You. You are sovereign, and we choose to place our trust in You, to trust in Your promise that You will bring good out of this situation and that You take care of our needs." As we claimed His promises of blessings, we chose to leave with Him what blessings He would choose to give us.

As we allowed God to give us His forgiveness and mercy, we experienced again His ability to change our hearts. We saw the evidence of God using us to draw others to Him. These blessings cannot be measured by human standards; they are blessings that will last for an eternity.

We also witnessed God's ability to provide for us financially. Summer is traditionally our slow time, but this July was anything but slow. We saw a dramatic increase in the quality and quantity of merchandise with which we were blessed—six hundred dollar sofas, seven hundred dollar entertainment centers, and on and on. Not only did we experience a dramatic change in our donations, but God provided the customers to purchase the abundance. It was going out as fast as it was coming in.

When the dust settled for the month, it was clear that God had returned all that was stolen. We expect that as we continue to allow God to teach us to walk in mercy, allowing Him to shine through us, the blessings will continue in our lives and those God brings across our path.

Tough Love

As Dennis was finishing the program at the men's center, he felt that God was directing him to ask to come back and work with us. He was able to come two afternoons a week, and when he graduated he planned to join us again full-time. The day Dennis graduated from the program he went out, had a drink—and broke into the store again! This time he only made it as far as the dumpster across the back alley, where the Eustis Police Department found him hiding with the money bags he had taken from the office. Just because we give mercy does not mean that everybody involved is going to choose the correct path.

When presented with the decision of whether or not to press charges, our first response was to say no. But as the morning progressed and we continued to be open to God's leading, it became clear that He was directing us to let the police department take Dennis in. Treating someone as if they are innocent is foreign to our nature, but as we are willing for God to give us His way of thinking, we become open to His leading, and He is able to impress upon us the direction He would have us take in each situation. Knowing this time that God was directing us to press charges, we had the assurance that it was for *his good* and that God would use this experience to continue drawing Dennis to the only Source of victory!

Dennis was released from prison and returned to the First Baptist Church's men's program. While there he completed one semester at a local seminary. Yes, Dennis broke into the stores a third time, but that is another story. Addiction is a powerful force; however, God is greater, and we trust that as Dennis continues to allow God to work in his life, he will see victory.

But the story does not end here.

Remember Tom and Jene? Jene continued to look for answers to life in the teachings of Buddha. She longed for the peace she saw in Tom's life; however, the battle for the mind is real. She experienced the tension for mastery of her soul, and while attempting to find peace, Jene decided to move out.

During this time Jene would occasionally attend church but made it clear that she had no intention of becoming a Christian. Tom and Jene had been separated for about six months when one evening Jene called Tom. During the conversation she asked Tom if he thought they could ever get back together. He answered, "As long as you are not a Christian, we would be unequally yoked, and we would have no foundation to build a marriage."

Jene responded, "I will *never* become a Christian!"

This conversation took place on a Thursday evening. That next week Jene found herself in church. At the end of the service when a call was made, she committed her life to Christ. She chose to accept God's offer to provide for all her needs. Praise God!

God has a thousand ways to reach a heart; however, we are humbled to realize He used our willingness to show mercy many months before. Our choice was for God to change our hearts. As this was taking place, He was able to shine His light to Tom. Tom began to make a conscious choice for God to change His heart, which led to Jene witnessing the peace in Tom's life. God used that peace to bring her to the point of yielding her heart to Him.

Jene said, "I now have the peace I was searching for, the peace I saw in Tom's life."

As we are willing to allow God to change our hearts and to put mercy first, God is able to shine His light through us more brightly. Only God knows the number of lives that have been touched and the amount of eternal good He will achieve through our experience with Dennis.

Thank God for His mercy to us, in that He has not given us what we deserve. Our choice is to continue to walk with God as He fills us with grace and mercy for our fellow man.

Chapter 14

HOPE FOR HURTING HAITI

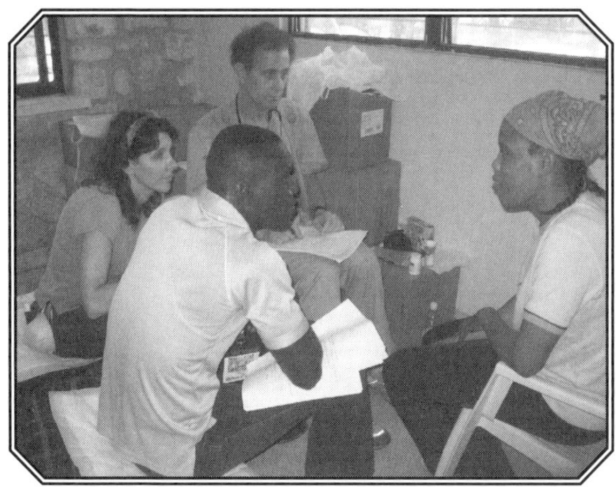

Dr. Tom Andrews, an ACTS World Relief psychiatrist, and his wife, Marie, came to Haiti after the earthquake, and he shares some of their historical perspectives to help you understand the background before the earthquake and how it affects them today. I would like to give a special thanks to Dr. Andrews for his stories and insights while serving in Haiti with ACTS World Relief.

> Those who responded to help Haiti following the 2010 earthquake agreed that this was probably one of the worst catastrophic disasters in history. It impacted them and thousands of responders for generations to come. [After the devastation, people found themselves asking questions like:] Why would anyone want to go to Haiti? Isn't it unsafe? Will it do any good to respond? Isn't the government corrupt?
>
> It is essential to understand the country that you are providing aid to, its history, and the cultural roots of its suffering. As a psychiatrist, it is an essential part of understanding the need of your patient. The same is true in relief work. Awareness of historically significant events will help the volunteers meet the challenges of that country and avoid

similar past mistakes. I'm providing this brief history to help [others] understand Haiti and to show the connection with our country.

The Pearl

Haiti was discovered and named Hispaniola in 1492 by Spain and became a French colony in the 1600s. The name was changed to Saint Domingue. The French developed a brisk trade with Europe by the mid 1700s. It produced 40 percent of the sugar and 60 percent of the coffee consumed in Europe—on the backs of nearly eight hundred thousand African slaves. At its peak, forty thousand slaves were brought in per year from Guinea, Congo, and Dahomey. Yet, because of its wealth it became known as the Pearl of the Antilles.

The French Revolution offered hope for the slaves. The National Assembly granted freedoms to the slaves in 1794. But the wealthy French landowners resisted, and armed conflict resulted. In 1802 Napoleon sent forty thousand troops to smash the rebellion. But with the pressures of the war with England and the British blockade of Haiti, Napoleon's fortunes in Haiti faded. The United States benefitted from the Haitian struggle. The Louisiana Purchase that added two million acres to U.S. soil was purchased at a fraction of its value to pay Napoleon's war efforts.

Haiti gained its freedom in 1804, but the road for the western hemisphere's second oldest republic was harsh. Haiti had to pay ninety million francs to France in 1825 to float the economy and pay reparations to France. It took one hundred twenty years to pay this back because of boycotts by slave holding nations that feared a similar rebellion.

The United States did not formally recognize Haiti until 1862 after the Civil War began. But the United States was later viewed as an occupier from 1915–1934 when troops were sent to restore order. This occurred again in 1946–1949. Powerful leaders took control for nearly thirty years and enforced their power with a strong arm. A republican form of government was revived in recent years with leaders facing many challenges to raise the standard of living. Such challenges are described in the following paragraphs. These are brief observations written by Mr. Harrison, who ran the United States Agency for International Development (USAID) mission to Haiti from 1977–1979 and now runs the Cultural Change Institute at the Fletcher School of International Affairs at Tufts University, and appeared in the *Wall Street Journal* February 6–7, 2010: "The Haitian experience—brutal slavery and the African culture—leave a value system shaped by these forces." The Nobel Prize–winning economist Sir Arthur Lewis, himself a descendent of African slaves, wrote that those who had experienced it "have inherited the idea that work is only fit for slaves.... Voodoo (a mixture between African religion and Catholicism) is practiced mostly by the poor Haitians...but all Haitians feel its influence." Wallace Hodges, an American missionary who lived in Haiti for twenty years, observed, "A Haitian child is made to understand that everything that happens is due to the spirits. He is raised to externalize evil and to understand he is in continuous danger."[1]

Breaking down these barriers and fears with a positive, caring Christian attitude with unselfish acts of kindness is essential for creating progress in the work in Haiti. One can also see the period of occupation of their country by the U.S. might bring recent cries of frustration that occupation is again occurring despite the altruistic motives. The Haitian people and their autonomy must be respected by a foreign volunteer, and this must be exemplified by a humble spirit when working with the population.

Haiti has seen emperors, kings, and presidents. Because of these many events in Haiti's history, 80 percent of the nearly ten million people living in the poorest country in the western hemisphere are living under the poverty line. This amounts to an income of less than two dollars per day. The needs have been great in Haiti. Then came the event.

The Event

On January 12, 2010, at 4:53 p.m., eight miles below the surface of the earth a massive shift occurred. Centered ten miles from Port-au-Prince, the capital of Haiti, its effects lasted for ninety terrifying seconds. Scenes on YouTube videos revealed an eerie 9/11-like dust-filled disaster not seen in our hemisphere in recorded history. Over three hundred thousand precious lives were lost. Two million people were homeless, and three million were in need of aid, food and water. One million children were unaccompanied, orphaned, or lost one parent in that minute and a half. Two hundred thousand homes were destroyed or damaged.

Terrified, the inhabitants refused to return to their homes following thirty-three aftershocks ranging in magnitude from 4.2 to 6.1. Tent cities emerged, with makeshift sheets, sticks, and twine supporting the fragile structures. Spots were claimed in precarious places, including roadway medians. Debris and refuse continued to accumulate in this scene of scattered lives. On this scene, ACTS appeared to help with five phases of care:

Phase I

ACTS: Operation Hope for Haiti deployed within three days of the earthquake. Over the next three months, more than 2,800 unpaid volunteers would respond. God miraculously provided 27 free jets landing in Port-au-Prince carrying these ACTS ambassadors, when most others could not even get in. Two very important executive board members of ACTS World Relief quickly volunteered their leadership as well. Christopher Biggs, who is an owner/operator of a major fast food chain and is used to professionally working with businessmen, coordinated all the flights; and Doug Lowe, who is co-owner of the Cuningham Group Architecture firm, kept morale high while groups were patiently waiting in the hangar for their flight out. Both men sacrificed substantially by paying for their own trips over the months to come. Doug brought in fellow employees and together inspected over eighty government, industrial, and school buildings, as well as hospitals and orphanages to declare them safe or unsafe to inhabit.

Gretchen Kerr, the director of emergency response from Northland, A Church Distributed in Central Florida (one of ACTS's strong partners) led out flawlessly by keeping the team focused by reviewing CERT training and chain-of-command procedures so the team was ready for action.

Haitian-born rapper Won-G came in on one of our first jets, which was a providential miracle of opening the doors to the executive airport authority, prime minister, president, and most importantly Dr. Jean Mathurin, who is the chief economic advisor to the prime minister. This favor of God produced many additional miracles networking together as a team approach, which is crucial in emergency response.

ACTS first deployed to a private Christian hospital that requested our help because most of their employees had gone to help suffering family members or fled to other countries. Dr. Jason Shives, who also volunteers on the ACTS World Relief executive board and led out in bringing many volunteers over the months to come, led out the surgeons, psychologists, anesthesiologists, nurses, EMTs, and physical therapists. Maintenance teams and cooks also came because the hospital could not afford to pay for the staff or ability to feed the thousands lying all over the front yard of the hospital. John Thomas, who led out in bringing several groups from Union College in Lincoln, Nebraska, brought in a search-and-rescue team who also worked with a K-9 unit.

Within the first week, cooks and food arrived with one of our long-time partners, Supreme Master Ching Hai International Association, producing ultimately 289,000 hot vegan meals over three months. Over 2.4 million dollars in medication was prescribed. Prosthetic evaluations with mental health and physical therapy needs numbered in the hundreds. Thousands of tents were donated and distributed. When the water dried up at the hospital because the city water pipes and cisterns were dry for three days, ACTS medical surgeons and non-medical personnel laid 2,700 feet of pipe to a spring from a private university up the hill. After one day, the hospital never had water shortage problems again. Can you imagine not having any water for surgery, toilets, showers, or cooking to care for thousands of dying patients?

Phase II

This phase, during the second month, included expanding across the street to a clinic where ACTS specialized in pediatric and primary care and mobile clinics to orphanages and the community, seeing between eight hundred to twelve hundred patients daily. Acute-care patients were sent across the street to the hospital. ACTS World Relief medical volunteers treated 72,000 patients with various medical and mental health conditions.

It was at this point that a very unique individual arrived. He became a temporary assistant administrator at the hospital where ACTS had been since the first week after being sent by a larger private hospital in the U.S. He said, "We appreciate all the help ACTS has been to aid our sister hospital, but we no longer need your help. I have come to build taller walls around this institution to keep others out and define each other's rolls." Politics had finally arrived. ACTS's philosophy is one hundred eighty degrees different from that philosophy. The only way to succeed in emergency response is by operating without walls and networking with others outside of your institution or denomination. Later, this same medical institution and others, requested to form an agreement to work together globally in emergency response. Miracles do happen!

This man's philosophy can never succeed, even if one had an endless stream of money and inside resources, but ACTS gladly expressed they would leave immediately, even ceasing to provide two vegan meals per day. It was a known fact that the hospital we were based from was identified as having the best food of any other hospital in Haiti. The other hospitals only provided one meal per day, which was very low in protein and vegetables. This prevented the patients from healing very rapidly.

"Oh no, please do not pull out entirely!" he pled.

Honoring our promise, ACTS now focused more on its medical clinic across the street and enjoyed sharing medical care providers as it expanded to mobile medical clinics to help the suffering, since all the hospitals were now turning away patients who could not pay. This also helped reduce the patient load at the hospital. The total donated value of supplies and transportation was in excess of $8.3 million the first three months.

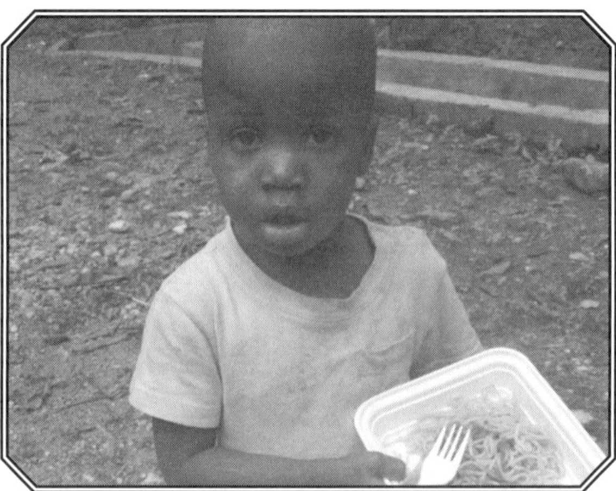

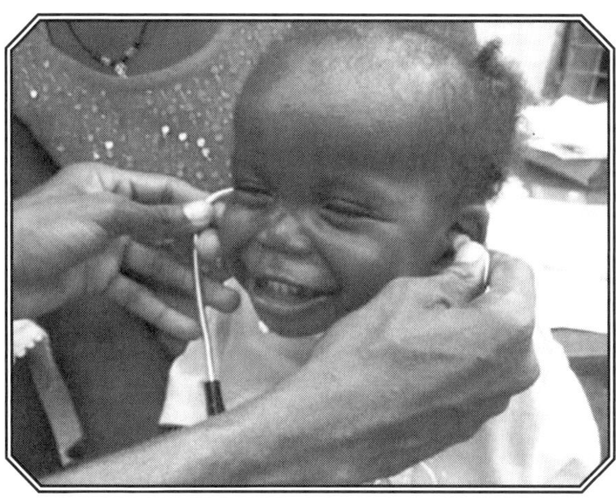

Phase III

This period, from the third to fourth months, involved training Haitian translators and medical providers to be certified in spiritual, emotional, and community health care, as well as emergency response. Facility and child assessments were utilized for prosthetic, medical, psychological, and educational needs. The Haitian department of health and education recognized the efforts of ACTS and gave them a leading role providing care for children's needs within the schools. A hot lunch program for schools and orphanages took place. Dr. Rebecca Thomley, an experienced disaster response psychologist, joined in bringing multiple groups over the months to come in, leading out in the emotional care needs of the many orphanage children.

Phase IV

The final phase, after eight months, was the most rewarding phase, because it capitalized on having met the needs of hurting people first, as Jesus did. Now ACTS began helping rebuild churches, schools, and houses. It was rewarding to watch thousands of smiling faces of children and adults as ACTS shared God's Word through puppet and drama ministry and singing at churches and in transitional camps. This is the most fulfilling part of emergency response!

A ADORATION
C CONFESSION
T THANKSGIVING
S SUPPLICATION

Grace

Phase V: ACTS World Relief Eden Garden Orphanage

Charles Le Morzellec, a great visionary, founded the Eden Garden orphanage seventeen years previously. He invited ACTS World Relief to assist with medical, emotional, and spiritual care. Because of our passion for the children of Haiti, our relationship grew to the point where both he and his board asked if ACTS World Relief would move our Haiti home base to the EGO campus and merge with one of the most beautiful orphanages of Haiti, which included buildings for medical outreach, dental outreach, a school for two hundred children, a church, and dormitories. All of this is in the setting of large trees, a water treatment plant, a place to teach agriculture within two hundred yards of the seaside. This miracle became a reality because of ACTS World Relief desiring to share acts of love and collaborate in changing the world through helping just one child at a time.

Haiti's Earthquake, through the Eyes of a Psychiatrist

A haze hung over Port-au-Prince. Fires were burning the remnants of the last few weeks of uncollected plastic bottles, debris, and unusable items destroyed in the event. The people of Haiti are colorful in attire, expression, and in spirit. The streets are astir with activity—women carrying belongings on their heads, men moving to reduce the tension of too much time, colorful burgeoning tap-taps carrying their load of human cargo, and the ever-present Haitian pigs wandering amongst the food stands and street gutters. The smell of rotting flesh soon permeated the bus. Our masks went on, but the people outside were accustomed to the deadly reminder of the event.

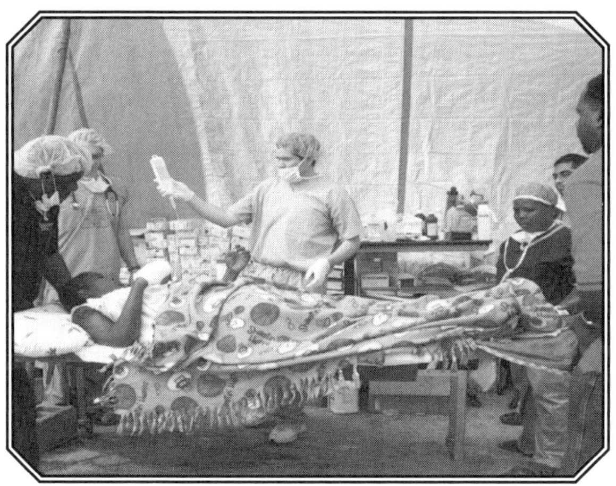

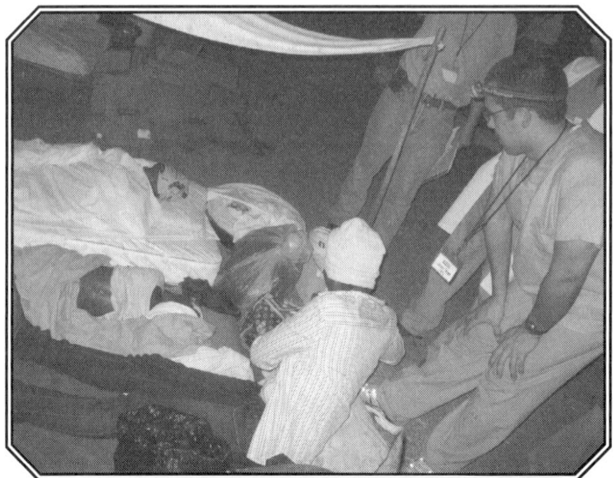

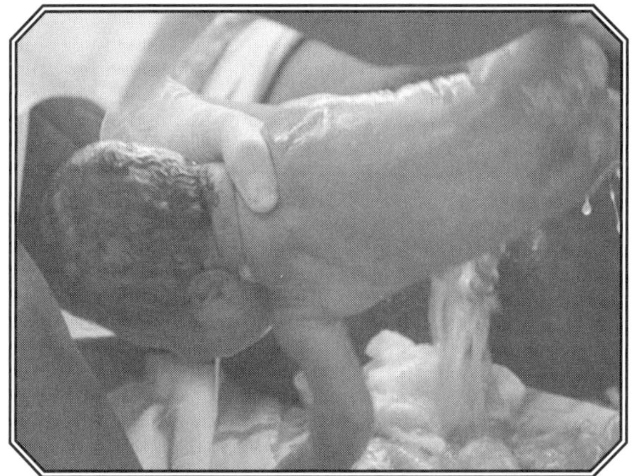

When I arrived at the ACTS headquarters, lines of people were near the hospital entrance. We quickly staked a claim for our tents, unloaded supplies, and had our first meeting. Here we learned of how God had miraculously provided for the ACTS first response team to arrive almost three weeks earlier, days after the earthquake, to stabilize the hospital, which only had a skeleton crew of staff because many had either fled out the country or were caring for their dead or wounded relatives. The first team had literally dug their way through the debris-strewn streets to enable their three-vehicle convoy carrying relief medical staff and emergency medications to arrive. Search-and-rescue teams at the airport told them the hospital was impossible to reach by vehicle because of it being too close to the epicenter of destruction. Within one hour of arrival, they had been performing surgery around the clock on hundreds of survivors whose limbs had been either severed or were cut off trying to free loved ones. There were times when they even ran out of anesthesia and patients pled for surgery without complaining. We were about to witness many of God's miracles of serving those in desperate need, including delivering babies.

No sooner had we finished the orientation when an American social worker by the name of Succoth who spoke Creole and English asked, "Can you come with me to see a patient who is experiencing deep emotional needs at the hospital?"

The Adventist Hospital was guarded at the entrance by South Korean UN troops. We entered the gate and were confronted with a maze of tents surrounding the hospital grounds. Succoth explained that the pre-op patients and families were first, the post-ops farther away, and the maternity wing was to the right. We walked quickly to the location where our patient lay sleeping in a Coleman camping tent.

Jasmine was covered with a once-white sheet, having survived many rain-soaked nights. Her mother looked on sadly. The neighbor, who had lost his left leg, gave us a bright smile. Jasmine awoke, and the social worker communicated in Creole. Jasmine was a gifted girl who was hoping to teach French or become a singer. She had been studying her college French literature on the third story roof of her home when the fourth story of the house next door came crashing toward her. She leapt in time to avoid being crushed, but she left the safety of the roof as she fell three stories. It crushed her left leg, and amputation was the only option to save her life. Her sister was not so lucky and died in the collapse of the home. She had three other sisters, but the sister who died was her older sister and the heroine she was bonded to. She was depressed, withdrawn, and nightmares filled her sleep.

Because of her post-traumatic stress disorder (PTSD), it would be important for her to "work through," as we say in psychiatry, the emotions and experiences she had recently suffered. She had been writing in her journal. The journaling of her precious thoughts was essential for her recovery.

I asked her, "Could you read us your thoughts from your journal?"

"The day that I had my accident is engraved in my memory. It's all as if it happened in a dream. Now, I am a handicap. I live in a world of handicap....It's thanks to their efforts that I'm still here, because life has no meaning. I have no house to live in. Five of my family members are dead. I live in a family not too rich and not too poor. But, I am miserable."

As we listened, we wept with her. We spent time offering encouragement, support, and validation for her. We formed connections with her father, mother, sister, and brother in-law. We would bring food items to her. But most of all, we listened.

She wrote again, "I have not lost all my hopes, for God is here during all my suffering, pain, chagrin, contempt, and humiliation. God my Father has sustained me, which is why I am not deprived. My Father, my Father, my Father..."

This biblical experience reminded us of Job 13:15: "Though He slay me, yet will I trust Him" (NKJV).

Fighting through tears, a smile of relief shone through the darkness. But the battle was not yet won. She then said, "One never knows. I know how I was born, I know how I will live, but I do not know how I will die. Sometimes we meet people who make sense of life, and sometimes we meet people that question life." Jasmine was struggling with both and commented on the therapy she was receiving. Would she be able to find meaning in her suffering?

She continued, "All my friends have the luck of happiness, except me. I am unfortunate. I live in a world of despair, chagrin, hate, sadness, and rancor. Almost all of our houses have been destroyed, and many of the people I love are already gone. It is hard to have lost a leg, and it's hard to see many people in my country are handicapped. Many children are orphaned. The tears in my eyes never stop running, because too much blood has been spilt."

This was a moment of realization. The Haitian culture can view life as capriciously controlled by entities. She assigns it to "luck of happiness," but it was not for her. The despair and shame for handicapped victims is great in Haiti, and many amputees stated such to us. But she was able to reach out and identify with the suffering of others and could cry in unison with them. Though the experience was painful, it allowed her to attach her hopeless feelings to others in despair. She too was "orphaned" from five near relatives, and she felt with Haiti's crying children she was not alone. "My dream is to become a singer. I always cry, I often think of incredible things. My deceased sister used to say, 'We must enjoy every part of life, because one never knows what is in your future.' We never know, we never know."

Jasmine was seeing a future dream and even using her sister's memory to give life to it. She lamented, "We live in a world of despair, regret, pain, suffering, and misery. For me, all my plans have crumbled." Her descriptions are so visual, like the crumbling building that changed her life. You see, when she lost her sister part of her dream changed. Her future dreams had included her. "My sister left me traces that make me sad...I cannot hope anything better for her because she has left me alone," she penned. How could she resolve this loss? A beautiful, sensitive soul is precious to our Lord, and He said, "Blessed are those who mourn, For they shall be comforted" (Matt. 5:4, NKJV).

"We are not responsible for what we have lost but for what we do. Sometimes love makes us suffer when it is sincere," Jasmine said. What a statement conveying the essence of Christ's suffering and the meaning of love, knowing that sincere love has depth of loss in death. She understood what survivors have: a gift of a life with dreams. Her survivor's guilt was met with the reality that she was not responsible for her sister's death but only for her feelings about it.

She realized that it was through others that her survival happened: "It is thanks to the Americans, the French, and the Chinese that gave us life. And it's thanks to them that many are still living. I give you many thanks for all this aid: the medicines, the food, the water, and tents. I don't know how to thank God because He sent you to us," Jasmine said. The divine providence in her rescue and that of her countrymen through the help of others gave her a sense of hope for the future. "I want our country to change, to become like other countries. I am proud to be a Haitian." And her hope is that one day her country will be strong enough to be able to send aid to others. Jasmine has a future dream. This is essential for long-term recovery in PTSD.

Our work involved helping many children. We used interview techniques like drawing pictures, connecting with the emotions of the event, and then focusing on their future hopes and dreams. Because our ACTS clinics saw nearly eight thousand people in a week, our time with the children involved brief interventions. We had them describe the presenting problem; had them draw a picture of the event; talk about their feelings, usually with parents present; and state their hopes for the future.

Skytue, who was twelve years old, came to the clinic with the chief complaint of fever and loss of appetite. She drew a picture of her and her mother running out of the home at the time of earthquake. The color of the house and occupants were earth tones, but when outside they were red and wildly waving their arms. She said, "My heart was beating so fast. I still sometimes feel that way. I was screaming when we ran out. I dream of it." She felt relief relating the story and became more animated. We offered medical treatment, prayer, and reassurance that we would continue to help. She left the clinic with more hope. Nezeirue was four years old and wearing his Rastafarian-colored hat down to his eyebrows. He seemed very depressed. Nezeirue was struggling with itching, not an uncommon complaint after not bathing for weeks and being exposed to the dust and elements living outside. He drew a picture of people outside with arms outstretched, wide-eyed, and conspicuously having no mouths. The story of fear and the destruction of the family home were related by his mother as he looked down, moving his feet nervously. His mother said, "We don't talk about the *tremblement*"—French for earthquake—"at all." I was told not to, it might be too upsetting." Now the picture made sense. The silence within the family about the event left this boy with no speech, and his drawing showed it in the mouth-less figures. We assured his mother it was very important for the family to share the experience and for reassurances to be given. A sense of family normalcy, security, fun time, and validation of feelings and meaning to the event were the counseling prescriptions given. The mother felt relieved. Nezeirue looked so much happier by the end of the conversation. We gave him medicine, prayed with him, and they left with hope.

Avril, who was eleven years old, was smiling. She came to be treated for an infection, which was quite common for women in Haiti after living outdoors for weeks. She drew a picture of her home falling down and said, "I hear screaming and crying a lot." We asked her to draw a picture of the future for Haiti. She drew a new, large home and an intricate flowering plant nearly dwarfing the house. There was also a pregnant mother with a large belly showing mouth-less child. Her mother admitted she was trying to be strong and didn't always show her feelings. Avril happily explained that the picture was of a beautiful Haiti with lots of flowers and that she wanted to live with her mother and the new baby. She was a lovely girl who helped you see the joy of the Haitian people, expressed in her bright eyes and beautiful smile. She was adjusting well to the trials. We asked her mother to share her feelings and allow her daughter to share in the new life about to emerge from this destruction. The flower Avril drew was a sign of hope.

Marie Anne was thirteen and refused to draw any pictures. She had come in feeling depressed. She was missing her aunts and had not heard from them. She lived on the street with her mother and older sister since their apartment was destroyed. They had no tent and only some sheets to lie on, yet they looked educated, and the clothing showed some sophistication. Her father had been a policeman (a better paid position in Haiti). Her father was murdered in 2004. Marie Anne remembered their last meal together. He would make corn with fish. "I don't like it anymore," she said. Her depression worsened, as her missing aunts, her dad's sisters, had not been heard from the last two-plus weeks. The mother's sad face revealed her concern about her daughter since this news. "She was close to her dad and her aunts," she said. They had lost many memories of her father in the event and now possibly two living relatives. We gave supportive therapy and recommended an antidepressant, giving samples and asking her to return in one week. "Would you like to have a tent?" I asked, handing them the tent we had been sleeping in. Light came into their eyes and heartfelt appreciation. One more day to provide a little hope.

Preparing to Meet Disaster

> Chance favors the prepared mind.
>
> —Louis Pasteur[2]

Be prepared. When disaster strikes on a national scale, the standard preparations would ideally have been made years in advance, but reality often dictates otherwise. There are three types of prevention:

primary, secondary, and tertiary. Joseph C. Napoli, MD, and V. Alex Kehayan, EdD, lay out important factors in their book *Resiliency in the Face of Disaster and Terrorism: Ten Things to Do to Survive,* from which this section receives insight in disaster preparation and psychological response.

Primary prevention is lessening or eliminating exposure to a danger.

Secondary prevention is stopping the consequences after being exposed to the disaster.

Tertiary prevention is stopping the long-term effects once short-term effects develop.[3]

In terms of the Haitian event, primary prevention might have included detection devices, earthquake-proof building codes, and routine inspections of facilities for the injured and non-injured. In secondary prevention, emergency personnel are ready and respond quickly, rescuing injured and stabilizing initial injuries. Tertiary prevention involves government and relief agencies providing assistance with water, food, shelter, and sanitation to prevent disease. In addition, mental health assistance to deal with the aftermath may help prevent chronic mental illness.

Planning, Training, and Exercise

Preparedness has three elements: planning, training, and exercise.

Planning means just that: determine which disasters may most likely occur in your area. This includes developing emergency evacuation routes, meeting with your team or family, and having communication networks phones/sat phones/walkie-talkies. Have names and phone numbers of important contacts not just on your cell phones but also in writing. Prepare disaster supplies and first-aid kits, along with food and water supplies.

Training especially emphasizes reading or attending seminars on how to be a first responder/volunteer to a disaster and how to care for themselves and their family.

Exercising is learning by doing and practicing what one has studied. This may include exercises at home, work, school, and rural areas. Develop escape plans for fires, earthquakes, and tornadoes and know how each differ. If you are going to serve in an area where an earthquake has taken place and aftershocks occur, you need to practice these survival skills. Rehearsing these activities can be invaluable.

Psychological preparation is important because you want to be able to help others and not be a liability. People who are unprepared to meet a disaster may become a disaster. Anticipating the worst and hoping for the best may be superficially helpful thinking, but understanding the response phase after impact to disasters is a must to be prepared. Expect disorder and chaos, damage and destruction. Roads and bridges will be blocked. There will be disrupted land and air. You should also expect:

- Hazardous materials
- Lack of water
- Loss of communication
- Mass casualties and injuries
- Outbreaks of fires
- Power outages and loss of air conditioning, refrigeration, heat, electric appliances, TV/radio/computers, water, and traffic lights
- Suffering in the extreme with emotional pain.

Recovery

The recovery phase follows with its own unique qualities:

- Economic hardship
- Huge financial costs for reconstruction
- Increased prices for goods because of shortages
- People displaced
- Waste accumulation because of disruption of garbage collection, spoiled food (lack of refrigeration), and sewage treatment plants unable to operate
- Health hazards and disease.

Workers need to develop skill sets that will allow them to be of service in specific areas. This will give the provider of care to the victims of disaster confidence that is much needed by the survivor. That is why it is most useful to be trained in emergency response work before coming and/or have well developed skills to be of service to the community. Limited training can be compensated for with group support and strong leadership. The psychological support from spiritual values, praying, and sharing is essential to adjusting to the hardships.

Coping With PTSD

This is a condition that is somewhat common in survivors of disasters. Approximately 61 percent of men and 51 percent of women in the U.S. are exposed to a traumatic event. Yet twice as many women will develop PTSD as do men. The range for men is about 14 percent of those exposed to a trauma and 24 percent of women exposed to trauma.

The symptoms include hypervigilance (this is an extreme form of anticipation), recurrent distressing thoughts and recollections of the event, increased irritability, avoidance of places associated with the event, and dreams of the event (impaired sleep).

Now that you know what it is and what you might look for in a survivor or yourself, what can be done to treat both victim and volunteer? Training volunteers to provide effective emotional support. The dos and don'ts are important. For instance, if a victim tells you they have lost a loved one, it is important to validate the loss and not dismiss it. Statements to avoid and those that would be helpful are listed below cited from Dr. Napoli's book.[4]

Avoid saying:

"I understand."—Only the person who is going through it can.

"You're lucky you survived."—Really, losing loved ones is *lucky*?

"The angels took your loved ones to heaven."—What if they believe differently and they could respond with anger for the "stolen" loved one. It's best to check the personal beliefs first.

"It could be worse."—This is not likely to be believed after such a trauma.

"Let me tell you what happened to me."—It may distract them for a millisecond, but the victim is not interested in your story.

"You need to get on with your life."—The person is not able to even think in the future. He or she is in survival mode in the here and now. And furthermore, it may rob the person of the necessary steps for grieving.

"You think this is bad? I've seen worse."—The person will feel they are in a competition for "who's the biggest victim/worst disaster."

Helpful sayings:

"What can I do to make you more comfortable?"—This shows you are a person who cares.

"I can only imagine how horrible this must be for you."—You are not trying to second-guess the person's exact feelings.

"This wasn't your fault."—Many victims feel guilty that they have survived and others have not. They think they should have done something to save other people. This response lets them know that they are not responsible. It may lessen their guilt.

"Things may never be the same, but they can improve with time."—This helps to put things into perspective and gives someone hope for the future. It can also start the healing process.

"Believe it or not, I might understand. Something like this happened to me."—There is an appropriate time and a proper way to let the victim know that he is not alone and that others have had similar experiences.

Children are particularly traumatized in natural disasters. The younger child can exhibit nightmares or regression to earlier stages of development (e.g., thumb-sucking or losing bladder or bowel control after having been toilet trained and showing increased signs of clinging behavior). It is important to be aware of the child's needs. Food and water are essential.

In the Haiti relief effort, children would eat a meal or less per day. When fed with a small item, it brought life to them and invigorated their spirit. Having parents who were emotionally unstable added to the child's distress. It was important for us to calm the parent so they could be more available to the child. In the short run the older child exposed to trauma may develop sleep disorders, persistent thoughts of the trauma, belief that another traumatic event will occur, conduct disturbances, hyperalertness, avoidance of any situation symbolic of the event, and mood changes (sadness/irritability). The following early interventions for children by parents and volunteers are listed by Napoli.[5]

Normalization of feelings—If a sixteen-year-old reacts poorly, you can say, "I see you're out of sync, but don't take it out on me." For a sad ten-year-old you might say, "It's OK to be sad. I'm sad sometimes too."

Kindness—Show kindness to neighbors and others. Children learn by example.

Spend time together doing family activities—This seemed to strengthen the Haitian community the most.

Individualism—One size does not fit all. Each child is different.

Meaning—Usually there are two meanings to trauma. One is what it personally means to the child, and the second involves culture and spiritual beliefs. When facing trauma, affirming the family's shared values or religious beliefs provides comfort and hope.

Questioning—Encourage your child to ask questions and make yourself available to them. Listen! Listen! Listen! It allows the child to process his or her experience.

Safety and security—Making the child feel safe is essential.

Understand—Try to understand what makes them tick and familiarize yourself with their personality.

Validate—There are two ways to validate someone. Test it by asking, "You looked worried to me. Are you?" The second is acknowledging an obvious feeling: "I hear how sad you are."

Exercise—Physical activity breaks the tension.

We found that storytelling and drawing pictures proved most useful in the young Haitian earthquake victims. Examples will be given in the next section. In the compilation volume *Post-Traumatic Stress Disorders in Children* the writers state that for children who suffered a traumatic death of a loved one, they use a three-phase interview techniques:

First, we engage the children, by having the child draw a picture and tell a story. This provides a link to the child's intrusive concerns of grief and trauma. The second phase explores these issues and concerns, attending to the child's perceptual and affective experiences. The third phase review's the child's present and future life plans.[6]

We used this in our interviews with the Haitian children and found immediate relief in most cases.

If untreated, other psychological disturbances can occur. For instance, following the Mount St. Helens volcano disaster, domestic violence rose 46 percent, stress related illness rose 198 percent, and the monthly average of mental illness increased by 236 percent. In children seven months after an event, increases of juvenile criminal arrests increased by 2 and 1/2 percent, vandalism by 24 percent, and disorderly conduct by 10 percent.[7] It is clear that trauma not treated can lead to a worsened state in Haiti. That is why it is imperative that ongoing help is provided. Part of the problem is the disillusionment that occurs two months to two years from the disaster, accompanied by anger, bitterness, disappointment, frustration, and resentment. Feelings of loss are noted particularly of the shared community. Various agencies leave, and some fail to meet the survivors' expectations. Out of frustration the youth may turn to aggressive or criminal behavior to release the pent-up frustration of financial and physical deprivation.

Techniques that help the provider not to suffer from trauma by helping the traumatized are noted below:

- Know your limitations and stay within them.
- Recognize and pull back when you are hearing information that is overwhelming to you.
- Recognize and pull back when you are getting beyond your training and abilities.
- Ask for help from your friends and relatives when dealing with others in a crisis.
- Use exercise and frequent breaks to relieve your own stress.
- Share your experiences as a helper by talking with others who are assisting disaster survivors.
- Accept that your reactions of stress, fatigue, or fearfulness are natural and valid.
- Seek professional help, if needed.

Stories of Hope and Care Serving in Haiti

Sam

Sam, a forty-six-year-old retired police officer with EMT experience came to Haiti to serve in a security capacity. He planned ahead with translation cards, back-up ID, basic maps, emergency numbers, embassy locations, and his own food and water to avoid getting sick. He had calculated his daily caloric needs and water intake. Clothing was a minimum. He brought extra

Deet, enough hand sanitizer for five hundred people, and enough food for fifteen people for one day.

On arrival, he was connecting with the locals for "intel" assessment. He took his job seriously and provided protection for the ACTS medical staff when the press of the crowd became too great. One day in the Cite du Soleil, known for being the most violent area of Haiti for gangs, he prevented a possible gang takeover of the medicine. "I used my politeness and respect as a tool during my trip," he explained. "We tried to treat women and children first, but in Haitian life deference to the sexes or youth goes mostly unrecognized."

In one tense situation Sam saw an older man beating a younger boy for moving ahead in line. He put himself between the boy and the man and did not use his hands, only his chest. He then spoke to those in the crowd: "I need the real men to show respect to have the women and children come to the front of the line." The crowd fell perfectly silent, the women nodding their heads in approval. Sam adjusted to the rigors of Haiti, avoiding danger or preventing it from escalating. He even resisted a political leader with greater ambitions who attempted to make him the head of his security force. After returning home he reported, "Home feels bittersweet…the job undone in our hearts…I want to turn around and come back." He did just that, bringing a group of EMTs and firefighters with him six weeks later at his own expense.

Marie

A homemaker, mother, wife, and French translator was able to change lives by her caring and gentle demeanor. Marie was neither adventurous nor trained in disaster preparedness, but her experiences in life made her able to reach out to the hurting Haitian family. You see, she had suffered loss as a child. Her parents' divorce and the later loss of her mother at thirteen years old helped her grow up quickly, and she knew this would be an issue for surviving children in Haiti when she heard the stories of the orphaned children on the news. Her family tried to dissuade her from coming.

She arrived the first night at the ACTS center in Haiti with apprehension, but the need for an interpreter at the hospital set her motion. She saw thousands of hurting people in hovels of makeshift tents around the hospital, and it only confirmed she was needed. While attending to a young girl of nineteen years old who had lost five family members, tears came to Marie's eyes as she translated poignant memories. Marie gave her hope again.

She was called to translate for a man who had sustained a displaced fracture of his upper right leg when a wall fell on him while selling sodas, which was his livelihood. While calling out for help, bystanders stole his product, his money, and his future income. He had lost something more dear to him—his wife. This struck a chord in her heart as she translated his fear of dying during the surgery and leaving his two daughters with no one to care for them. He was assured of the doctor's abilities and asked what it would take to help his business start up again. He sadly said, "Two hundred dollars." After he came out of recovery, we were able to help him financially, and this money helped him start life again. He had hope.

Marie gave a soccer ball to a little boy who had lost his leg when a wall of his house fell on it. His stump was healing rapidly because of the vegan meals the ACTS kitchen crew had been feeding patients, staff, and refugees by the thousands. It was a known fact that this hospital was seeing patients heal twice as rapidly than any other medical facility because of the highly nutritious meals ACTS is known well to provide. Marie helped the boy with his new crutches and said, "I know of a little boy in Africa who also lost his leg but plays soccer now. Would you like to kick this ball?" His broad white smile told her yes. Within minutes of giving him the soccer ball he was playing on his crutches with his parents, brothers, sisters, and friends.

Susan Bartlett's Story

I boarded a train to Miami on April 24 with six other members from Northland, a Church Distributed, and the following morning, we flew to Port-au-Prince, Haiti, for a seven-day relief mission trip.

Before my departure, friends praised me, family called my act "noble," and one group even took me out for dinner. To some degree, I found it embarrassing. The earthquake happened more than three months before, and I was not one of the first responders. Two members of our group were, and this was a return trip for them. There was no way I was going to experience the same devastation.

When we landed and were greeted on the tarmac by a couple of men wearing fatigues and carrying machine guns, my senses went into overdrive—and they stayed that way for the next three days.

Where we had strip shopping centers, they had cities of tents. Where we had grocery stores, they had poultry, livestock, and fruit displayed on blankets by the side of the road. Concrete rubble lay everywhere, and the nights were lit by candles, not streetlights.

By the third day, I was simply going through the motions expected of the "medical person" on this journey, as I became more and more conscious of the physical elements that made me so uncomfortable. I traveled for hours on the back of a truck over bumpy roads in ninety-four-degree weather, which left me sore, sweaty, and dreaming of my air-conditioned house.

In order to distract myself, I developed an overly stoic attitude, distanced myself, and labeled this a sort of survival fitness camp without celebrities. When I met the group of Haitian translators working with ACTS World Relief, our non-profit host agency, that all changed.

The thirty [Haitian] translators consisted mostly of displaced college students and young adults volunteering—not working for pay—in order to take on a leadership role in their community. These were well dressed and well spoken young people who showed a passion for making a difference and spent days away from their families to help us as we traveled to orphanages with medical supplies, activities, and fun lessons to teach the children.

When we left, they had each written a letter sharing their personal experience of the events of January 12, and at our request, they included a few items of need.

It was when I got home and walked into my house that it hit me.

The translators too lived in the tents we passed, and not once did they describe their life as one filled with hardship. Their letters all ended with reference to their faith and gratitude for whom and what was spared on that day.

Gratitude is a fleeting emotion often only expressed when blessed with good fortune or material gain. The volunteers' ability to express appreciation when they have so little humbled me.

I thought at forty-five that I had reached a level of maturity, but the character of the volunteers proved otherwise. The next time I start to grumble about my day, I am going to flip through the photos of the trip and remind myself that I don't have it so bad.

Hope for Haiti

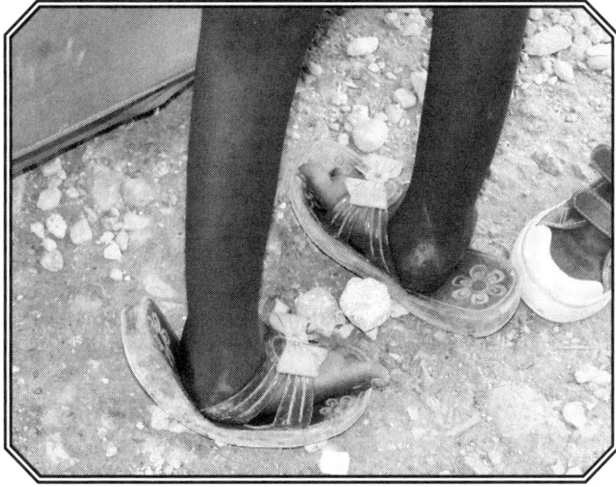

Hope is why Haitians are so resilient and strong. Because they have been without so much for so long, they are hopeful that the future must be better than the past.

Through years of watching money and resources taken from them, they have learned to live just one day at a time. Some simply say there is no hope for Haiti; the government is too corrupt, they have no desire to change, and they have no desire to clean up garbage piled up all over with no apparent sense of pride to live in a cleaner environment. But new industry is being created to turn even their garbage into creating something great with new housing construction materials. Haiti has more natural resources than most places of the world, including, oil, gold, fishing, and rich agriculture. The best way to describe Haiti is "organized chaos."

Haitians desire to change if they see a new role model of someone they trust who is not simply out to take away more from them. If you go to Haiti thinking that you are going to just give something, watch out, because there is a good chance that you will receive more good and be blessed more than you can give away.

Acts 1:8 says we receive power when we demonstrate a lifestyle of Christ's power in us. What hurting Haiti needs most is for Christians to demonstrate a practical, unconditional kind of love. Galatians 5:6 says it best: "Faith working through love" (NKJV).

Food Perimeter Control

I have watched many come into the country and blame the people for rioting, being out of control, and selfish, because they had no concept of perimeter control. They merely bring in a truck filled with food and think they can distribute food in the middle of an open area without any true logistical plan. When distributing food to starving people with medical needs, you must clearly define a setting where there is a gate or area that has perimeters of definition to keep people feeling safe and maintain clarity of vision and order, serving a few at a time. Before beginning you must instruct them that before you will even open the back end of the truck or set up for medical care, you need their help; you need them to help you in keeping everyone in order and only allowing a few to receive help at a time in a line.

Some mistakenly think success is having enough armed guards on hand to use brunt force and being demeaning and cruel, but this is not necessary with proper perimeter control.

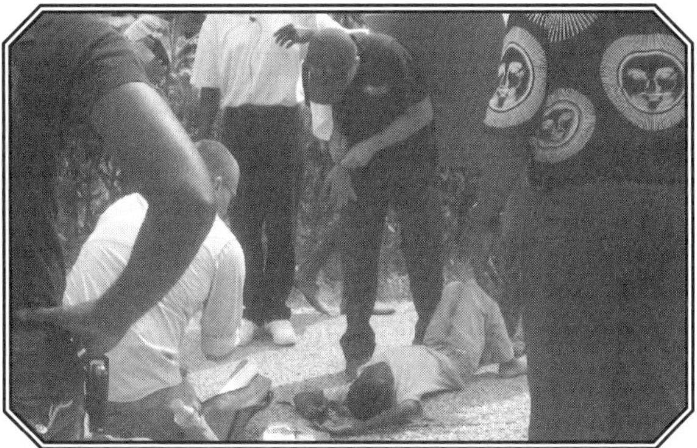

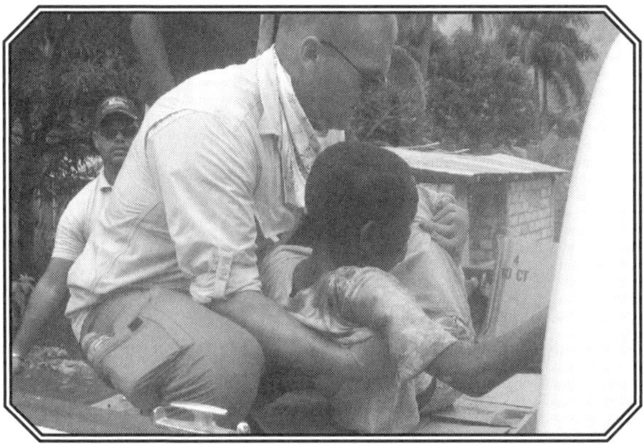

Screeeeech! The jacked-up four-wheel-drive pickup truck in which were riding looked like a "tap tap" on steroids and came to a sudden stop in the middle of the road. We had just finished pushing it out of deep mud where it had gotten buried after crossing a river in order to get to a remote village. Crowds quickly formed around a little boy about seven years old who was having seizures after being struck by a passing pickup. This sight was not uncommon. We witnessed many motorcycle and pedestrian accidents that killed people instantly. It seemed in Haitian culture the way to drive was to act like you are being chased by a gang of assassins ready to kill you! Whoever has the largest vehicle wins the crash-car derby race of life. The value of life is quite low, because if you think the police or ambulance is soon to come, think again. After about fifteen minutes of gawking, bodies and body parts are either just covered up or dragged off the middle of the street, and life continues on. There are no tickets and few laws.

District fire chief and paramedic Mickey Agostini, who had volunteered to train our translators and older teen Haitians at an orphanage, and three others who were riding in the front of our truck with me jumped into action! It was clear the little boy forgot to look as he darted out in the road, where they often played. There was a large pool of blood forming on the road from the gaping hole and gash in his forehead. Mickey had his trusty, big red medic bag loaded with life-saving bandages, IV fluid, and gloves. He began seamlessly moving into action. The rest of us did what we have been trained to do in emergency response by setting up perimeter control and assisting him. No one bothered to stop and ask if this boy had AIDS, as his blood was now soaking most of our shirts and all over our arms and legs.

All too quickly, we began to realize that there was a new problem developing. There was growing resentment and a look of anger in faces of the crowd. As outsiders to their small rural village in the mountains, we were viewed as the ones who caused the accident by those arriving late to the scene.

As the boy began to regain consciousness, he became increasingly combative, making the insertion of an IV impossible. Continuing medical treatment on the scene became an exercise in futility. After finding that we exhausted the supply of gauze and tape, Mickey said, “Let’s load him into our truck and get him to a hospital.” With limited emergency medical supplies, we improvised by placing a flannel-covered piece of cardboard we were using to illustrate Bible stories under his head in preparation to load him up in our truck and rush him to the nearest hospital, which we found out was miraculously only about an hour away.

The situation was rapidly growing worse, because the crowd around us was becoming increasingly emotional. Ladies screamed and men hollered every time they caught a glimpse of his gaping, bloody wound. Plus, the boy was fully conscious now and very frightened and agitated.

Turning to our Haitian driver, I asked, “Please find out who the mother or father is of this little boy, and get one other relative to ride with him to the hospital.” Our driver found the mother and said to her, “Get ahold of yourself and stop screaming so you can be of some help to your son and ride with him." It was imperative we got ourselves and this boy away from the situation in order to save all our lives. Our director, Andy, a former Marine and body builder, quickly reached down and picked up the boy (flannel board and all) in his arms and carried him to the back of our truck. He sat down on the tailgate, holding the boy closely to his chest, providing the comfort he needed most in that moment of fear.

Later that evening, we debriefed on this unique accident and how we could have been more effective. Mickey shared that in all his twenty-three years of responding to similar accidents, this one was the most unique in a number of ways. Perimeter control, normally essential to the safety of emergency medical/fire crews, was virtually impossible because of language barriers and the excitability of the Haitian people. Even if effective communication were possible, being viewed as an "outsider" because of the color of his skin was unique, because he never considered that an issue when he risked his life while being soaked in a victim's blood.

Lesson Learned

Remember, Jesus was beaten and soaked in his blood for you, as He says to you today, "When you have helped a little child in Haiti, you have really helped Me too.")

In Haiti, most do not understand how God's wonderful gospel plan actually prevents them from many hurtful consequences. This is healthy perimeter control. God's commandments are like a fence at the top of the Grand Canyon trying to keep us safe. Some people are determined to climb over the fence, which God allows us to do, but there are consequences we should not have to experience. God also provides an ambulance called forgiveness at the bottom of the cliff to restore us and brings us back up to the top of the mountain once again.

When we no longer understand truth from error, lying from truth, and mix superstitions of voodoo and Christianity together, this leads to self-destructive lives. When ACTS's medical and emotional care providers observed countless children who were raped by their relatives, neighbors, friends, or strangers, they were at first overwhelmed. They then understood that the word *rape* is not something used, but rather such actions are often justified or rationalized because punishment or consequences to the perpetrator are rare. Because it is so common in the country, children are so resilient they try hard to quickly rebound if not continually abused. When God's principles are practiced by role modeling rather than threatening that God is punishing them now by an earthquake, they are confronted with the reality of a God who desires to love them from their sins if they choose Him. ACTS World Relief believes that the best way to change a nation is to train the next generation of youth by example one person at a time. By teaching them how to fish, hope is created. Then meet their immediate needs by providing them a fish as well. By giving them ownership of the pond, change becomes realized. That is why we are committed to training translators to become teachers in spiritual and emotional care, community health, emergency response, and English literacy.

Emergency Response Training in Haiti: by Rich Wales

As the assistant fire chief of Orange County, I thought training a group of ACTS Haitian translators in Community Emergency Response Training (CERT) would be essential, as the professional certification would empower Haitians to help each other save lives. Leo, one of the translators, shared, "If we only had known this information before the earthquake we could have saved the lives of hundreds of our friends and relatives." As we were helping them change their lives, it was changing mine! Now they have many tools to train others in reoccurring catastrophic events, giving them a new-found confidence.

Preparing to deploy to a disaster-burdened country was something new to me, but dealing with the aftermath wasn't. Working in harsh environments and dealing with death, injury, and tragedy was common during my twenty-year career as a firefighter and paramedic, but nothing can fully prepare the soul for the experiences we facedafter "The Event." The conditions and resources available in Haiti were nonsensical. The capabilities and outreach of stateside volunteers from ACTS World Relief are inspirational to say the least.

My goal was to provide a base level of knowledge and skills for future disaster preparedness now that the hurricane season was upon them. Never did I expect to have the level of admiration for the Haitian people as I did. The translators with whom we worked absorbed everything we taught. They demonstrated each skill back to us, and then they participated in a final scenario with a mock medical and collapse disaster. Each person in this new group stepped up, like a member of a well-trained incident management team from a seasoned search-and-rescue team! I could not have been more proud of the ACTS team who helped me teach the program or of our incredible Haitian translators who developed the aptitude for disaster response.

Aftermath: How Do We Respond Now?

I give you a big thank you for everything because you have helped me so much. You give me much strength. If you had not been here I don't know what I would have done. I was humiliated before by Haitians like me. They scorned me and made me feel like trash. But now I don't need to be ashamed because you have given me much hope and [let me know] that I continue to have value in this world. I was dead in the beginning, for I had no one to give me advice, to joke, to make me laugh, to console me. But since you arrived you made me feel alive and that I am part of this world. You make me feel like I am a human being who deserves everything. I don't know how to thank you. Tell me what you want from me, and I will give it to you to make you happy. I have nothing to offer you but my writings to thank you. If you had not been here I would not be here today. Sometimes I could say that many Haitians are...very insensitive—many have no heart. It's as if the end of the world is coming. We never know with life. I am a little bit ashamed to see that the Americans, the French, and the Chinese left their own countries just for us, to save our country.

—February 6, 2010

This is a note from a Haitian who expressed his appreciation for ACTS World Relief helping after the earthquake. (A book titled *My Experience of the Haiti Earthquake* was produced as an ACTS fundraiser and was written by our ACTS Haitian translators. It is available for more stories.)

As one provider stated, "I have been a Christian my entire life. But I have never experienced God's majesty and power that led the Israelites through the Red Sea and brought water from the 'Rock' until now." It is with profound humbleness that we thank the people of Haiti for allowing us to feel, to hear, and to see the power and awesomeness of God in action as the God of Abraham, Isaac, and Jacob.

Haitians teach us how important relationships are in life. It seems that in places where the need is greatest is where we learn what is really important in life; that which you cannot buy. The best relationships are gained by serving others; relationships that will last throughout eternity!

Through our response in Haiti, we can begin to understand how Christ loved us unconditionally by coming to save us from self-destruction. Romans 5:8 says, "While we became victims of selfishness, Christ died for us" (author's paraphrase). The question is: Are you willing to help save others when they need you?

Chapter 15

HOPE FOR HELPERS—RESILIENCY IN THE FACE OF DESPAIR

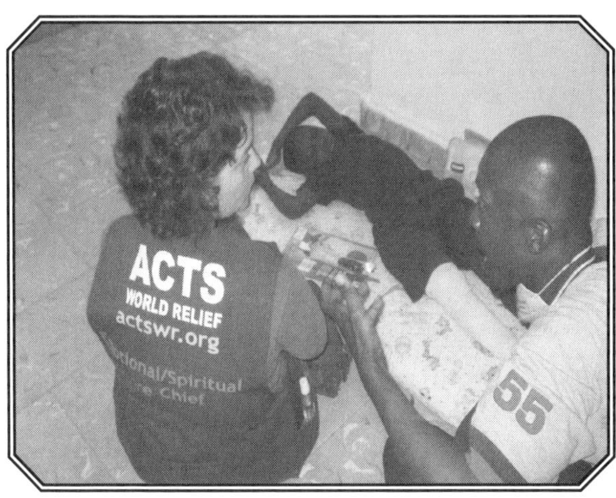

EVEN THOUGH HEALING comes through helping others, you might need only to be given appropriate levels of responsibility and leadership based on the level of immediate or past trauma you have experienced. As you gain your healing, your level of responsibility grows based on the opportunities God provides.

The following section was graciously authored by Dr. Jeanne M. LeBlanc, PhD, ABPP, R. Psychologist.

"The young psychology graduate student put in a long week of volunteering with ACTS World Relief, supporting both Haitians and volunteers, normalizing understandable feelings of stress, providing relaxation training, and battling her own illness during the last day there. She had remained strong and focused throughout the deployment, and her smile and determination was a source of inspiration to those she encountered. However, when she was placed in a wheelchair (due to her physical weakness with the illness) at the Miami airport, she dissolved into tears. Between her sobs, she looked up at me and said, 'After having done this…seeing all of these things…hearing all these stories.…how could anyone not go do this again?'"

Much has been written about trauma and even the development of psychiatric illness after a significant disaster or life-threatening event, but it is also known that God has given most people the strength to move forward in face of desperation and despair and that the majority of us do not develop post-traumatic stress disorder after trauma. For those individuals who do experience long-term emotional consequences, personal growth can still occur, as they strive to regain their sense of stability and meaning. This resiliency of spirit is a gift of courage and growth that can help both the individuals who experienced the event but also those who are fortunate enough to be in the position to help or assist others in their journey to recovery.

This chapter will highlight key aspects of resiliency and growth—both for those impacted unexpectedly by horrific events, as well as those who willingly volunteer for service in the midst of these stressful and challenging situations. In particular, information increasing awareness of how "normal" people respond to disasters will be provided, practical tools for promoting the emotional well-being of survivors of disasters will be described, methods of encouraging resiliency will be noted, and finally, self-care for responders and volunteers will be discussed.

Who Is Touched by a Disaster?

It is a well known saying in the disaster behavioral health community that "no one who confronts a disaster remains untouched." This adage is true for many more people than you might think. Let's take the 2010 earthquake in Haiti, for instance.

The earth trembled and shook violently on Tuesday, January 12, 2010, at 4:53 in the afternoon as Haitians were going about their day-to-day routines, preparing to go home after a long day at work, thinking about dinner with their family, playing with their grandchildren, or sharing conversation with friends while sitting in a park. Suddenly schools, homes, businesses, and churches collapsed. Roads were filled with falling debris. Families were separated—some by location, some by death. Coworkers were pinned in buildings and children trapped or killed in daycares. As a friend of mine would often say, "Seconds and inches…life is about seconds and inches." For the people of Haiti, this was indeed true, as their lives were irrevocably changed by ninety seconds of tremor, with inches often literally making the difference between those who walked away and those who were terribly injured or died.

When it comes to disasters, most people first think of the initial trauma that people living in the affected area experience. However, like a pebble dropped into a still pond, the ripples of disaster impact spread outwards and touch many. On my way to Miami International Airport for deployment along with a medical team to Haiti within days of the earthquake, my cab driver, a kindly, middle-aged Haitian woman pleaded,

"Please find my nephew, if you can... He is a smart student—attending the university and planning to be a doctor someday—a fine young man. His mother is worried sick. Please find him... Please have him call..." She scribbled down her phone numbers and email, said a quick prayer, and wiped away the tears coursing down her cheeks as she thrust the paper into my hand and hugged me briefly. Thanking me profusely for my willingness to help, I found myself feeling awkward and powerless as I saw the despair and desparate hope in her eyes. It practically moved me to tears as well. Gently I promised that while I would do my best, I could not guarantee an outcome. She grasped my hand again and let me know that she just was grateful for being able to give her message to someone—the rest was "up to God." Suddenly the sights and sounds of Haiti broadcast on TV over the past few days had now become very human and very real to me. Her grief-stricken plea and concerned filled eyes etched themselves onto my mind. Without a doubt, I knew that this disaster response would be different from all of the previous disasters I had worked with, and a vague sense of apprehension hit me for the first time as the full enormity of the situation invaded my consciousness.

Thus the impact of a disaster is vast. The immediate impact is obviously upon those who physically experience the event. But who else is impacted? Friends and families trying to contact their loved ones, fellow countrymen either living elsewhere in Haiti or abroad, people who have experienced earthquakes elsewhere themselves who know only too well the difficulties the Haitians will soon face, disaster responders who nervously listen for their phone to ring with the call-out for response, and people with love and compassion for those around them, saddened and grieving over the news and images shown. All of these individuals are touched by what they see or hear, and all will have some type of emotional reaction as they take in what has occurred.

Normal Reactions to Abnormal Events

So you may find yourself wondering, What exactly *is* the normal way to feel after a disaster or catastrophic event strikes? How *should* you feel when you are suddenly surrounded by chaos and change? How do *most* volunteers feel when they do this type of work? What do *most* people do when they see these scenes of destruction on TV and their heart goes out to the people shown?

The quick answer is that it differs for everyone. Some people may feel a great deal of distress right away; others get busy working or putting their energies elsewhere and don't give themselves time to feel anything for a while. Other people stay strong in front of family and friends but dissolve into tears or anger when someone takes their parking place at a grocery store. Regardless, it is clear that disasters increase the stress in our lives, and stress can result in changes to the way we think, the way we feel, and the actions that we take—at least for a short while.

It is important to remember, though, that *most people don't experience all of the stress symptoms possible, and many times what they do experience is mild.* For most people they decrease in strength as time passes and healing occurs. With this caveat in mind, you may recognize some of these common reactions to significant stress:

Emotional changes:
Anger and irritability
Loss of interest in activities or things you usually find enjoyable
Feeling numb or distant from things
A sense of fear
Grief
Guilt or shame

Susan was deployed to Haiti soon after the first earthquake happened and was jolted awake by a strong aftershock. She ran from her sleeping quarters, her eyes blurry from the cloudy contacts she had been sleeping in, frantically trying to remember which way to run out of the building when confronted with four corridors all leading in different directions. She safely found her way out, her heart pounding as she stood outside.

Afterwards she laughed with fellow volunteers about their "adventure," and was grateful that she had not been in Haiti during the first one. A few days later, while flying home, she found herself having no interest in chatting with the person next to her—an activity she usually enjoyed. She saw an article about Haiti in the newspaper she was holding but could not bring herself to fully focus on the content or relate to the story. Suddenly the plane began to jerk violently as it went through significant turbulence. Susan's heart began to race. With both hands she grasped her armrests tightly, and she looked around frantically as she quickly reminded herself, "This is not an earthquake. You are in the air. This is not an earthquake." After the turbulence passed, tears came to her eyes, and she chided herself for reacting so powerfully to a minor event. After all, the people of Haiti appeared to be so very strong after a much bigger trauma. How could she have let herself panic or be disturbed by just an aftershock?

Cognitive changes:
Confusion
Impaired concentration
Disorientation
Indecisiveness
Intrusive thoughts
Memory loss
Self-blame
Decreased attention
Preoccupation with disaster

Michele's niece and nephew were staying late at their school in Port-au-Prince when it collapsed upon them in the earthquake. Both lost their lives. They usually came to her house after school, but unfortunately, this afternoon was different. Rather than grieve openly at that time, Michele threw herself into helping her neighbors and friends, seeking resources and assistance for them day and night. Her friends became concerned when Michele began coming back to their temporary tents and shelters, again and again, with no recognition that she had been there a few hours ago, asking them what they needed. They tried to sit her down and encouraged her to take a break, but Michele would agree one minute and then change her mind the next. With further discussion, it became apparent that Michele was avoiding sleep and rest, as she was haunted with thoughts about what she imagined the children must have experienced in their last moments. She blamed herself for not insisting that they leave school at their normal time of the day. She found herself revisiting the site of their school again and again.

We visited with Michele about six weeks after this tragedy. She had continued to overwork until an intestinal ailment forced her to stay home. It was at this point that she finally began to actively grieve. When she was able to resume her relief efforts, things had changed for her. While she still clearly grieved for the loss of the children, she no longer had difficulties thinking, guilt, or the intrusive thoughts that she experienced earlier. Occasionally she would experience pangs of regret and blame but would quickly remind herself that she had been a very loving aunt and that the children had peace and were in God's hands now. She was still a strong advocate for services for the people who were now homeless, but she returned home every night, and even took some time for herself.

Physical changes:
Body aches
Change in appetite
Diarrhea
Difficult sleep
Fatigue
Nausea
Racing heartbeat
Startle response to noise
Shaky hands

John's wife was volunteering in Haiti. He got emails from her periodically, but phone contact was not possible. He found himself watching all the news he could about the situation there and tried hard not to think about how dangerous it all appeared to be. He tossed and turned at night and worried that he might be getting the flu or something. The dog was gaining weight as John got thinner, for John had no interest in what he cooked, giving it to the dog instead. When a knock sounded on the door, John jumped up from his seat abruptly, knocking over the glass-top table, while his dog looked on curiously.

Behavior changes:
Increased conflict
Increased use of controlling behaviors
Withdrawal from social support

Terry was volunteering with a medical team in Haiti. She had worked for many years as a secretary and had excellent organizational skills that she planned to use to help the team there. Once she arrived in Haiti, nothing went as planned. Since they arrived after dark, there was no transportation from the airport, and the team had to literally sleep on the tarmac, adjacent to the noisy jets landing and taking off from the airport all night. The next day, when she and the team arrived at the hospital, all the forms she had worked on and copied had been misplaced and were nowhere to be found. Electricity came and went, and what she was told was important to help with one moment changed and became something else the next moment. As it appeared no one seemed to understand the importance of following through on her requests for help, Terry's irritation with her fellow volunteers (whom she was supposed to be helping) grew. The one person who had been helpful to her was no where to be found. When he did return, Terry angrily confronted him and told him that it was very important that their planned schedule be followed—no matter what. The helper glared at her and quietly walked away. The chaos continued, and Terry found herself withdrawing from others, going to bed early, and choosing to eat alone.

What these stories and examples show us is that many people—even those not directly there— are touched by the stress of a disaster. It may come out in thoughts, feelings, behavior, or in physical symptoms. It may happen all at once; it might not happen for a while. Regardless, these are all normal responses to abnormal events by normal, everyday people. The time it takes to process through these experiences can vary quite a bit, as everyone is unique.

When "Normal" Becomes a Concern

While most people are resilient and get through stresses adequately in the long-run, for some people the stress can be just too much for them at that time, and they may benefit from professional and/or spiritual assistance. This is more likely to be true for people who have been severely traumatized in the past, who may have very limited social support, who may have other significant stresses in their lives, who have a history of emotional difficulties and/or mental illness in the past, or those who have experienced the death or loss of a loved one. Nonetheless, the wrong combination of events and stressors may result in longer-term effects of stress in anyone; thus there is no reason to be hard on yourself if you find yourself unable to break out of the post-disaster, post-stress range of difficulties on your own. Symptoms of concern are those that impact your ability to participate in typical activities such as work, relationships, and leisure activities for a month or more, with an increase in severity or frequency. They may include:

Ongoing and severe stress reactions:
Phobic avoidance of reminders
Out of the ordinary level of grief
Frequent episodes of intense anger
Severe sleep disruption or frequent nightmares
Severe and ongoing anxiety
Clinical depression (lasting more than two weeks straight)
Impaired problem-solving which persists
Severe, distressing, intrusive thoughts

Warning signs:
Abuse of alcohol/drugs
Social isolation
Spiritual despair
Inability to work
Suicidal thoughts
Persisting departure from reality; tendency to live in the past

For a very small subset of people, the strong experience of grief and despair can lead to thoughts of suicide or self-harm. In this case, the person should not hesitate to get professional mental health support as soon as possible—even going to their local emergency room if necessary.

Risk Factors for Increased Distress

When considering the potential impact of being exposed to a disaster or very large stressor, there are a number of key factors that are helpful in identifying who may be most in need of long-term intervention or may have difficulty coping. This includes the following:

- Those most severely exposed to the trauma itself
- The bereaved (parents who have had the death of a child; sudden, violent death of loved one; those who have not been able to locate the bodies of their loved ones; those with poor relationships with those who had died and no chance to ask forgiveness; those who witnessed the deaths)
- The injured (inability to perform previous work or social functions; disfigurement; lack of social support or financial opportunity; confrontation of fears related to dependency, loss of control, fear of rejection)
- Those who physical and social resources have been destroyed
- Dislocation from home and community

- Separation from family members, neighborhood, community, place of work, or school
- Social networks, which usually help with stress, are interrupted
- Populations that have been previously traumatized (refugee populations; those exposed to previous disasters or conflicts; those abused in childhood; those with pre-existing mental illness; those who have difficulty coping prior to disaster will likely show the same impaired coping skills, at a higher level, after a disaster; many external coping resources—medical, family, community—may not be available)
- Those with preexisting physical disability (those with an increased risk for homelessness or increased hospitalization due to lack of support)
- Those exposed to prolonged uncertainty and possible ongoing threat (lack of safety; risk of re-exposure; uncertainty of being able to move forward)
- Helpers and emergency responders (informal first responders may be particularly vulnerable because they lack the training and normal systems of support)

A Note Regarding Haiti

When the list of risk factors for future difficulties is reviewed, anecdotally it appears that at least 95 percent of all of the Haitians encountered during the deployment met at least one of the risk factors listed in the previous section, and many of them met multiple factors. This would suggest, then, that the vast majority of the population of Port-au-Prince, for example, would be highly at risk for the onset of mental illness.

However, there are cultural considerations to be kept in mind. Providers of mental health services in long-standing centers in Port-au-Prince and throughout Haiti have reported a figure of closer to 4 percent of Haitians meeting the criteria for PTSD, two to three months following the earthquake, of the hundreds they have seen.[1] The resiliency of the Haitian people have been noted by various authors, and this in fact appears to be an advantage for many of them as they strive to move forward. (For an excellent review, see "Weathering the Storms Like Bamboo: The Strengths of Haitians in

Coping with Natural Disasters" by G. Nicolas, B. Schwartz, and E. Pierre, in *Mass Trauma and Emotional Healing Around the World*.) This does not mean that the Haitians aren't suffering psychological effects following the earthquake—just that it appears that cultural factors, such as family, religion, community, and group culture, assist them in their resiliency and perhaps are increasing the odds of individuals avoiding the onset of significant mental illness despite these multiple stressors.

Psychological Phases of Disaster Recovery

We have now reviewed a number of individual traits or experiences that can impact people's stress and emotional well-being following a disaster. However, it is important to also realize that the emotional challenges following a disaster can vary, depending simply upon the time that has passed since the disaster occurred and the stage of recovery the community is in at the time. These phases of disaster recovery include the Heroic, Honeymoon, Disillusionment, and Reconstruction stages:[2]

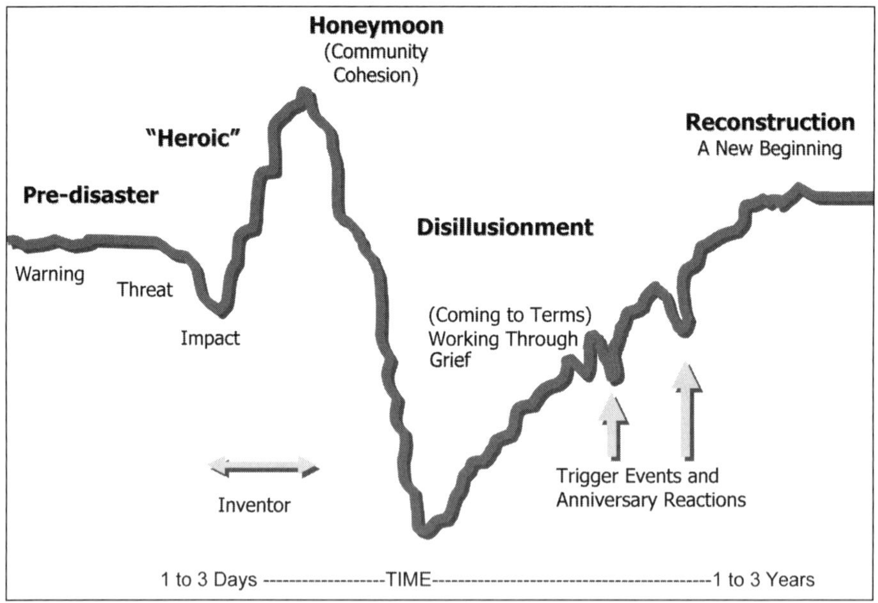

Heroic

In the Heroic stage, survivors and the community put forth a great deal of energy and activity into rescuing, assisting, housing, emergency repair, and clean-up of debris. This stage lasts anywhere from a few hours to a few days. Emotionally, this is characterized by a great deal of altruism and long hours of hard work without complaint. During this stage, people who have lost a loved one may be in shock, actively grieving, or on the other hand, fully putting aside their grief as they attempt to help or save those around them.

Let's once again look to the case of Michele. Initially she was very much in the Heroic stage. She found families tents or sheets to help give them a temporary shelter, acted as an impromptu clinic manager for a nearby medical clinic, coordinated and translated for a number of US relief agencies, and took the time to listen to the problems of patients and friends alike. Michele went without sleep for three days, insistent that she could not rest due to the needs of those around her.

Honeymoon: Community Cohesion

This stage usually lasts until about the third week to a month following the disaster. The community and those affected tend to be hopeful and upbeat about the likelihood of assistance. Aid and donations pour in, the media is present, and celebrities and/or important politicians visit and try to reassure people that their lives will get better. At this stage, survivors are very hopeful (and are likely to believe) that their lives will get back to a "new normal" somewhat rapidly and easily. People continue to work hard to get their lives back together.

However, by around week three, the donations tend to slow down, the television and news are not reporting their struggle anymore, and celebrities and politicians often are on to other areas of interest. The survivors, however, are surrounded by the enormous task in front of them every day, and the tremendous task in front of them becomes more and more apparent. At the same time, people's energy levels begin to decline, and they grow weary.

Philippe was a student at a university that collapsed during the earthquake. He was excited by all of the relief agencies he saw coming into Port-au-Prince and made it a point to note that he had met a famous US actor who had been in town a few days prior. Philippe volunteered as a translator for various aid agencies and felt fairly certain that his hard work with these groups would help him get to Canada to continue his studies. However, as time passed, Philippe became more somber, and he struggled with motivating himself to continue his volunteer work. He sadly told me that he did not know how young men such as himself would ever be able to have a future as long as they stayed in Port-au-Prince, and the paperwork it took for him to go to Canada seemed impossible to overcome.

Disillusionment: Coming to Terms—Working Through Grief

In the next weeks to even years later (in the case of large-scale disasters such as Haiti), the symptoms of stress increase while the initial hope and optimism begin to fade. Survivors begin to realize that the temporary aid often does not offer the long-term solutions they hoped for, and the full extent of their loss of family, home, community, and/or church fully sinks in. Fatigue continues, and what used to be easy completing simple demands, now have become burdensome tasks (i.e., in Haiti, having to stand in lines for food or medical care, having no home to live in). The politics of the disaster response become more of a focus.

At this stage, survivors can easily become more irritable, and patience is decreased. They may complain of feelings related to being betrayed, abandoned, treated unfairly, or the victims of government incompetence as it becomes clear that no one can fully save them from the difficulties they face.

Mr. Aube had been a successful owner of a small contracting business in Port-au-Prince. He had two homes and was married with three teenage daughters. He had worked hard for his achievements, but fully believed that he—and many like him—could eventually rebuild Haiti into a stronger and more profitable nation. He had attended a number of meetings with various relief groups, and willingly shared his property with small relief agencies helping his community. However, gradually Mr. Aube's sleep had been disturbed, and he had found himself arguing more and more with his family (who were also growing irritable with the lack of school and social opportunities). While initially happy to host various relief agencies, he was now losing patience with the attitudes of some of the volunteers and felt that he was no longer respected as he should be. Many of his employees had died in the earthquake or their whereabouts were unknown. He had many choice words to say about his perception of the Haitian government and was frustrated that there was no agency that would help him begin the very much needed task of rebuilding Haiti and also rebuilding his life.

On the other side of this process, though, is a gradual coming to terms with the obstacles that survivors of a disaster face and a gradual working through their grief with a charting of a new course for their lives.

Reconstruction/Recovery: New Beginnings

The hard work performed early on begins to bear fruit. Reconstruction takes place around them, and government processes begin to flow again. Most people return back to their pre-disaster level of emotional well-being, but there is a lot of variation, as some are back to their "old selves" within about six months while it may take eighteen to thirty-six months for others. Most survivors relate having a new appreciation for intangibles, such as spiritual connectedness, relationships, and life and have improved self-confidence about their ability to confront significant difficulties.

Yuan Yin was working on her bachelor's degree in psychology at the time of the Sichuan earthquake in Chengdu, China. She and her other fellow students were initially recruited to assist with search and rescue. However, they were then put in the position of assisting with the coping and well-being of the hundreds and hundreds of survivors who were placed in temporary shelters, despite their very basic level of education at this point. Yuan Yin, herself, did not know the status of all her family members for a number of weeks and had also been traumatized by what she saw and experienced during search and rescue. Regardless, she worked tirelessly for many weeks but eventually became exhausted, feeling guilty about her poor energy. She then found herself being more and more irritable about the lack of coordinated services and limited number of trained people to help the emotional well-being of so many. As the months passed, her anger and depression about the lack of skilled providers shifted such that she was driven and focused on facilitating the future training of as many people as possible on the effects of disaster and providing support as needed. She worked with people in the Foreign Experts Bureau and the local psychiatric hospital and coordinated a number of visits and workshops by worldwide experts in the field of disaster response. When Yuan Yin was visited for the second time—a year after the earthquake— she said, "I would never have wished for this earthquake, but when I think about how it pushed me to do something I never thought possible for our citizens, I have to believe it was for a purpose. I am now the chief administrator over continuing education for our province's healthcare providers, and we are no longer unprepared for future events."

Promoting Resiliency in Those Impacted by Disaster

We know that disasters impact many people at many different levels. There are a number of suggested approaches to help people regain a sense of themselves and normalcy, despite the chaos that surrounds them, and a few are reviewed here.

Education: As we have discussed in this chapter, it helps survivor and responder alike to have their stress-related experiences "normalized" so that they do not misunderstand their normal feelings as being a sign of psychological illness and increase their sense of stress and worry.

Encourage engagement in productive work or social activities: This is important in all stages of disaster recovery, as the individuals who have been affected typically are looking for ways to contribute to the improvement of their situation to counter feelings of helplessness and hopelessness. ACTS World Relief sees this as an important and primary organizational goal, encouraging and facilitating volunteerism from the locals being served in all of their disaster responses.

Impromptu self-help groups: These groups are led by peers and allow members to share stories and provide support. (These groups are generally productive and encouraging to most individuals, but it's also important to pay attention, as those who seem most distraught may benefit from being more active first, as hearing other people's stories may re-traumatize people. *If in doubt, ask a mental health professional!*) Peer groups can be helpful, as they provide benefits such as emotional support, reassurance, relationships and can assist with ideas about services and ways to meet needs. This also provides role-modeling and guidance and encourages a sense of belonging, validation, and feedback.

Self-care: For both responders as well as those impacted by the disaster, it is very important to remind people to not overlook the very basic activity of self-care. This can include positive coping skills, such as prayer, exercise, eating regular meals, receiving and giving social support, relaxation, and meditation. It is also important to encourage a sense of playfulness and humor at times.

Wanted:

Currently looking for ambitious, community-minded individuals to assist a team of skilled workers in a variety of ways. This is a once-in-a-lifetime opportunity to assist people all around you. Hours are flexible. Ability to perform assigned tasks and creativity are assets. Travel and people skills are a plus! Benefits are numerous, and compensation is immeasurable. This is guaranteed to be different than any other employment opportunity available. Many find they do not want to leave work at the end of the day! Please contact 604-555-1212 immediately if interested!*

****Warning: Participation in this work environment may involve exposure to hazardous chemicals, diseases, and dangerous work and living conditions. Psychological and physical distress is common. Profound sadness, grief, and anger are frequent side-effects, although you may attempt to counter your feelings of stress with increased dedication and commitment.***

Resiliency and Self-Care for Responders: Considerations Before Leaving Home

Dr. Gordon has a busy family practice and very much wished to volunteer in Haiti after the earthquake, as he knew that his skills were needed and would be of great use. However, his father was in the final stages of a chronic disease and was being considered for hospice care. Furthermore, he had never been to a disaster site before, and his wife was very concerned about his welfare if he went to Haiti (they had two small children under the age of five, and she told him clearly that she did not want to take any chance—even if small—that he go to a location with known dangers, such as what she saw each night on the television news. Dr. Gordon tried to educate his wife about the reality of Haiti as he understood it, but she just looked at him with a mixture of exasperation, fear, and anger and would leave the room. After spending some time in deep introspection, Dr. Gordon had to admit that his blood pressure had been high for a bit and that he never really had dealt with heat well. (And he definitely never did enjoy "roughing it" or even camping in state parks.) As much as he wished to go, he decided the personal costs outweighed the positives. Thus Dr. Gordon decided to instead volunteer his time providing free medical care in a local clinic instead and assisting the organization in Haiti by providing crucial medical supplies from hospitals in the United States.

Disaster response—although extremely rewarding—can be one of the most stressful activities in which a volunteer and/or professional chooses to participate. The simple truth is that a responder who is not functioning well is not only placing himself or herself at an emotional and physical risk, but he or she is also taking away much needed resources from the survivors and fellow volunteers they agreed to assist. While it is understandable that most volunteers will have an "off day" or get ill despite their best attempts to remain well, it is critical that all volunteers take the time to fully assess their readiness and personal traits in respect to the future demands of the situation at hand *before they volunteer for deployment.*

Volunteerism does not happen in a vacuum. Volunteers have families, jobs, friends, and lives outside of the disaster zone. Without the support of your family and employer, for example, you may find yourself returning to another "disaster" once you come home. It is essential that potential responders be aware of their emotional, physical, and situational readiness at that time in their lives to volunteer. The checklist below reviews these issues more fully.

Volunteer Pre-Deployment Self-Assessment[3]

Please take the time to review the following questions prior to agreeing to volunteer. It is easy to get caught up in the moment when the need is so apparent and volunteer. However, sometimes it is better to put your energy in assisting from home or nearby, or even letting this volunteer opportunity pass, rather than going to the stressful disaster site.

If you answer "yes" to some of these variable questions, it can help you determine whether the timing may be best for you to volunteer. Experienced disaster responders know that there will always be another disaster and that before going to help others you have an obligation to yourself and your family to ensure that you are physically, financially, and emotionally healthy.

Disasters are very demanding, and if you are not in good health, not only may you jeopardize your own health, but you may further tax the already stretched resources of the local community to respond to your health issues.

Yes	No	
		Are there any particular health hazards associated with this disaster response (e.g., smoke and poor air quality in forest fires) that would exacerbate any pre-existing health conditions?
		Have you had a recent surgery or recently undergone any extensive medical treatment?
		Are you on any medications that may make working long hours without regular sleep and/or meals difficult?
		Is acquiring sufficient medication to take with you on this disaster assignment a problem?
		Would you have any difficulty working long hours or walking a fair distance if regular transportation is not available?
		Would an inability to acquire tobacco and/or alcohol create a stressful situation for you?
		Have you had a recent medical check-up? Would your doctor disapprove of you going on this disaster assignment?
		Have you had a recent dental check-up? Is there any reason to suspect any dental problems may surface?

Circumstances can change—sometimes very quickly. Everyone has times when one's life situation is more stable than during other times. Going on disaster assignment as a volunteer is demanding enough without having to worry about what is happening at home or leaving when things have been very stressful (either positively or negatively).

Yes	No	
		Has your life situation changed recently? For example, have you recently experienced a separation, divorce, or a period of marital discord? Have you recently married? Has there been a recent birth in the family? Has a family member been seriously ill, and/or is anyone in your family undergoing medical treatment?
		Have you returned recently from another disaster assignment?
		Have there been any recent traumas and/or critical incidents in your life?
		Have you recently moved?
		Have you recently lost your job or been laid off work?
		Are there any significant financial stresses in your life?

Yes	No	
		Are there any important family occasions in the near future, for example, a graduation, expected birth of a grandchild, significant wedding anniversary, or birthday?
		Do you have plans for a family vacation or anticipated trip?
		Have you made any important commitments (family or organizational) that would be difficult to change and/or postpone (e.g., providing child care, caring for an elderly parent)?
		Has it been a long time since you have had time off to yourself and/or simply relaxed and enjoyed life?
		Will volunteering be welcomed as an escape from having to cope with ongoing problems at home or in the workplace?
		Will your family disapprove of you (or be uncomfortable with) you volunteering?

It is also important to ensure that financial matters are looked after while you are on assignment, as regular life and responsibilities does go on even while you are away.

Yes	No	
		Will your employer be reluctant to allow you to volunteer?
		Will volunteering jeopardize your job in any way?
		Are you in midst of any projects that would make it difficult for you to leave the office?
		Have you recently been promoted?
		Have you applied for another job, and is it likely that you would be asked to an interview in the near future?
		Will your employer pay for your time away from your job? If not, will it be financially difficult for you to volunteer?
		Have you talked to your colleagues about volunteering, and will volunteering create difficulties in terms of work coverage?
		Will you have to take vacation time to go on assignment? If so, will this disrupt any vacation plans with your family?
		Will there be any problem paying bills while you are away?
		Will there be any problem depositing checks or making bank deposits during your absence?

Resiliency and Self-Care for Responders: Considerations While Deployed

Dr. Reid is a psychologist working at a hospital. She heard about the earthquake that afternoon at work, and the more she heard, the more she knew she was going to do everything she could to help. When she was asked to deploy, she gladly did so, rapidly rearranging her schedule and preparing to go. Once there, Dr. Reid began working day and night. She would leave the hospital with mobile medical teams and would also spend time with fellow responders each night after they returned. She assisted with surgeries since it was needed, and helped people connect with their families. She consoled individuals who had lost their loved ones and those who had been through difficult medical procedures. She directed people to shelters and food. Days turned into weeks and weeks turned into a month. The scope of the disaster was enormous, and Dr. Reid felt as if she did not even have time to sleep or eat—there was so much need, so much to do.

By the end of a month, the "helper" found herself being uncharacteristically irritable and definitely not wanting to stop working. Dr. Reid was arguing with her colleagues and having difficulty keeping track of what she was going to do next. She began having vivid nightmares and felt exhausted most days. She found herself crying at small things, unexpectedly. When she made a mistake with a family one day, she felt like she could never overcome the guilt of sending them to the wrong location for help.

While disaster health services may provide an excellent means for fulfilling a psychologist's or medical professional's ethical obligation for social responsibility, disaster settings can thoroughly challenge professional skills and personal resources. Personal qualities important to a mental health or medical professional engaged in a disaster response include self-knowledge, openness to supervision, ability to perform job demands capably, flexibility, and dedication. Self-care is a critical aspect of successful disaster mental health or medical service provision, as you must do this to be able to continue to help others. Every disaster volunteer should also be alert to the potential for his or her own trauma as a result of being exposed to stories, sights, sounds, and smells associated with the event.

Once deployed, there are a number of ways a responder can maximize his or her impact and promote self-care (both for themselves and for fellow volunteers).[4]

Management of workload:

- With your fellow volunteers, set task priority levels and create a realistic work plan
- Ask for assistance and be willing to delegate when needed
- Balanced lifestyle
- Exercise and stretch muscles when possible
- Eat nutritionally, avoiding junk food, caffeine, alcohol, tobacco
- Obtain adequate sleep and rest
- Maintain contact and connection with primary social supports (family, friends, community) through phone calls, email, etc.

Stress Reduction Strategies

- Reduce physical tension by deep breathing, meditating, walking
- Use time off for exercise, reading, or listening to music
- Talk about emotions and reactions with fellow volunteers
- Spend time with others
- Look at situations or difficulties with a sense of humor, when appropriate

Self-Awareness

- Recognize and heed early warning signs for stress reactions
- Accept that you may not be able to see the problems well in yourself, so listen to the feedback of others when they say you need a break
- Be careful not to identify too much with survivor grief and trauma

Your job is to assist the best you can. This does not mean you can do everything. Take comfort in doing your part.

- Understand the differences between professional relationships and friendships.

- Examine personal prejudices and cultural stereotypes
- Be vigilant not to develop trauma from the stories you hear from others or compassion fatigue. Recognize when your own disaster experience interferes with effectiveness.

It is unreasonable to expect that you will not experience stress from participating in a deployment. Volunteers usually have compassionate hearts, and these hearts respond to the distress of others. As a consequence, the questions really are *how* much stress you will have and in *what way* it will show up in your life. A productive and valuable disaster responder takes this into account and strives to balance self-care with productivity and seek outside counsel or support whenever needed.

Resiliency and Self-Care for Responders: Considerations Once Back Home

Jesse spent two weeks in Haiti providing nursing care. She formed close friendships with the team of volunteers with whom she worked and woke up each day excited about the opportunity to use her knowledge and skills to help people. She truly did not want to leave, despite sleeping in tents, eating food she didn't particularly like, and being sweaty and smelly each day with only cold showers being available (when she took the time to take them!). She shed tears were shed as the plane took off and she glanced down upon the island, already missing the Haitians she had befriended and her team.

When Jesse returned to Calgary, she found the superficial trappings of many people's lives to be annoying—no... downright disrespectful. People panhandling in the streets who had all of their limbs, as well as shelters, food banks, and free health care, seemed to be ignoring their obvious opportunities, which also irritated her, and she fought the urge to walk up to them and tell them so. Jesse re-evaluated her life's choices, and seriously considered whether it made sense to follow through on her and her husband's plans to begin a family in the next year. How could she continue volunteering in disaster response if she was pregnant or had young children? Her husband was supportive, although a bit confused by his wife's sudden change of view. He also had to admit he was a bit jealous of her conversations with other returned volunteers, as they laughed and discussed the deployment and views on life, which he had no way of really understanding, despite his best efforts.

When Jesse returned to her job at the hospital, she felt that she really wasn't needed, as there were so many others available to provide care and the resources were so plentiful. She was often caught daydreaming about how she could find a way to return to Haiti, despite the very real, negative effects it would have on her job and her relationship with her husband.

Fortunately, Jesse had been given the advice of not making any significant life choices for at least six weeks to two months upon return, which she followed despite her desire to do so initially. With reflection and return to her normal life, Jesse began to appreciate just how much she loved her husband and the preciousness of their lives together. She saw how her work in Haiti made her more compassionate toward the struggles of the patients in the hospital and was more forgiving toward the excesses and privileges that life in Canada provided to others. She knew that Haiti and those she volunteered with will always have a very special place in her heart, but she also knew that God placed her in a life that allowed her to serve others and share love every day, and that this was just as important and needed.

Jesse's story points out a number of considerations for responders once they return back home. We have already discussed a number of the typical stress responses, but her story illustrates the life-changing aspect of disaster volunteerism. The joy of service has been described by one volunteer as, "The purest work I've ever done—it is work just for God…just for the betterment of others. No insurance companies, no focus on numbers or quantities…just working from your heart." Thus returning home requires adaptation from both stressful and trying circumstances to the reality of day-to-day life, with all of its normal, mundane, and even superficial qualities.

People who are experienced disaster responders generally learn to develop a routine of self-care when they return back home. This can come in a number of different forms:

"I always give myself at least three days to just be home and to be totally useless. I think because I am constantly on the 'go' for so many days in a row, my brain just gives up working for a number of days. I can't even decide what to order on a menu if there are more than three items listed! I now know that this tends to happen, so I don't pressure myself to go back to work, socialize, or do much of anything. If I need to cry…I cry. If I need to sit and watch stupid comedies on TV and not think about

anything, I do it. Whatever the case, I'm kind to myself and treat myself gently as I get back into life."

"I have learned to have a 'disaster-buddy.' I'm fortunate enough to have a good friend who also volunteers for disasters and such, so I always schedule a breakfast or lunch with her right after I return. That way I can talk to her nonstop about what I experienced, and she can be a sounding board to all of my various thoughts and feelings and understand the laughter through the tears. After my first deployment, I tried to use my husband for this, but he just got protective of me, as he didn't understand the joy I felt in the midst of the struggles and pain. He wanted me to promise to not volunteer again and worried that I had put myself through too much."

"I always schedule a day or two at a hotel at whatever city I'm flying in and out of, before I return. A hotel with room service is best! Although I do miss my family, I know that I need some time with just my thoughts with no demands from others. I hate losing my temper, but I can just be a bit too irritable at first from all the overstimulation, I think. So this way I get the chance to refocus and not take it out on others."

"My wife has always been a great source of support for me. She used to work as a missionary in Africa and has a great understanding of the challenges I faced. I look forward to returning to normal things—dinner with the family, going to church, and taking the dog for walks. The funny thing is that after every disaster deployment, I go through a period of having a cold or symptoms almost like the flu—my body is just letting me know that I've done a lot, I suppose. My wife is encouraging of whatever way I try to go (as sometimes I just need to throw myself back into work, as I'm not quite ready to sit and think things through), and I don't know what I would do without her."

The important thing to remember is that everyone is different, as is every disaster experience. There is no one "right" way of returning back to your typical life—just be aware that you will experience a period of adjustment and plan accordingly.

Concluding Thoughts

In this chapter, we reviewed normal responses to disasters, tools for promoting the well-being of survivors, methods for encouraging resiliency, and self-care for responders. While disasters clearly have numerous severe and significant challenges for all concerned, they also have a way of encouraging personal growth, developing tools for resiliency, and increasing the wisdom of all who have lived through them.

The preceding section was graciously authored by Dr. Jeanne M. LeBlanc, PhD, ABPP, R. Psychologist.

Our mission to offer mental health support and to assist those affected by disaster led us to the ACTS organization and to Haiti. With ACTS, our team benefited from working in a Christian environment, allowing the grace of God to be openly received and accepted.

For many volunteers, the trip was religiously inspired and spiritually fulfilling: "My trip to Haiti in July was the most amazing experience of my life. I feel grateful for the opportunity and the individuals I met in Haiti. It was amazing to see how the Haitian people are so giving and caring…The best part about my trip was hearing and sharing stories with the Haitian people. I believe that God brought me to Haiti for a reason, and I feel inspired to go back again."

Other volunteers have expressed how they were personally changed. As one volunteer explains, "This trip meant so much, and it changed me. As with other disaster trips, I experienced a lot of team building with other employees that I don't typically work with, and it [allowed] me get to know the people I work with on a regular basis on a more personal level. But this trip was so much more. I think the biggest thing that I have changed is I now try to slow down and focus on really connecting with people. There were people in Haiti that I couldn't talk to because we didn't speak the same language, but despite that, we somehow connected in a very personal way. Most of the people we met have been through unimaginable things, have little or no food or shelter, and yet they are hopeful, faithful, and seem to be fairly happy."

Another volunteer expressed her appreciation for the ACTS World Relief organization: "I have had a very soul-filling and amazing experience volunteering my time in Haiti while under the care of ACTS. Through ACTS I was able to have a safe opportunity to help those in need."

Our work in Haiti included visiting a number of orphanages and working with the children using structured intervention and play therapy. Our experiences with the children had a profound impact on us. When we returned home, our team members felt we must do something to help the children at one particular orphanage. We truly felt that it was a matter of survival for the children. We sent a description of the orphanage and the conditions there and asked that our past volunteers sponsor twenty-five children at fifteen dollars each a month. Our goal was to raise enough money to support feeding the children for six months. Within twenty-four hours, the generous

Headwaters volunteers pledged over thirty-two hundred dollars, exceeding the goal we had set and allowing us to sponsor twenty-five children for nine months. We continue under the ACTS umbrella to look for ways to make a difference in Haiti by assisting a school with textbooks, connecting a young musician with a producer, and helping an interpreter pursue his education in the United States.

Team building and team support were extremely important to the groups that traveled to Haiti. As an organization, we have become skilled in developing teams and team leadership. We work with teams that are primarily made up of volunteers that have either never worked together or have never met. We blend experienced volunteers with those who are less experienced. We build teams within teams and work to blend people in other ways, such as creating other partnerships. Prior to any deployment, the teams have opportunities to meet and work together and support each other through fundraising and planning. In that way they get to know each other and each other's individual skills.

After returning from Haiti, one volunteer made this observation about the team: "Although the Headwaters team was comprised of a mix of people that worked for Orion companies and volunteers external to the organization, the group members came together as a team quickly. It matters who the group members are individually, but I think it was the service work itself that brought out the best in us—and made us a team. It was humbling to be in Haiti, where the need is so great and the resources are so few. Team members cared deeply about working with the children and about giving of themselves during the short time that we were there. We needed each other to make it meaningful for the children, so everyone did their part. It made us appreciate each other and value each other's contributions."

Most importantly, the team supported each other when the work was difficult. "Working with the children was always meaningful and a happy experience—but at times it felt like our contribution was too small compared to the enormity of the problems there. I think it was through our team's shared experiences that we gathered strength and were resilient."

Through our organization's volunteer work, we have seen camaraderie and trust increase among staff across organizational departments and between staff and senior management. The feelings of shared purpose in the service of others truly brought us together when we were back at work. There are those among us who haven't been able to travel due to family, school, or other commitments. Their contributions become part of the cause, whether they are helping with fundraisers or sharing the workload so that others can travel. Most of all, there is a sense of pride in working for an organization that goes above and beyond in service of others. It has helped us recruit top people in our field and has created leaders at all levels in the organization.

No diversity training we could provide would have given our staff anywhere near the depth of understanding on issues of race, poverty, and culture in America than the experience of working in the Ninth Ward's poor, mostly black neighborhood. As we oriented new volunteers to our work in the Ninth Ward, we had to assimilate, examine, and articulate our own experiences and biases.

In Haiti we were confronted by poverty and the lack of resources, which provided the opportunity for additional insight into the privilege we experience. One volunteer was moved to examine his life in light of the destruction and poverty he witnessed: "I have a greater appreciation of how good I have it—my financial situation, job, law enforcement, health care, and all the comforts I enjoy (house, cars, streets, electricity, furniture, food, Internet, water). Many people focus on what they don't have, but you realize just how much you do have after spending time there."

The organization has changed and benefited from our desire to serve. We have become more goal conscious and outcome oriented. More recently we raised funds to defray the cost of our trips to Haiti and to feed the children in the Haitian orphanage.

Our employees who give to the community are far more capable of giving to the company's clients, their co-workers, and to the organization as a whole, serving all with the skills they have acquired through their work on volunteer projects. The complex problems they have had to face while engaged in this work has helped our employees to develop skills as creative, innovative thinkers. As a result, when they serve, they are able to do so generously but also prudently, understanding far more intelligently where they may need to focus their efforts. Assuming leadership over a group of volunteers has helped them to become true leaders. They return to their work in the organization with those honed skills, benefiting all whom we serve.

Chapter 16
CHANGING MY WORLD

My mother, Shirley, was an encourager who knew no limits when it came to adventure, and she endeavored to encourage me in just about anything I wanted to do. Her father, Victor, was a professional clown, well known for his adventurous accomplishments in the circus. I share this same adventurous spirit.

When my mother was seven years old, her father was killed in a tragic car accident while driving his new 1940 Hudson. They were following behind a flatbed truck when all of a sudden, with a deafening sound, a pipe flew off the back end and came through the windshield, splitting Victor's head in half and puncturing a hole in the rear seat next to Shirley's shoulder. Both her sister and mother were frozen in shock. She leaped forward and lovingly held her father's head until he passed away an hour later.

The family priest visited their home and declared that if a sizeable amount of the insurance settlement were given to the church, then Victor could be released from Purgatory. Understandably, the family did not want Victor to suffer any longer, and as they now had the financial means to do so from insurance, the money was paid.

Unfortunately, this totally drained any means of financial support from the family, causing them to be divided. The two sisters and the mother went to live at separate homes. Their mother, Pat, later remarried an alcoholic named Clifford. Needless to say, due to his addiction, compounded by many personal issues from which he was trying to escape, the two girls did not feel welcome. My mother observed the abuse in this dysfunctional home for many years.

My father, Jerry, grew up with parents, Forrest and Pearl, who quit attending church because of someone seeing them come out of a movie theater together. This was against their church doctrines at that time. Instead of being censored, they volunteered to leave and never set foot back in a church for many years. One day while my parents were dating, my mother found a free Bible study course card at Jerry's parents' house. This ultimately led all of them to find a loving, caring church family. They enjoyed serving in many capacities, from children's ministry to a ministry for older teens, called Pathfinders. This led to their healing of past hurts.

At the age of forty, my father decided to attend college and become a certified X-ray technician; something he had been doing for many years previously. It was only through sheer perseverance and God's grace that he graduated. Less than half of his class graduated with him, because they were primarily uncommitted young people who hadn't quite figured out what they wanted in life.

Together my parents determined to commit their lives to loving others through youth ministry and overseas mission projects on the Bay Islands of Honduras, where they were instrumental in building a school. It was there that my father trained others in the use of X-ray technology at the local medical clinic. They left a legacy of serving others to my brother and me as well as other people.

My parents, grandparents, and God gave me a vision of serving others throughout life. This has been the key to keeping perspective on what is important and maintaining spiritual health. When I was five years old, Dennis, my older brother by eighteen months, and I could often be found leading out in worship and singing with groups such as the Happiness Singers. Music has always been an important part of my life.

It was through our shared love of music that I ultimately met my wife, Sherri, while on a singing tour that included her church in Orlando, Florida. She was in high school, and I was in my first year in college. After she graduated from nursing, we were married. She was eighteen, and I was twenty-one. To this day, my lovely wife glows in the presence of God as she worships in music, and her talents have enabled her to direct many worship teams over the years. I praise God for bringing Sherri into my life, for she has been unusually supportive of my big dreams and visions for ministry throughout the years.

Upon my completing seminary, Sherri and I began serving others in ministry full-time. Our ministry vision included ideas of how churches could reach out in love into their hurting communities or how love meant living in harmony with each other. We were in for the shock of our lives when we came to realize that the majority of churches' energy was not spent in reaching out to truly help others; they were more focused on defending whatever they believed to be right, hurting each other, and fragmenting a team spirit. Individuals are highly influenced in their direction from the vision cast by their leader. A clear vision from the leader determines more than anything else what motivates you to want to rise up and become a movement for good in your community.

Early in our ministry, Sherri's parents, Bob and Betsy, were dynamic training leaders in our church denomination. Because they were a little too radical in the approaches they used for outreach ministry, they were removed, or disfellowshipped—whichever terminology one chooses—and they left the church. Some paid church leaders felt threatened by the idea of empowering lay leadership in too significant of ways. Bob and Betsy also challenged many of the traditional doctrinal perspectives. Through the years, my wife's and my position was to minimize blaming anyone and try to be as positive as possible with our family, emphasizing forgiveness toward those who hurt our loved ones and showing our love to them through their pain.

Due to the pain endured by our extended family, my wife and I became very determined that lay leaders and volunteers are the keys to individual and church growth and that the church can save no one. Satan is seeking to destroy God's people through backbiting and self-centeredness, and we refused to let Satan have the last word on how he wanted to destroy God's love from flowing through us. A denomination's primary role is to be a facilitator of encouragement by demonstrating God's love to the hurting and choosing to overlook politics. We chose to overcome the deep hurt, seeing the challenges ahead as opportunities for God to miraculously show Himself strong, by serving others—and being loved by many. We were about to begin a radical journey in shaking up traditional denominationalism, as well.

Forgiveness

To unlock the power of the gospel (especially within church), be determined to forgive others who do not understand that Christianity without God's power, practicality, and miracles is only religion.

> People will love only themselves and their money. They will be boastful and proud, scoffing at God, disobedient to their parents, and ungrateful. They will consider nothing sacred. They will be unloving and unforgiving. They will slander others and have no self-control. They will be cruel and have no interest in what is good. They will betray their friends, be reckless, be puffed up with pride, and love pleasure rather than their God. They will act as if they are religious, but they will reject the power that could make them godly. You must stay away from people like that.
>
> —2 Timothy 3:2–5

Through the years we discovered church members who had no desire of developing a relationship with their pastor but only with their clique of political friends. They had either been hurt or neglected by former pastors or others in life. Some thought their denomination would ultimately save them once they joined. Most individuals we found, though, when loved, would give love in return in a bountiful way!

Our family has been blessed to serve others in ministry through the years, which has developed many life-long, cherished relationships with people. Some of the things we enjoyed doing to put our love into action has been to work alongside members and non-members in their gardens, help them pack and move in and out (this really shows who your true friends are), be with them at their hospital bedsides by the hour, or to just plain listen to their needs. We endeavored to create environments that produced a place for the hurting to gain healing, rather than shooting the wounded. When love is expressed in laughing, crying, and sharing with each other through good times and bad, you become as one. You can then come to understand the saying "Tears taste the same regardless of the color of the cheeks they roll over."

Through our commitment to meeting people's needs, we developed close friendships with people outside our church walls as well. How can you develop healthy relationships with "outsiders" if you see them as inferior or evil? We are *all* equal at the foot of the cross and in need of a Savior who loves to give good gifts to His children! We are *all* challenged to grow the most when we learn from individuals in all walks of life. I praise God for many wonderful, rewarding years serving Him in pastoral ministry with plenty of opportunities for character development that ministry brings. There were so many loving individuals who reached out to our family and blessed us. Many of our church members "adopted" our children and loved them as only an effective church family can do. Above all, I am extremely proud and blessed for the love and support shown wholeheartedly to my family by both my parents and in-laws.

Our children, Autumn and Andrew, are probably more on the adventurous side, like I am, and have been involved in everything from feeding and homeless ministries to emergency response outreaches and block parties where you help inner-city youth. This provided opportunities to model serving others in love.

Autumn loves helping in international medical brigades in Spanish-speaking countries like Nicaragua and Mexico. She has been inspired to attend medical school in Argentina and to learn Spanish fluently in order to help others around the world.

Andrew loves working more with his hands and is especially gifted in making broken things work. He also likes taking fast cars and making them even faster. My guess is that I had something to do with that, since we raced a number of muscle cars we had restored together over the years and he might have gotten a little tainted. He sees things not for what they are but for what they can become. He believes in a very practical-sided religion. If he hears a sermon or hears one speak of the Bible, he is quick to assess whether they are applying it to real-life situations. He watches how you live more than he listens to what you say.

Through the difficult times in our family's history, the solution for healing came by loving others in spite of the pain we experienced. One thing we have learned is: remember to focus on the positive, or the negative will overwhelm you. When you do this, you will grow through the gospel of serving others. You will be better equipped to help someone else in need because of sharing the way God gave you victory from the challenges of life.

Pastoral Progress

During the first ten years of my pastoral ministry, I primarily focused on teaching the doctrine of justification without a plan of love in action. The focus was on receiving what Christ had done for you. Through many seminars, crusades, and sermons, I disseminated vast biblical knowledge. Most of my congregation loved being made to feel "comfortable," and they truly believed they were the only ones worthy of salvation. I focused on John 3:16, "For God so loved the world that He gave His one and only Son." I thought we were meeting people's needs by intellectually sharing what we believed everyone wanted to know. Was the truth we were trying to share accurately meeting their needs and making a difference in their lives? We claimed we had "the truth." Yet, when new members were taught this truth, they rarely stayed in attendance for more than a year. There seemed to be a constant turnover of followers without much sustained growth. Some tried to act holier than God in an attempt to reassure themselves of being the true remnant. Others stressed an even stricter diet than Jesus practiced, thinking that if they didn't, they might jeopardize their justification and definitely their sanctification. This kept our focus and energy inward, maintaining an institution instead of encouraging revelation.

Then God told me it was time to put what I believed into action. By combining justification (receiving) and sanctification (releasing), salvation is received. This is the recycling or growing process of becoming God's real treasure and living fulfilled lives. During the last twenty years in ministry, I have emphasized both justification (receiving what Jesus has done for you) and sanctification. Sanctification is the process of releasing what God has done for you with love in action. Now there is a connection between John 3:16 and 1 John 3:17, "If I see a brother in need and do not do something about it, how can God's love be in me?" (author's paraphrase).

When we become involved in living to love others through serving, it brings healing to both our past and present. The greatest blessing I have experienced is to speak, pray, and if possible, to live to bless those who have hurt me the most. Why? Because it releases the toxic animosity in my heart toward those who have caused me pain.

Pastor Transformed by a Broader Vision

Choosing to focus less on what I thought the community needed to know doctrinally, I began to utilize our youth, finding out what our community's needs were and then meeting them. This process of helping others changed us from who we were and made us into who we needed to become. That is when ministry became fulfilling not only for myself but for the congregation as well. Our church exploded with growth and resources. The median age of our church continually decreased, whereas the trend of my denomination and most others was to increase one year older per year. We began to focus on training and empowering our youth through the gifts of those who were retired. Our focus shifted to:

- Church and worship, meeting the needs of our community.
- Empowering youth leadership through mentorship from our older and more experienced leaders.
- Opening a chain of thrift Stores and food pantries to see if we could out give what we had been given. We implemented eighty-seven different outreach ministries in our community.

Before long, we began to realize that as the occurrence of natural disasters increased (400 percent over the past twenty years), the needs of thousands of suffering victims grew. After four historic, disastrous hurricanes hit Florida back-to-back in less than two months, practical need was at an all time high. Hot meals and donated food needed to be distributed, along with water, diapers, and baby formula. This led to the birth of a ministry called ACTS (Active Christians That Serve) Disaster Response, which later developed into ACTS World Relief, which focused on empowering youth in worldwide service, or love in action!

God leading me into ACTS World Relief wasn't according to any career plan of mine. When some mistakenly thought that I was now in the fast lane of success, receiving millions from donors and enjoying a comfortable lifestyle, this was far from reality. I have never worked so hard in my life to receive so little personal financial return. Yet, I have never been blessed so much as now!

God has revealed to my wife, Sherri, and I that greatness is really all about giving away what He has entrusted to us. There were months that Sherri was confident God would somehow provide but stressed out when there was not enough money from ACTS donations to pay any salary to me. We were constantly reminded that God would never fail us because of seeing so many of His constant miracles just one day at a time. It was at this greatest time of financial need that she came down with cancer and went on medical leave. Giving of charitable donations to ACTS was at historic lows, yet miraculously God smiled upon us. He never gave us or ACTS more than what we needed at the very time we needed it most.

I experienced greatness when Sherri let me know how blessed she and our now grown children are to know what unconditional love means at home. My wife thanked me for loving her at times in her life when she wasn't at her best. To me, she is more beautiful then when I met her in college, because I know her inside beauty is just as breathtaking as her outward appearance.

Challenge

Do you have enough faith to feel secure if your financial portfolio doesn't keep growing while you're serving others in ministry? What if you don't become the big millionaire? What if your spouse becomes unsightly, changes in careers, or becomes physically disfigured? As we move through our journey of life's mistakes and choices, greatness is only a breath away when we are ready to focus on giving instead of receiving and when we are willing to seek forgiveness. God sees you for what you can become in Him, filled with more love and greatness than you ever dreamed possible! This message should bring ongoing hope, encouragement, and set a new vision, definition, and standard of how God is calling you to a journey of power-packed living!

> The greatest among you must be a servant. You can either exalt yourself and experience a lot of hurtful consequences in life, or humble yourself to serve and be exalted!
>
> —Matthew 23:11–12, author's paraphrase

When disasters occur in your life, choose to capitalize on these situations as opportunities. Choose to focus on solutions to every challenge in life. You will view these as opportunities to stretch your personality and relationship with God. By loving and serving others, you will grow and gain healing through your pain. God will then be glorified as you grow in Him. You are becoming transformed with new life in His resurrection power with new life through helping others. This power is available to you today, so reach out and take it!

Appendix–
STUDY GUIDE

THIS STUDY GUIDE is presented in a format that can be used in an accelerated program during which the curriculum can be completed in as little as three months or up to seven months, with each session lasting one to two hours. The slower pace will allow it to fit into an academic year and be useful for students or faculty as an elective study. The group coordinator should decide which is best, considering the availability of participants.

Before the first group session:

- The group leader(s) should be identified and should include, if possible, someone trained in behavioral science if in an academic setting.
- A meeting place should be conducive to having group discussions (i.e., all participants should be in a circle with the ability to make eye contact with each other). A chalkboard or other similar device would be helpful.
- Students should read the "About the Author" section at the end of this book to get acquainted with the author of the book.
- Each participant would benefit by completing a spiritual gifts assessment tool. This should be shared with the group leader. (These can be obtained on-line or through your local Christian bookstore.)
- Participants would benefit by completing a personality profile assessment tool, such as the Myers-Briggs personality inventory. This should be shared with the group leader.
- Participants should write a personal mission statement and motto.

FIRST SESSION: Introduction

General introductions of each coordinator and participants helps you get to know each other. The question should be asked of each person, what can you do to make a difference in serving others unconditionally?

The goals of the course should be identified and discussed. Among other things, the following are primary goals:

- Recognize that one of the noblest experiences in life is the opportunity to serve others.
- Share some ideas that are out of the box or nontraditional ways of thinking that could help someone else in need.
- Help the participants to develop an idea of how to fit into the gospel of serving. A review of the spiritual gifts assessment tool and the personality evaluation tool should be discussed.
- Begin to identify the personal changes or further development of personality traits that is required to be able to love unconditionally. (Discuss whether or not there is a personality profile or spiritual gift that is required in order to have unconditional love.) Does one start serving first and in the process of serving develop unconditional love?

A part of serving can include participation in a disaster setting. Therefore, understanding the incident command structure (ICS) is essential and will be part of these sessions.

Homework

- Read Chapter 1, "First Response"—Emergency Personnel
- Share ways that John 15 can be applied to "lay down your life for your friends or enemies."
- Visit the ACTS World Relief website and begin the training in levels one and two curriculums.
- Share how the four key texts that illustrate "love is action" apply to our lives.
- How is it possible for you to have a first response (knee-jerk reaction) to want to become involved in acts of love when most people like to just be comfortable and hope someone else helps others?

SESSION TWO:
Chapter 1, "First Response"–Emergency Personnel

PRAYER FOR TODAY

Ask each participant to thank God for one gift in his or her life.

Group Discussion

- Describe your homework experiences. (Each person should respond to the following questions.)
  - What feelings surfaced while asking for help or with helping others with their chores? Was there hesitancy in asking for help or offering help?
  - Which were positive feelings and need reinforcing?
  - Which were negative feelings and need changing?
- Discuss ways you could be a "First Responder" in meeting the needs of others.
- Review the contents of Chapter 1 and discuss the miracle of change, the miracle of self-realization.
- Would you feel comfortable in doing prostitution ministry or bar ministry? What are the limits you would go to, to demonstrate unconditional love?

Homework

- Identify community service organizations that are available in a context outside your comfort zone. (These may be in your immediate neighborhood or within the broader community. This organization should be one that challenges your negative feelings.) One of the goals in this exercise is to identify organizations that challenge your feelings of working with groups that have cultural, ethnic, or religious concepts that conflict with your personal values or views.
- Read Chapter 2, "Having a Healthy Identity.
- Continue the ACTS World Relief training online. When available, bring your ICS ACTS World Relief online certificates of completion to class.

SESSION THREE: Chapter 2, "Having a Healthy Identity"

PRAYER FOR TODAY:

John 17:1-4, My Prayer to Jesus (repeat together)

Glorify me today so that I can give glory back to You. You have given me authority over all circumstances. Thank You for giving me eternal life, because I know how much You love me! In everything I do, I want to bring You glory!

Group Discussion

- Discuss the homework project. Identify the community service organization you selected, and explain how this organization will challenge the personal traits that interfere with your willingness to offer unconditional love. Identify the areas of your pain.
- Leaders, begin to insert the idea of teamwork and group interdependence. (Chapter 8 has a lot to offer on this subject. The entire chapter should be reviewed as the group develops into a team.) The idea is to have the group functioning as an effective church board, visionary board, or any other team that is discussing and planning evangelism, youth retention, out-reach activities, or mentoring. Of great importance is the acceptance of each person in the group with unconditional love. We all have our "scabs and barnacles" and need acceptance in spite of them.
- Discuss Chapter 2.
    - Focus on the section titled "Personal Identity Crisis," inserting yourself into these pages.
    - Understand that change, powerful change, is possible. You may wish to change your personal mission statement into a personal visionary mission statement. Have you recognized the difference between the two? Read Chapter 10, "Big Vision and Big Faith" for further insight into these differences.
- Answer the question, Given resources available through the power of the Holy Spirit, what would you like to accomplish during your lifetime? (Review Chapter 11, "Prayer Is Your Source of Power!")

Homework

- Select and join a community service organization that will challenge the negative concepts identified you in the homework assignment in Chapter 1's exercise.
- Should you think that you have not identified any negative concepts, etc., ask the group coordinator to choose a community service organization for you.
- Read Chapter 3, "Overcoming Fear Factors and Discovering Self-Worth."
- Continue the training sessions at ACTS World Relief's website.

SESSION FOUR: Chapter 3, "Overcoming Fear Factors and Discovering Self-Worth"

PRAYER FOR TODAY:

Hebrews 10:22-23 (repeat together)

Lord, I come into Your presence with:

1. A sincere heart,
2. Full assurance of faith,
3. Freedom from guilt because of Your sacrifice.

I thank You that because of Calvary I am born again! I hold fast to the hope I profess because You are faithful, according to Your promises!

Group Discussion

- Identify the organization that you chose, and the coordinator will keep a list of these for later discussion. So far, as a member of that organization, what have you done? If you feel comfortable in discussing you choice and the identified characteristics that lead to this choice, discuss them with the class.
- Chapter 3 is all about integrity. One must understand how integrity functions along with congruence, ethical behavior, and "tough love"—all the while relating to unconditional love. (Hopefully you have exercised your personal integrity in

choosing your service organization and in discussing it with the group.) Answer the questions below as a group:

- How is integrity related to unconditional love, along with ethical behavior and "tough love"? What is congruence, and how does it function in the setting of integrity, "tough love," and ethical behavior?
- Discuss concepts of integrity regarding relationships with a special person in your life, such as a close friend, spouse, parent, or God.

- The chapter describes multiple interactions that require integrity. Discuss them all, if time permits. However, focus on the section titled "Love in Action: Finger-Lickin' Good." Incorporate the concepts of integrity, unconditional love, "tough love," and ethical behavior in each situation discussed.

Homework

- Review your visionary mission statement for congruence in thought, plan of action, and actions taken. Are your plans and actions reflecting the concepts of integrity? Seek divine guidance for the ongoing fulfillment of your statement.
- Read Chapter 4.
- Use any spare time you have to become more involved with your community service organization.
- By now you should have completed several of the courses offered at ACTS World Relief.
- If available and appropriate, choose a younger person to join with you in your work with the community service organization. Information regarding mentoring is found in Chapter 9.

SESSION FIVE: Chapter 4, "Getting Dirty"

PRAYER FOR TODAY:

Matthew 6:6-9 (repeat together)

Father, You alone are my majestic, holy and loving God. I want to experience Your power today, and may Your miraculous, perfect purpose spread throughout all the world, as it is in heaven. Because You are My provider and sustainer, You have promised to supply all my needs according to Your riches in heaven. Today, I forgive ______, who has intentionally or unintentionally hurt me, and now I thank You for forgiving my intentional or unintentional sins. When I am tested and tempted today, I thank You in advance that Your promises will give me strength to overcome all the power of the enemy!

I will glorify Your name forever, for You are an awesome God!

Group Discussion

"Getting dirty" is about releasing and giving. Releasing is ridding oneself of baggage that interferes with giving. The first homework assignment prepared you in a small way for this chapter. Remember, you asked for help and volunteered to help in the context of relating to a person you didn't know. Now we will broaden that experience by providing principles of engagement. Understanding others' needs and thus being able to help involves being alert to the situation. Keep your eyes open, ears unstopped, mind in gear, and tongue unengaged. Remember that opportunities sometimes appear unexpectedly.

Four criteria are mentioned in the text: ask, resource, give, and practice. We will discuss each.

- **Ask:** Ask for help and empowerment and gain by asking and doing. Review the story of Sam in the section titled "What Sex?" Who has the most "trash" to release in that story? Sam, David (the author and counselor), the senior pastor, or you? Make a list on the board of each person in the story and his baggage, and then make a list of the thoughts/baggage of the people in the group. Remember, baggage interferes with being open to serving and having unconditional love.

- **Resource:** Putting yourself in Sam's situation, what resources could you muster in order to give Sam the feeling that you cared and were willing to be involved? Spiritual empowerment? Friends? Professional people? Willingness to be a friend? Role play and express your plans for future contact with people like Sam.
- **Give:** Continuing to think of Sam, what do you have to give? Time? Money? Knowledge? How about self and your unconditional love and support? (Remember, you do not have to agree with a person in order to be supportive of the person.)
- **Practice (what you preach):** Does the term congruence apply in this situation? If something interferes with your ability to demonstrate unconditional love in Sam's situation, then you may wish to revise your visionary mission statement. Also, ask, has anyone in the group experienced a feeling of guilt over doing good? Has anyone broken some long-embedded rule in order to be helpful or giving? (Review the section titled, "The Perfect Pastor?")

Report to the group your progress in selecting a younger person to join with you in your work with the community service organization. What questions do you have regarding mentoring?

Homework

- Volunteer to be responsible/accountable for some small or simple project for which you have minimal or no qualifications that comes up in your community service organization or in your social setting.
- Read Chapter 5, "Faith, Focus, and Following Through."

SESSION SIX: Chapter 5, "Faith, Focus, and Following through"

PRAYER FOR TODAY:

Psalm 5:1-12 (repeat together)

Help, Lord. I need You this morning and expectantly bring my requests to You! I ask forgiveness from sins, like lying, pride, deceiving, and whatever else You convict me of right now. [Take

time to ask for forgiveness for other specific sins.] I refuse to be separated from Your presence, which brings healing to my life right now, in Jesus' name.

Because of Your unfailing love, I love to worship You!

Lead me in the right paths today, or my enemies and challenges will conquer me. Tell me clearly what to do and where to turn today.

May any potential enemies be caught in their own traps today. Some of them are trying to flatter me. Chase them away from me today. I release any animosity or anger against them. I pray blessings on their lives instead.

I take refuge in Your presence, and I sing joyful praises to You forever!

Protect me today, all my loved ones, and those who love and don't love You yet.

Send someone across my path today who is hurting or does not yet know You, to whom I can be a living, loving Jesus.

Lord, bless me today with Your shield of love!

Group Discussion

- Review your homework assignment from the last session. Discuss your activities. Not only was it important to emphasize the content of that chapter, but now we get to analyze your focus and following through. If you have accepted that assignment, you have already demonstrated the faith part. If you completed the project, you will now realize that your faith has been rewarded with victory.
- It is now time to sort and sift your priorities. Sometimes this is referred to as making a searching and fearless personal inventory of your ideals and goals. It is an honest approach to your visionary mission statement in that this statement should identify your goals. (Allow for a quiet time in the class, with each person focusing on his or her goals. Each person is to make a list of these goals and all necessary accomplishments that are needed in order to achieve these goals. A timeframe should be inserted. Over time, the items on this list may change or there may be a shift in the order of importance. In contemplating this exercise, review the "Lessons Learned" section.

Homework

- Between now and the next session, review your goals and priorities. Arrange them in their order of importance. Pray over this list on a daily basis and review the list during your prayer sessions. Feel free to change your priorities as you are impressed to do so. This list is your list; it should be kept to yourself unless you choose to discuss it with anyone. This list should be congruent with your visionary mission statement.
- Read Chapter 6, "Impossibilities Become Possibilities"—Looking, Listening, and Learning.

SESSION SEVEN: Chapter 6, "Looking, Listening, and Learning"

PRAYER FOR TODAY: Ephesians 1:17-20 (repeat together)

Thank you for giving me the spirit of wisdom and revelation of who Christ is and what He has done for me. I pray that my heart will be flooded with light to see the inheritance promised to me. I understand how incredibly great Your power is to me as a believer. It is the same mighty power that raised Christ from the dead and caused Him to sit at Your right hand in heaven.

Group Discussion

As you did your homework, you will have experienced the basics of looking, listening, and learning while seeking contact with God and His Spirit. We now wish to use those same principles in relating to others. Again, the term *congruence* may be applied; your actions must be consistent with your words. Falseness is readily apparent to most people, particularly those who are hurting.

Review the story of Gwynne; you probably know someone like her. That person may be a close friend you wish to reach with your unconditional love or a neighbor you would like to develop a friendship with. Learn the lessons of effective interaction as outlined in this story. *(You may wish to set up a role playing exercise to illustrate this.)*

- By observation ("looking") one can usually identify something in common with that person or something that is unique or special about that person. Sometimes that person has a special gift or talent. Loneliness or depression may be recognized. If nothing is apparent that offers an opening wedge, initiate the conversation by observing the weather or mention some recent event.

- As the contact is made or conversation is initiated, listen to the person's story; everyone has one. What does he or she wish to talk about? Find out if he or she is hurting or depressed.
- Learning how to make contacts and maintain contacts is vital in the gospel of serving.

Homework

- On campus, your community service organization, or anywhere else, identify a person who is unknown to you and find out how you can be of service to that person.
- Read Chapter 7, "Timing, Impacting, Maximizing, Eliminating."

SESSION EIGHT: Chapter 7, "Timing, Impacting, Maximizing, Eliminating"

PRAYER FOR TODAY:

Numbers 6:24-26, the Prayer of Aaron

Bless and protect me. Smile upon me and be gracious to me. Show me Your favor, and give me Your peace.

Group Discussion

- Report on your homework assignment of serving a person in your community.
- Time is the greatest gift God has given you. Multi-tasking can be both a blessing and a curse. Try only accomplishing as many things as you can do in excellence. Share one way you are efficient with your time and one way you waste time.
- Review the four key words, *timing, impacting, maximizing,* and *eliminating,* to see how effectively you are applying each of these principles in your life. Have your group share which

key word each might choose to be their greatest strength or weakness.

This is the final session, should this be part of an academic year curriculum. The remainder of the guide can be used for those parts of the book that are included in the academic sessions or for use if the book is used in other settings.

Homework

Read Chapter 8, "Multiplying, Motivating, Movements, and Building Healthy Teams."

SESSION NINE: Chapter 8, "Team Work—Multiplying, Motivating, and Movements"

PRAYER FOR TODAY:

John 17:20–22, Jesus' Prayer for Unity as a Team (repeat together)

As believers we are united in demonstrating Your perfect love. This will cause others to believe in You. Thank You for giving us Your glory now so that we are becoming perfect in unity. Thank You for promising to reveal Your full glory to us when we go to live with You forever!

Group Discussion

- Nothing breeds success like success. We all want to learn the keys to a healthy, growing team! What are the four do's to a healthy marriage team?
- Music can either be a powerful ingredient for church growth, or it can be the most divisive and controversial issue. What are the twelve principles to insure it is multiplying, motivating, and creating a movement?
- Name the three principles of developing a team spirit:

1. ______________________________

2. ______________________________

3. ______________________________

- Answer, what are the nine keys to changing your world through acts of love? This sequence is the most important key for growth in effective team building. If you miss only one ingredient, you will not succeed.

Homework

Read Chapter 9, "Building Loyal Relationships."

SESSION TEN: Chapter 9, "Building Loyal Relationships"

PRAYER FOR TODAY:

I praise You, Lord, for experiencing blessings today, for this is the day that You have made. I will rejoice and be glad in it. Holy Spirit, move in a mighty way in my heart today. "Now-faith" comes by hearing and submitting to Your Word. Faith rests on Your power, not man's wisdom. I am a believer, not a doubter. Your Word tells me that faith is speaking of those things that are not as though they were, those things invisible as though they were visible. I chose to put You first in my life, and I live in a relationship with You, Lord. I speak words of life and not death, faith and not doubt, encouragement and not criticism.

The weapons I use have divine power to demolish every stronghold of evil in my life. You have given me authority to overcome all the power of the enemy! You are my Deliverer. I walk in Your favor and in the power of the Holy Spirit. Abundant life comes to me now! You are my Shepherd; all my needs are met according to Your riches in glory. Because You have promised to never leave me or forsake me, I can be sure that You are here now, and because You are here, the power to heal is here.

I am a hearer and obey Your Word. I am more than a conqueror through Your love for me. I trust and depend upon You by casting all my cares on You. I praise You, Lord, that You have equipped me with all I need to stay strong in my day of adversity!

You will keep me from falling, because no weapon formed against me shall prosper. In Jesus' name, amen!

Group Discussion

- Share ideas of how you can use Jesus' model of meeting the needs of others first in order to develop loyal, lasting relationships.
- Share how long it took to develop a deep relationship with someone when you met their need. (Be sure to observe how the greater the need was met, the quicker the relationship deepened.)

Homework

Read Chapter 10, "Big Vision and Big Faith."

SESSION ELEVEN: Chapter 10, "Big Vision and Big Faith"

PRAYER FOR TODAY:

Jabez Prayer of Big Faith (repeat together)

Oh that You would bless me and increase the possessions entrusted to me! Please be with me in all that I do, and keep me from all trouble and pain!

Group Discussion

- Share your mission statement and your vision or passion of what God is calling you to do now with your group. Ideas might be shared that even sound a little too radical!
- Share an example of how God is leading you to think big, start small, and act now.
- Share a personal challenge related to how the three keys to overcoming animosity are crucial to keeping your dream alive.

Homework

Read Chapter 11, "Prayer Is Your Source of Power."

SESSION TWELVE:
Chapter 11, "Prayer Is Your Source of Power"

Begin with conversational prayer by going around and thanking God for one of the most important blessings in your life right now.

Power in prayer comes when we use faith by thanking God for answering our requests before we see how He chooses to do so. Claiming His promises activates His Word in answering our requests, because faith comes by speaking and hearing what He has promised (Rom 10:9; 17).

Group Discussion

- Is there a difference between praying, "If it be Thy will," or "Thank You, Lord, for Your will being done?"
- Answer, What is God's will for our lives? (See John 10:10, 3 John 2. Be sure to emphasize that it is for us to glorify Him.)
- Share ideas of when it is applicable to pray (e.g., making decisions, priorities of each day, relationships).

If you do not pray, will everything be the same anyway?

Homework

Read Chapter 14, "Hope for Hurting Haiti."

SESSION THIRTEEN:
Chapter 14, "Hope for Hurting Haiti"

Group Discussion

- Why is it important to understand the history of the country or area that one is providing relief efforts to? (Answer: cultural awareness and roots of suffering, attitudes to outsiders, America's history with the country, beliefs unique to that country [e.g., voodoo in Haiti], needs of the persons helping in the context of the history and culture of the area [e.g., history of poverty or affluence and expectations])
- What are the three areas of prevention to limit a disasters impact and examples of each?
- What are the three elements in preparedness? Which one do you feel you need the most help with?

- Why is it important to understand the response phase and its expectations and stress, and what are they?
- What is the incidence of PTSD in the general population? Give examples of untreated PTSD after the Mt. St. Helens eruption.
- What are examples of statements to avoid with disaster survivors?
- What are more helpful examples of helpful statements or questions to ask disaster survivors?
- What do kids need after the basic needs are met?
- Practice role playing in disaster training. Create a story and have two or three people play the roles of victim and helper. Change stories and reverse roles. After the exercise is finished, rate each person according to how each did as a helper (the "victim" gets an "Oscar" for best performance). Criteria for consideration may include, were they knowledgeable? Did they calm the victim? Did they seem confident? Did they have an action plan? Could they think on their feet? Did they show compassion?

Homework

Read Chapter 15, "Hope for Hurting Helpers."

SESSION FOURTEEN: Chapter 15, "Hope for Hurting Helpers"

Group Discussion

- There are many times in one's life when stress rears its head. Stress cannot be avoided but must be recognized and attenuated. Discuss the information regarding stress and PTSD.
- Open the floor for group discussion of the course content and how it could be changed. Inquire as to the practical ways in which the course has been helpful to the individual participants. Encourage each person to make themselves available for deployment into a disaster situation.
- Take and then share your results of the pre-deployment survey. Compare why these questions are important to understand how good and bad stress affect your life.

NOTES

2: Having a Healthy Identity

1. Website: about.com (accessed October 29, 2010).
2. Ibid.

3: Six Keys to Changing Your World

1. Quote from website: http://www.quotelady.com/subjects/mistakes.html (accessed October 29, 2010).
2. David Canther, *Experience Big Faith* (David Canther, 1999).
3. "Faster Than Fema," segment on *CBS Evening News*, available for viewing at http://www.youtube.com/watch?v=BCChT46kjpo.

5: Faith, Focus, and Following through

1. *American Heritage Dictionary*, 2009 edition, s.v. "faith."
2. *Merriam-Webster's Dictionary of Legal Terms*, 1996 edition, s.v. "faith."
3. Website: answers.com (accessed October 29, 2010), s.v. "emunah."
4. Ellen G. White, *Review & Herald* article, May 28, 1895.

10: Big Vision and Big Faith

1. Ellen G. White, *My Life Today* (Hagerstown, MA: Review and Herald Publishing Association, 1980).
2. Jim Cymbala and Dean Merrill, *Fresh Faith* (Grand Rapids, MI: Zondervan, 1999), 16.
3. Copyright unknown by author of oft-quoted passage.

14: Hope for Hurting Haiti

1. Lawrence Harrison, "Haiti and the Voodoo Curse," *Wall Street Journal*, Feb. 6–7, 2010.
2. Louis Pasteur quote found at ThinkExist.com, http://thinkexist.com/quotation/chance_favors_the_prepared_mind/214449.html (accessed October 29, 2010).
3. V. Alex Kehayan and Joseph C. Napoli, *Resiliency in the Face of Disaster and Terrorism* (Personhood Press, 2005).
4. Ibid.
5. Ibid.
6. Spencer Eth, M.D. and Robert S. Pynoos, M.D., M.P.H., *Post-Traumatic Stress Disorders in Children* (American Psychiatric Press, 1985).
7. Ibid.

15: Hope for Helpers—Resiliency in the Face of Despair

1. Dr. N. Aube, Medicins Sans Frontiers, personal communication, (April, 2010).

2. Nebraska Disaster Behavioral Health, "Nebraska Behavioral Health All-Hazards Disaster Response and Recovery Plan," http://www.disastermh.nebraska.edu/files/Appendix-D.pdf (accessed October 29, 2010).

3. The following checklists have been adapted from the British Columbia Disaster Worker Care Committee. See the Government of British Columbia, "Worker Care Materials and Cards," British Columbia Emergency Social Services, http://www.ess.bc.ca/pubs/workercare.htm (accessed October 29, 2010).

4. Centers for Disease Control and Prevention, "Disaster Mental Health for Responders: Key Principles, Issues and Questions," http://www.bt.cdc.gov/mental-health/responders.asp (accessed October 29, 2010).

ABOUT THE AUTHOR

David Canther has been a pastor for twenty-seven years. He is also an inventor, with seven registered patents, an author, and the president and founder of ACTS World Relief. He has been married for thirty-two years to Sherri Canther, a registered nurse. They have two children: Andrew, who is pursuing engineering/construction management, and Autumn, who is pursuing a career in medicine.

Books by David Canther

Experience Big Faith by David Canther, Copyright 1999 (self-published).

TO CONTACT THE AUTHOR

David Canther
600 Citrus Ave.
Ft. Pierce, FL 34950
david@actswr.org
www.actswr.org
888.336.7119

To order books, visit our website or contact us at our 800 number.

***First Response* is also available in Spanish.**

ACTS TRAINING:

Orlando International Airport
November 2010

LANET
CITY OF ORLANDO
POLICE
ORLANDO
POLICE

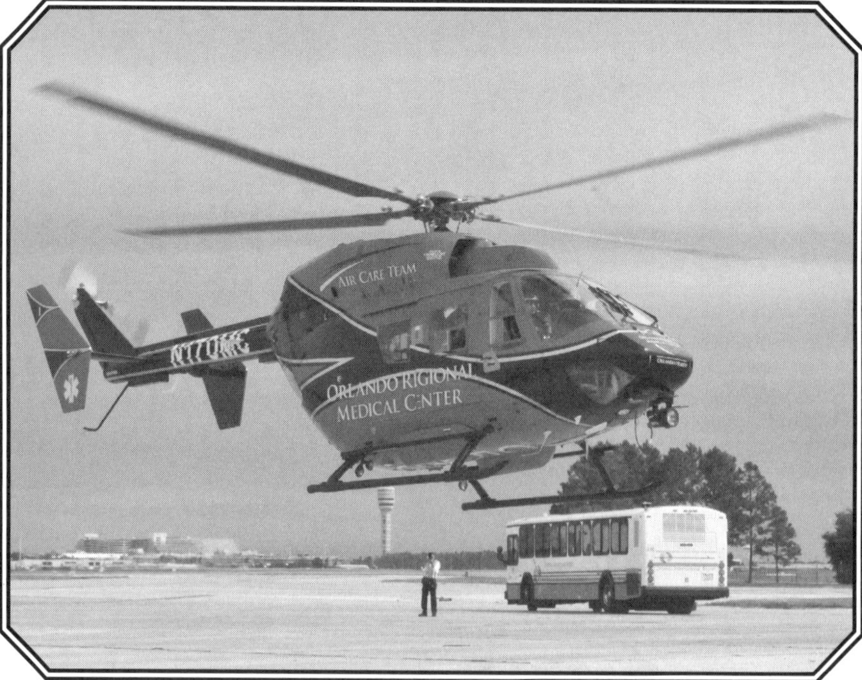
AIR CARE TEAM
N170MC
ORLANDO REGIONAL
MEDICAL CENTER

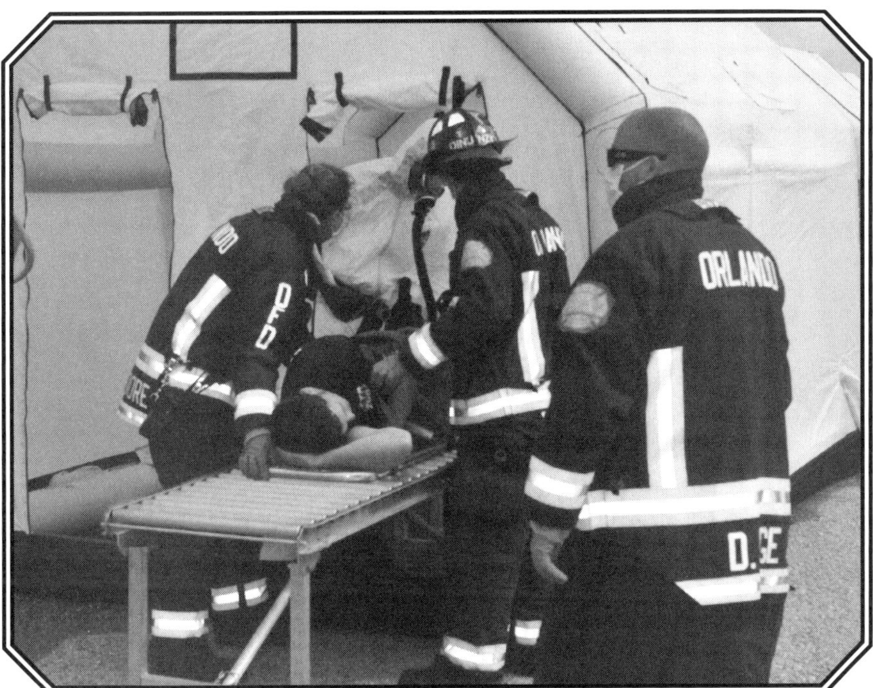
OFD
ORLANDO

R. ALLEN

ACTS
World Relief
www.actswr.org
Medical
Response
NORTHLAND
Disaster Response Team

SCOTT
AIR-PAK

PLANET

RANGE COUNTY FIRE RESCUE
TECHNICAL RESCUE
RESPONSE

Airways
MSA
MSA

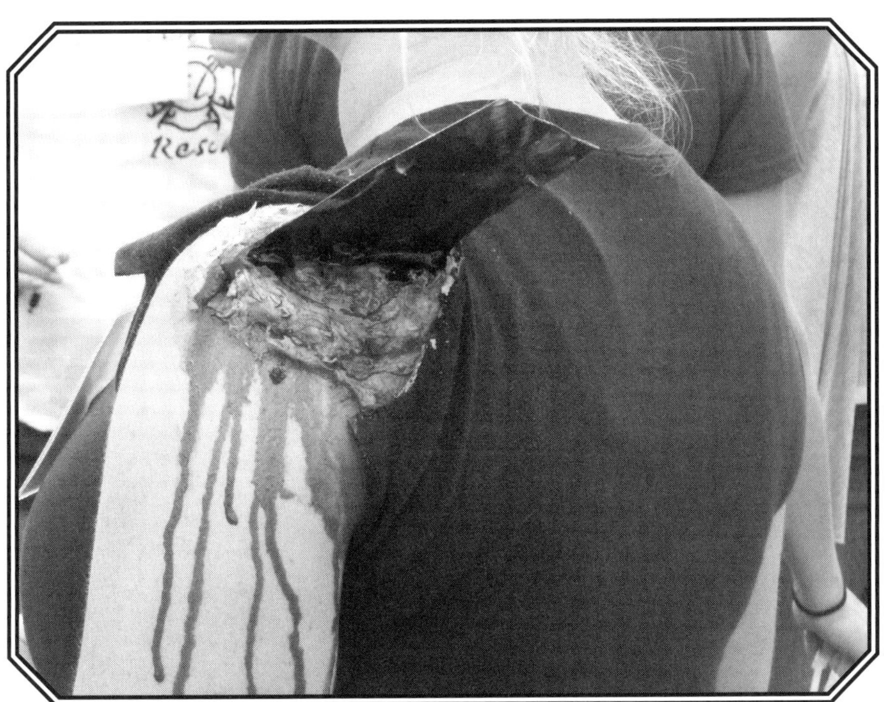

Become an ACTS World Relief "First Response" Faith Partner and receive a newsletter and pin or patch free.

Donate now: www.actswr.org
Or send donations to:
ACTS World Relief
600 Citrus Ave.
Ft. Pierce, FL 34950
888.336.7119